ENLARGED & REVISED THIRD EDITION

ROLLS-ROYCE SILVER SHADOW

BENTLEY T-SERIES

CAMARGUE & CORNICHE

First published in 1996; revised and updated edition 2000; enlarged and revised third edition 2004, by Veloce Publishing Limited, 33 Trinity Street, Dorchester, Dorset DT1 1TT, England. Fax: 01305 268864/e-mail: info@veloce.co.uk
web: www.veloce.co.uk or www.velocebooks.com/
ISBN: 1-904788-25-4/UPC 36847-00325-8

ENLARGED & REVISED THIRD EDITION

ROLLS-ROYCE SILVER SHADOW

BENTLEY T-SERIES

CAMARGUE & CORNICHE

MALCOLM BOBBITT

VELOCE PUBLISHING
THE PUBLISHER OF FINE AUTOMOTIVE BOOKS

Acknowledgements
&
Introduction

Acknowledgements

When I began to research the first edition of this book I quickly realised what a vast subject the Silver Shadow and Bentley T-Series cars is. Fortunately, I had the assistance of Peter Baines, General Secretary of the Rolls-Royce Enthusiasts' Club, who directed me to a number of individuals who readily agreed to help. Among them was Ian Rimmer, who not only gave me background information about the cars, but also read my manuscript and offered much in the way of technical advice. At the time, Ian was Quality Engineer at Crewe, before Rolls-Royce and Bentley were sold; Rolls-Royce to BMW and Bentley to Volkswagen. Ian's enthusiasm for the marques resulted in him being elected to the R-RREC committee, and as well as being a past Secretary of the Club's Northern Section, he continues to play an active role in club affairs. Ian will be known to many for his splendid book on Rolls-Royce and Bentley experimental cars, and I thank him sincerely for his support.

Ian put me in touch with many people who were involved in the development of these fine cars, and allowed me to search company photographic archives. One of those Ian suggested I meet was Martin Bourne who, until taking retirement from Rolls-Royce, spent his career in the styling department, initially working with John Blatchley, then Fritz Feller, and latterly Graham Hull. I cannot thank Martin enough for his wholehearted help, and the considerable time he spent answering a stream of questions. Martin arranged for me to meet the stylists, design and body engineers, and test drivers, as well as senior personnel responsible for the Silver Shadow and its Bentley sister car.

I am indebted to Richard Charlesworth who, at the time the first edition of this book was published, was Head of Public Affairs at Rolls-Royce Motor Cars Ltd. Richard provided specification material and production details, and gave permission for me to use original drawings. Chris Ladley assisted enormously in the provision of photographs, and Mark Whitaker was instrumental in making other specific images available. Graham Hull, at the time Chief Stylist at Crewe, gave me the benefit of his styling expertise, and explained the design methods employed at Rolls-Royce.

It was through Martin Bourne's efforts that I was able to talk to many retired personnel. John Hollings, Technical Director at Rolls-Royce, provided much in the way of the cars' development, and I was saddened to learn of John's death only a few days before the first edition of this book appeared. Chief Stylist, John Blatchley, who showed such foresight in shaping the Silver Shadow and Bentley T, talked to me about his career and the fine cars he created, at Rolls-Royce and before he joined the company. As this new edition of the book was under preparation I learned that John was celebrating his ninetieth birthday, still taking an active interest in motorcar design.

Other members of the Rolls-Royce team who gave their help and support include the late Bill Allen, a senior stylist at Crewe who assisted with many of the designs, including that which emerged as the Corniche; Eric Langley, Body Engineering Designer, who created the original full-size body layout; J. (Mac) Macraith Fisher, Derek

Men of style. On 13th May, 1996, John Blatchley, Chief Stylist at Crewe until 1969 when he took early retirement, was reunited with his deputy, Bill Allen (left), and styling engineer Martin Bourne (centre). This emotive picture was taken by the author outside The Hunt House, headquarters of the Rolls-Royce Enthusiasts' Club at Paulerspury, when the three gentlemen became honorary members of the R-REC. Bill Allen died on 23rd December, 1999, at the age of 87, and John Blatchley celebrated his ninetieth birthday in summer 2003. Martin Bourne continues to play an active part in motoring and motor sport, and, as a pilot, likes nothing better than to be at the controls of an aeroplane. The Silver Shadow pictured is SRH 18616, a late Series 1 model. (Author's collection)

Coulson, and Jock Knight, all of whom spent endless hours designing and perfecting the cars; John Astbury, who worked on engine design, and John Cooke who had the task of dealing with many of the design regulations; John Gaskell and George Ray, test drivers who spent innumerable hours behind the wheel of experimental cars; Dave Tod, sales representative, who took the first production T-Series to Scotland to sell the Silver Shadow; the late Roger Cra'ster who, as Export Manager, negotiated vehicle sales to the royal family and other heads of state. Peter Hill, Nick Colbourne, Dave Preston, Barry Greenwood, and the late George Moseley, all added much general information.

Much assistance has been provided by the R-REC and the Sir Henry Royce Memorial Foundation, courtesy of Peter Baines and Philip Hall. I am also grateful for the support given by the Bentley Drivers Club at Long Crendon in Buckinghamshire.

A number of specialists have also given their support, and I am indebted to the following: Rhoddy Harvey-Bailey at Harvey Bailey Engineering; Rob Jones, Benver Services, Crewe; John Bowling of Bowling-Ryan in Bolton, Lancashire; Bill Bateman; Michael Hibberd, Langley, Buckinghamshire; Reg Vardy plc; Appleyard Rippon; Murray Motors, and Bentley Ribble Valley.

Thanks, too, to the following kind people who have given their time and enthusiasm: Andrew Minney, Robert Vickers, Andrew Morris, Brian Drummond, Bill Wolf, David Rizzo, Richard Mann, Martin Bennett, and the late Roger Lister.

As always, I would like to thank the librarians at the National Motor Museum for their help in sourcing relevant information and photographs.

My thanks to Rod Grainger and Judith Brooks at Veloce. It was Rod who suggested I write this book originally, and who commissioned this new edition.

Finally, a word of thanks to Jean, my wife, who has provided so much in the way of encouragement.

Introduction

When the Silver Shadow and T-Series Bentley were introduced in the autumn of 1965, they were not only the most innovative cars to wear, arguably, the most famous emblems in the world, they also indicated a new direction for Rolls-Royce. Though the saloon models gracefully withdrew from production fifteen years later in 1980 (the Corniche and Continental derivatives remained until 1996), they still today have a contemporary appearance, plus that presence so characteristic of all Rolls-Royce and Bentley models.

In 1965 the Silver Shadow was a sensation; bristling with technology, it was easily the most up-to-the-minute bearer of the Rolls-Royce marque for more than fifty years. Bentley enthusiasts, who remembered those fabulous cars built at Cricklewood by the firm's founder, W. O. Bentley, and successive models marketed as The Silent Sports Car, which were assembled by Rolls-Royce at Derby, might have been hoping for a dedicated sports saloon in the best tradition that the winged B emblem could offer. It's understandable, then, that loyal Bentley customers were disappointed that the Bentley T, despite it being a most magnificent motorcar, was nothing more than blatant badge engineering. Had the T-Series Bentley appeared without a direct Rolls-Royce equivalent, the car would have met with universal acclaim.

During a time when directors and engineers at Crewe were discussing plans to replace the Silver Cloud and S-Series Bentley, there was certainly provision for a Bentley model, intended to be a totally different car to the Rolls-Royce that was then proposed. The period was the early to mid-1950s, when Britain was experiencing a spell of austerity following World War 2. The cost, in terms of finance and resources, of developing a new car (and one that incorporated - for Rolls-Royce - such new technology),

Pictured in 2002, this Silver Shadow II exudes elegance and successfully disguises the fact that it is twenty five years old. (Author's collection)

was enormous, especially for a limited volume manufacturer.

The only practical course was to combine development and market a single design as two models; one carrying the prestigious Rolls-Royce radiator adorned with the Spirit of Ecstasy, the other the famous Bentley wings once so familiar at Le Mans. In retrospect, we can be thankful that the Bentley marque, which Rolls-Royce acquired in 1931, was not allowed to fall into obscurity.

The decline of Bentley sales during the Silver Shadow era has often been the subject of acrimonious debate. History has shown that the sixties and seventies were decades of growing prosperity, a time when ownership of a Rolls-Royce, in preference to all other luxury cars, was more desirable and more affordable.

The Silver Shadow and Bentley T introduced new design and build techniques which allowed Rolls-Royce to build cars in relatively large numbers. Production figures show that, following the start of car production at Crewe in 1946, fewer than 24,300 cars had left the factory, including coachbuilt and Phantom models, by the time the Silver Shadow and T-Series made their debut. In contrast, the Silver Shadow and Bentley T range of models accounted for more than 40,550 vehicles.

The decision to revolutionise the production process at Crewe resulted in substantial profits for Rolls-Royce, and throughout this transformation, thankfully, the foundation upon which the company built its reputation was never undermined.

Only now, when reviewing the four decades which have elapsed since the unveiling of the Silver Shadow,

can it be appreciated just how big a technical leap the company took. After years of building and designing bespoke motorcars, Rolls-Royce was faced with a formidable challenge: accept modern engineering methods, build in large numbers - or die ...

Luckily for Rolls-Royce, the company was rich in expertise and foresight and its personnel - people like Dr Llewellyn Smith, Ray Dorey, Harry Grylls, and John Blatchley - were not afraid of change. That the Silver Shadow and Bentley T appear as fresh today as they did in 1965 is tribute to John Blatchley's prudence and skilful styling, making the cars timeless classics. It was this same attitude and approach that carried the company through a turbulent era when many time-honoured traditions were consigned to history, and the foundation of what had become a national institution was badly shaken.

This book is not just about the cars produced over a fifteen year period from the mid-sixties to 1980, and beyond, but also the company - and the people in it - that was the very bedrock of British industry. Tradition is an intrinsic part of Rolls-Royce, and to examine the Silver Shadow and Bentley T in detail it has been necessary to burrow back in time and talk to those people who conceived the cars, those who styled them, modelled the prototypes, designed, engineered, built, and tested the definitive vehicles.

Well in excess of 36,000 Silver Shadow and T-Series cars were produced; with Cornice and Camargue derivatives the figure swells to 40,556. Happily, a large number of examples have survived worldwide, due not

only to excellent design and quality of manufacture, but also the care and attention of their owners, who appreciate driving such fine machinery. It is nearly a quarter of a century since the last Silver Shadow was built, and almost a decade since the Corniche and Bentley Continental derivatives disappeared from the company's catalogue; a tribute indeed to the cars' original design and engineering.

Silver Shadows and Bentley Ts enjoy an enthusiastic following among marque devotees, and sought-after by those motorists seeking an affordable classic car, who often, to their pleasure, discover a whole new meaning to motorcar ownership.

Writing this book has been a uniquely pleasurable experience, as it has brought me into contact with the very people responsible for the Silver Shadow and Bentley T. It is through my researches, and since, that I have made many friendships, all because of motorcars - and very good ones at that.

Malcolm Bobbitt
Cumbria
England

Author's note

Throughout the text, individual names appear in italics, e.g. Harry Grylls (*Gry*). This practice was very much part of the established tradition within Rolls-Royce and I have used it for this reason. Rolls-Royce's factory at Crewe is referred to as being in Pym's or Pyms Lane, depending at which end of the road one views the street name. In the interest of consistency I have used Pyms Lane, the most recently preferred spelling. The name of the coachbuilding facility within Rolls-Royce has changed over the years from H. J. Mulliner, Park Ward to Mulliner, Park Ward, and then Mulliner Park Ward. More recently the facility has been referred to simply as MPW, which, again in the interest of consistency, I have used. Now that Volkswagen owns Bentley, the coachbuilding facility is known as Mulliners.

Contents

1

The best car
in the world

There was no doubt what the main attraction was at the 1965 London Motor Show at Earls Court: lamps high above the array of gleaming cars seemed to shine on two stands in particular - Rolls-Royce and Bentley - where a constant stream of visitors gazed in curiosity and pride at the models making their first British appearance.

A new Rolls-Royce or Bentley model has always been something of a sensation, and the Silver Shadow and T-Series were no exception.

The Silver Shadow was unveiled at the Paris Motor Show in the autumn of 1965, and had its British debut at the London Motor Show a couple of weeks later, where this picture was taken. The Silver Shadow and T Series were the first Rolls-Royce and Bentley models to have unitary construction, and Rolls-Royce took the unusual step of displaying the car without doors in order to show the build structure. (Courtesy Rolls-Royce Motor Cars Ltd.)

The two cars had already enjoyed an enthusiastic reception at their European debut two weeks earlier at the Paris Salon, which opened on Thursday 7th October and continued until Sunday 17th October. It was now the turn of British motorists to see for themselves the latest models to earn the reputation of "best in the world."

There was some doubt whether the Silver Shadow and T-Series cars would be prepared in time for the Paris Motor Show, especially as activity was already frenetic in order to produce the cars in time for the British launch. There's evidence that some commentators considered that the cars on show in Paris might not have been driveable, as the bonnets were kept firmly locked and rumour had it that the cars were without engines; hardly likely, considering that the models on show had been demonstrated to Rolls-Royce and Bentley agents at Crewe on 30th September and 1st October.

Whereas some manufacturers might have seized the unveiling of a new model as a chance to introduce a little *razzmatazz*, Rolls-Royce - with customary sophistication - resisted the temptation. *The Autocar* described the appearance of a new Rolls-Royce or Bentley as 'the event of a decade' and this was especially so with the Silver Shadow and T-Series, which the magazine acknowledged as by far the most advanced and intricate cars the company had so far produced.

The cars from Crewe were certainly revolutionary; Rolls-Royce claimed them as the most radical new cars in 59 years. The specification was impressive and included monocoque - integrally chassied - construction, all-round disc braking, independent front and rear suspension with hydraulic self-levelling, and much more. The resultant design was a car more compact in size, lower and shorter than previous models, but losing nothing in the way of interior space and comfort.

Rolls-Royce and Bentley cars retained their own identities at Earls Court and were featured on separate stands. Stand 112 was graced by three Silver Shadows: one was finished in Regal Red and another in Dawn Blue, whilst the third was presented in Shell Grey. In spectacular contrast to the new model, and virtually dwarfing it, was displayed the majestic Phantom V Limousine which, like all Rolls-Royces and Bentleys, was built to special order. Unlike its predecessor, the Phantom IV, of which all 18 models built had been reserved exclusively for royalty and heads of state, the Phantom V was available for general purchase; in total, 516 examples were produced.

Bentley - a marque established by W. O. Bentley in 1919 - cars adorned stand 141. Famous for its motor racing successes at Brooklands, as well as five-times winner at Le Mans between 1924 and 1930, Bentley was acquired by Rolls-Royce in 1931, after which the cars bearing the winged B emblem acquired the accolade 'The Silent Sports Car.' Two elegant T-Series, one in Caribbean Blue and another in a striking two-tone colour scheme of Sage Green over Smoke Grey, represented the marque, along with two special-bodied S3 Continentals by Mulliner, Park Ward (by this time absorbed by Rolls-Royce as a subsidiary company and referred to simply as MPW). Although the T-Series Bentley superseded the S-Series cars, the Continental version was still listed as a special order, and the two vehicles - one a dashing white convertible with scarlet leather upholstery, and the other a Flying Spur, finished in Shell Grey and Blue - appeared quite generous in proportion to the new model.

It could not be missed, however, that, as separate marques, Rolls-Royce and Bentley had gradually grown closer together and had been sharing designs. This was even more apparent with the new generation cars, and the T-Series Bentley - as noted in the pages of *Motor* and *Autocar* - had become, essentially, a badge-engineered version of the Silver Shadow. The price difference between the two cars was so slight as to be non-existent, and the future of the Bentley version seemed less secure than that of the Rolls-Royce. To many, an additional £60 to acquire the prestigious Rolls-Royce badge would have seemed a bargain, and there was a danger that, due to Rolls-Royce-preferred sales, the Bentley marque would become extinct.

Whilst many would recognise and appreciate the Bentley emblem for its associations with motorsport traditions, it was the famous Spirit of Ecstasy mascot designed for Rolls-Royce by Charles Sykes in 1911 that commanded the most respect for British engineering at its best. Not only had Rolls-Royce become synonymous with motoring excellence, but the company's aero engines now powered some of the world's best-known aircraft, including the D. H. Comet, the first jet airliner.

A late model R-Type Continental, chassis number BC51D, in 2003. It was delivered to its first owner in February 1955. (Author's collection)

Although the Silver Shadow and Bentley T-Series had almost identical styling features, the cars nevertheless retained their own distinctive radiator shells. The difference in price between the two was £60.00. (Courtesy Rolls-Royce Motor Cars Ltd.)

BC51D (registration PXM 926) as seen several years ago at a Bentley Drivers Club event. The car in the foreground is the R-Type Continental prototype model, universally known as Olga due to its registration number OLG 490. (Courtesy National Motor Museum)

Rolls-Royce and Bentley motor cars were synonymous with engineering excellence. The company's aero engines powered the world's first jet airliner, the De Havilland Comet, seen here with a Bentley R-Type Continental. (Courtesy Rolls-Royce Motor Cars Ltd.)

Those who gazed in awe at the new Rolls-Royce and Bentley cars at the 1965 London Motor Show could be forgiven for their amazement; the beloved Silver Cloud, ten years old and carrying with grace its majestic razor-edge styled coachwork, was no more and the new car was, for Rolls-Royce, a totally new concept in design. The Silver Shadow was sleek, its coachwork smooth, and there was a large glass area. More than anything else, it exuded a degree of dignity and sophistication that could only be had with a Rolls-Royce.

The ten year old Bentley S-Series and Rolls-Royce Silver Cloud design was not without its critics within the motor industry. For long enough harsh words had been uttered about the cars' handling and, if the Crewe factory's design team was affected by such criticism, it was not shown publicly, such was the team's loyalty to and pride in the company and cars it produced. Instead, the design team worked diligently to produce a car that made full use of the latest technology available to the motor industry.

The Silver Shadow and T-Series cars were the first Rolls-Royce and Bentley models to use a chassisless construction. This was sensational enough, and yet the cars also had all-round disc-braking, which ensured better than adequate stopping power, and a radical suspension system that gave the most comfort for driver and passengers. The cars were seen as an important departure from traditional production methods, a brave move which coupled advancing technology with the need to be more accessible to a wider and increasingly more discerning market.

Criticism of the Silver Cloud and S-Series cars was replaced by an enthusiastic, if perhaps slightly cautious, reception for the new generation models. Some enthusiasts were more than a little reluctant to accept the company's new direction, and saw it as a departure from a tradition steeped in history. The decision to proceed with a radically different design of car was not taken lightly but, ultimately, it was survival in a competitive market which was the deciding factor.

Whilst it might appear that traditional coachbuilding techniques had been discarded in favour of volume production methods, the change to unitary construction was no more than a process of evolution. Some aspects of Rolls-Royce manufacture could, understandably, never change. The company's legendary attention to detail and refinement continued as always, and both Rolls-Royce and Bentley cars retained that very special quality which was second to none, of which the marques were justifiably proud. Ironically, the styling of the Silver Shadow allowed a return to traditional values in respect of the famous Rolls-Royce radiator: the lower profile of the car meant that radiator height could revert to the proportions established during the pre-First World War era.

The Silver Shadow was Rolls-Royce's most radical car in over 50 years. Its chassisless construction meant that external dimensions could be reduced without compromising interior space or comfort. Note the difference in radiator size between the Silver Shadow on the left, and the Silver Cloud. Owner R. Allwright stands between the two cars.
(Courtesy Rolls-Royce Enthusiasts' Club)

The postwar period

The changes to Rolls-Royce manufacturing methods which resulted, ultimately, in the Silver Shadow and T-Series cars was the culmination of many years' painstaking development. The programme can be traced to the period immediately prior to the outbreak of the Second World War, and it's understandable that the decisions taken at that time were considered quite extreme. This was a period when automobile design was undergoing serious change; streamlining was becoming popular, and there was a move towards producing small and economical family cars, a good example of which is the Volkswagen concept and Ferdinand Porsche's endeavours to produce a car for the people. When the political situation in Europe deteriorated and the likelihood of war became very real, Rolls-Royce - along with other manufacturers such as Rover and Austin - was forced to alter its role dramatically. Car production was put aside and manufacturing concentrated on the war effort.

Rolls-Royce's factory at Crewe had been constructed as part of the

At one time all Rolls-Royce and Bentley cars were built with separate chassis. This is the chassis of a prewar Corniche, which is similar to the short-lived Bentley Mk V. The Corniche would have been displayed at the 1939 Motor Show, had the event not been cancelled, and the entire project was abandoned.
(Courtesy Rolls-Royce Motor Cars Ltd.)

Shadow Factory Scheme introduced in 1936 to produce aircraft components in preparation for war. Work began on the Pyms Lane site during the second half of 1938 and, within eleven months, the first Crewe-built Merlin was running. By the end of the war the plant had produced 26,000 Merlins of various marks, and 2000 Griffon engines. During the war years development of the site continued with the addition of machine and assembly shops and test rigs. Shadow Factories, which were often camouflaged for protection from aerial attacks and painted to look, from the air, like housing terraces, now provide an interesting area of industrial archeology. Incidentally, signs of the camouflage were still faintly visible in the early seventies. Once their wartime use was over many Shadow Factories were turned over to car building and, as with the Rover Company, which had adopted a Shadow Factory at Solihull as its car manufacturing plant, so Rolls-Royce concentrated motor production at Crewe.

Traditionally, Rolls-Royce made bespoke motor cars of the highest quality, which earned the accolade of best in the world. Whilst Rolls-Royce hand-crafted the chassis, bodies were prepared by the most famous coachbuilders who applied their exacting standards and degree of refinement. The cars were supplied to customers who demanded only the very best and graced some of the most influential motor houses around the world. The history of Rolls-Royce and Bentley as separate entities has been well documented. Rolls-Royce continually lived up to its formidable reputation. Bentley, prior to 1931 revered as one of the finest sports cars - to use W. O. Bentley's words: a fast car, a good car, the best in its class - lived up to its Silent Sports Car accolade. In 1931 Bentley was absorbed by Rolls-Royce in what, at the time, was a controversial acquisition. Napier, manufacturer of luxury cars between 1900 and 1924, and highly regarded for its aero and marine engines (especially the Lion engines used in connection with the Schneider Trophy air races), saw the chance to gain control of Bentley and re-establish itself in the motor industry as a producer of quality vehicles. Rolls-Royce considered that Napier's engineering prowess, coupled with Bentley's automobile experience, would pose a serious threat and out-bid Napier at the last moment.

The Second World War had a dramatic affect on Rolls-Royce as a company. Prewar, car output had never been huge and virtually half of all cars produced were exported. When car manufacturing resumed in 1946, there was a potentially huge market for motor cars, but it was left to manufacturers of the popular makes to meet that demand. Even though the cars produced were, essentially, of prewar design with only a minor face-lift, there seemed no shortage of buyers except for luxury cars. With home sales deeply depressed in this market, it was to export sales that Rolls-Royce turned its attention.

Decisions taken when reviewing some of Rolls-Royce's manufacturing methods were the result of plans drawn up at the end of the 1930s by W. A. Robotham (Rm) who, at the time, was head of chassis design. Having joined Rolls-Royce as an apprentice in 1919, Robotham was appointed to the company's experimental department in 1923 and soon made a name for himself working with, and testing, chassis. His brief called for standardisation of designs which would have the consequence of lowering production costs without any loss of build quality. Some of the ideas that Robotham suggested were far-reaching and, had they been allowed to fully materialise, might have drastically affected the whole structure of the company. In 'popularising' the Rolls-Royce and Bentley marques to the extent that he had foreseen, the demise of the company as it was, and as it is now, might have been a distinct possibility. According to John Blatchley, who was responsible for the Silver Shadow's styling, Robotham was keen to forge a relationship with the Rover company. Any such plan, of course, did not materialise.

Demonstrating the company's willingness to consider new ideas, Rolls-Royce experimented with the design of a small car known as the 'Myth,' a vehicle of diminutive proportions - by Rolls-Royce standards - which weighed 22 hundredweight (1118kg) and was equipped with an engine of just 1497cc. Decidedly problematic, the prototype car was continually beset by overheating problems and was dismantled after just 407 miles (651km) had been completed.

Standardisation of chassis design and the introduction of component interchangeability was a realistic venture first seen on the Bentley Mk V, a very short-lived model which was abandoned due to the outbreak of war and after only 11 cars had been produced. The series was not revived when, postwar, production was resumed.

The Mk V Bentley was the first car to receive a standardised chassis design. Pictured here in London's Richmond Park is one of only 11 cars built. (Courtesy Rolls-Royce Motor Cars Ltd.)

For bespoke motor cars such as the Rolls-Royce and Bentley, it might have seemed somewhat unnecessary to introduce standardisation, especially when annual output of vehicles amounted to around only 1000 cars. It was, however, low volume production which demanded standardisation: with fewer than 100 cars a month being built it was likely that as many as three chassis designs, all quite different, would be needed.

A rare Bentley MK V in splendid condition photographed at an enthusiasts' rally in Yorkshire during 2002. (Author's collection)

W. A. Robotham foresaw that the bespoke bodywork crafted by leading coachbuilders, so usually associated with Rolls-Royce and Bentley, would, eventually, become a practice of the past and that the company would either produce its own bodies or buy in from a volume supplier. It was accepted that such a change of direction would have to be a gradual process, and the first steps towards standardisation went almost unnoticed.

Rolls-Royce selected a number of coachbuilders who could produce bodies specifically for standard chassis designs, and it was to these that customers were directed. This presented little problem, especially as the customer had been assured that the coachwork was specifically approved by Rolls-Royce and Bentley. These companies included James Young of Bromley, Park Ward of Willesden and H. J. Mulliner of Turnham Green, Chiswick. The association between Rolls-Royce and Park Ward developed to such an extent that the latter company was absorbed by Rolls-Royce in 1939. H. J. Mulliner was taken over by Rolls-Royce in 1959 and, in 1961, the two coachbuilding concerns of Park Ward and H. J. Mulliner were merged and became known as H. J. Mulliner,

After the war, Rolls-Royce resumed car production with the Bentley Mk VI. Here, a Park Ward convertible is given its final inspection at the coachbuilder's Willesden factory. (Courtesy Rolls-Royce Motor Cars Ltd.)

Park Ward Ltd. The close association with Rolls-Royce did mean that 'in-house' coachbuilding methods of the highest quality could be maintained. James Young, however, remained as a separate company and continued to supply bodies for Rolls-Royce and Bentley cars from its Bromley premises.

After the war ended the Bentley Mk VI heralded the return of car production at Rolls-Royce. The detail and design of the car was not dissimilar to that of the Mk V Bentley; the classic semi-razor-edge styling clearly having an influence on the postwar car. Standardisation, it seems, had arrived at Crewe ...

Even though car production ceased during the war years, development and research on W. A. Robotham's ideas nevertheless continued. Rolls-Royce played an important role in the war effort, and it was fortunate that the company had the means to also carry on with experimental work and produce some prototype vehicles. The Rover company at Solihull was in a similar situation and Maurice Wilks was able to try out a number of particular designs on 'company business and time.'

Standard steel bodies

Convinced that the future lay in a chassis design capable of accepting a standard body format, Rolls-Royce went shopping for the best quality product. The company it approached in January 1944 was Pressed Steel of Cowley, Oxford.

Pressed Steel, with premises opposite the Morris factory, provided bodyshells to much of Britain's mass-produced motor industry, and had the potential facilities to supply to Rolls-Royce.

Pressed Steel readily agreed to produce bodies to Rolls-Royce's own specification (the prestige was enough to secure the deal) and it was Ivan Evernden (*Ev*) and John Blatchley (*JPB*) who undertook the styling. While Evernden produced the

Of the 5201 Bentley Mk VIs built, 4202 carried Pressed Steel coachwork. Produced from 1946 to 1952, the car illustrated is a later version, evident by the design of the side lamp nacelles and the pleated seats.
(Courtesy Rolls-Royce Motor Cars Ltd.)

basic engineering principles, it was Blatchley who took responsibility for the detailed design.

H. Ivan F. Evernden's career with Rolls-Royce and its design department began when, as a young man, he joined the company in 1916. Six years later in 1922, he found himself a protégé of Sir Henry Royce when he was appointed to the design team, at that time based at West Wittering on the south coast of England. Extremely conscientious by nature, Ivan Evernden built a reputation for precision (amongst the cars he helped design was the R-Type Bentley Continental, one of the all-time great sporting cars). Following his retirement in 1961 he continued for a period of time in a consultantcy capacity, and even, in a moment of meditation, designed his own headstone in the shape of a Rolls-Royce radiator shell!

John Blatchley was no stranger to Rolls-Royce either as, prior to the Second World War, he had worked for J. Gurney Nutting, coachbuilder of considerable repute. The company,

The driving force at Rolls-Royce: this photograph was taken in the early fifties at a Clan Foundry reunion dinner. Seated from left to right are: W. Robotham, Harry Grylls, John Reid (chief designer at Clan Foundry), and John Blatchley.
(Courtesy John Blatchley)

Chief Stylist John Blatchley at work styling a wax model of the Phantom V Limousine. (John Blatchley)

established since 1919, had been building bodies on Rolls-Royce chassis since 1925. Generally favoured by Rolls-Royce in its standardisation programme, Gurney Nutting was acquired by Jack Barclay Ltd. in 1945. Whilst John Blatchley's design followed the fashion of the immediate prewar period, it also incorporated the latest styling ideas, which were considered to be in keeping with the new Rolls-Royce and Bentley models.

John Blatchley's early career is of immense interest. As a boy he suffered from rheumatic fever and did not have a proper schooling. He was educated at home by a private tutor, and his thoughts were often not on his studies but motor cars. His early drawings, sketched before he had reached his teens, were clearly advanced and show some very elegant coachwork styling. At the age of 18, John's father thought it appropriate for him to go to Cambridge University and, after some intensive tuition, he was ready to sit the entrance examination. The young Blatchley was less keen on an academic career, however, and, after sitting at a desk for 20 minutes (in which time he had not written a word), he put away his pen and left the examination room.

Instead of going to university, John enrolled at the polytechnic for motor body building, a course which lasted for 18 months. A friend of his worked for Gurney Nutting and it was through him that John was able to get a job. Assigned to Gurney Nutting's chief stylist, A. F. McNeil, John Blatchley's talents were soon recognised and

some of his first styling exercises were based upon Duesenberg and Lagonda chassis for an Indian Maharaja. At the age of 24 he was promoted to take over from McNeil on his retirement.

In 1944 or 1945, John sought a position with Rolls-Royce and was offered a job in the company's aero engine division. He disliked designing aero engine cowlings, much preferring to work with motor cars, and eventually went to see W. Robotham at the car division. Robotham welcomed him with open arms and Blatchley soon found himself working alongside Ivan Evernden.

One of John Blatchley's first assignments was to prepare some drawings for the proposed 'Junior' Bentley and a small Rolls-Royce, the Silver Ripple; these designs did not materialise but John's watercolour sketches of these cars are a delight. He was then given the task of tidying up the design of the Mk VI Bentley which, at that time, was less than pretty. John restyled it so that the door hinges were concealed. He was then responsible for the R-Type Bentley and later generation Rolls-Royce and Bentley models.

A new era began for Rolls-Royce in spring 1946 when the company announced its first postwar models: the Bentley Mk VI and the Silver Wraith. This was something of a frustrating period as components

and materials were still in short supply after the war and production severely affected. As a result, delivery of cars did not commence until late in the year. Decisions made prewar in respect of standardisation meant that the two cars had certain similarities, although the Bentley was some 7 inches (178mm) shorter. Whilst the Bentley was built at Crewe as a complete car, the Silver Wraith was constructed more in the Rolls-Royce tradition with the chassis being made to accept custom-built coachwork. It was three years later, in 1949, that greater standardisation was achieved when Rolls-Royce announced the Silver Dawn, which shared both the chassis and dimensions of the Bentley Mk VI. Whereas the Silver Wraith had been designed to accept a coachbuilt body the Silver Dawn was specifically intended to carry standardised steel coachwork.

The difficulties experienced during early postwar production were not unique to Rolls-Royce. All British manufacturers were at the mercy of a motor industry starved of raw materials, which, even when available, were often of indifferent quality. The

government of the day ordered a massive drive to earn much needed foreign currency and priority was given to export sales. As a builder of luxury cars Rolls-Royce's market was extremely precarious. Major business came not so much from home sales but the more lucrative markets abroad. In order to build cars with specialist coachbuilt bodies, Rolls-Royce would have had to continue to endure very low production figures, unacceptable if the company was to stay in business. Likewise, it would have been impossible for specialist coachbuilders, which were usually small businesses, to invest in huge outlay in order to raise production levels. Of the relatively few coachbuilding specialists only Park Ward was able to produce a standardised body. Even so, it was still only possible to achieve a maximum production figure of 10 bodies a week.

Adoption of standard steel bodies did, as can be appreciated, draw some criticism and traditionalists feared that the unique appeal of the bespoke Bentley or Rolls-Royce might be lost forever. Conversely, the company's policy also attracted a new clientele

The first postwar Rolls-Royce specifically designed to carry a standard steel body was the Silver Dawn, which, apart from the radiator shell, minor mechanical differences, facia layout and badging, was identical to the Bentley Mk VI. (Courtesy Rolls-Royce Motor Cars Ltd.)

and it was evident that, ultimately, the design of the standard steel saloon was as elegant as its forebears and the finish just as 'superior.' For Rolls-Royce, the change to utilising bought-in bodies meant the establishment of a completely new industry. This enabled the company to finish the bodyshells delivered from Pressed Steel to acceptable Rolls-Royce standards, and to erect production areas which accommodated the processes necessary to fit out and trim the cars. For the committed traditionalist, however, which standardisation could never satisfy, it was still possible to specify a custom-built version of either car, prepared by one of a number of firms to include Hooper, James

When the R-Type Bentley superseded the MkVI, the re-styled Silver Dawn retained its appellation. Note on this Rolls-Royce the styling differences from the B-C posts rearward, including the larger boot which was hinged at the top. The occasion is the R-REC Northern Rally, held in August every year at Harewood House, near Leeds. (Author's collection)

The Silver Cloud and its Bentley equivalent, the S-Series, were introduced in 1955, and became popular abroad, especially in America. Here, a Bentley SI is being exported and is carefully loaded aboard the SS Brandager. (Courtesy Rolls-Royce Motor Cars Ltd)

Young, Freestone and Webb, MPW, J. Gurney Nutting, and Abbott of Farnham. Continental coachbuilders were also able to offer their designs for Rolls-Royce and Bentley, and amongst the more favoured were Franay, Pininfarina, and Graber.

America loved the Silver Cloud and this first series car makes a handsome companion to a Piedmont turboprop airliner. The aircraft appears to be a Fokker F27, built under licence by Fairchild, which makes it an FH227. The significance of the photo is that the aircraft was powered by Rolls-Royce Dart engines. (Courtesy Rolls-Royce Motor Cars Ltd.)

The Mk VI Bentley and Rolls-Royce Silver Dawn evolved into a new generation of models with deliveries beginning in June 1952. The R-Type Bentley superseded the Mk VI but the Silver Dawn name was retained for the new Rolls-Royce. Both cars shared modifications and these included a larger boot and the option of an automatic gearbox, the latter initially supplied for export models only. There were some important chassis modifications which accounted for the enlarged bodywork; therefore the springs were made both longer and wider.

Possibly one of the most elegant, charismatic and desirable of all postwar Bentleys was the R-Type Continental, the performance and looks of which successfully revived the marque's sporting tradition. Only 208 examples of this superlative car were built and, fortunately, a healthy number have survived.

The Silver Dawn and its Bentley equivalent, both with ancestry traceable to the immediate prewar era, remained in production until the early part of 1955 when two new models were unveiled, the Rolls-Royce Silver Cloud and the S-Series Bentley. Matters concerning future new models cannot be hurried at Rolls-Royce and, as the new cars were being acclaimed, in the design department attention had already turned to a successor for launch a decade ahead.

Commendation for the Silver Cloud came particularly from America where it enjoyed considerable popularity. The Bentley marque, sadly, never achieved the same recognition from that side of the Atlantic, even though both cars shared an almost identical profile, apart from the radiator shell

Bentley S and Silver Cloud in front of the main extrance of the Rolls-Royce factory in Pyms Lane, Crewe. The styling differences between the two are evident. (Courtesy Rolls-Royce Motor Cars Ltd.)

and bonnet line. There was, however, a significant detail difference between the two cars: the bonnets were not interchangeable due to the shoulder radius which, on the Silver Cloud, was sharper than that of the Bentley.

John Blatchley was responsible for the styling of both cars, with their reputation for being particularly handsome. Some enthusiasts would argue that the Bentley was more aesthetically pleasing than the Silver Cloud, and the S-Series was especially sought-after in Britain. This may be why more Bentleys were sold, despite the Silver Cloud's prestigious radiator and mascot.

As was to be expected, the finish and trim on both cars was exceptional and, in standard steel form, their elegance could hardly be bettered. Specialist coachbuilders, however, did offer some exotic designs and Freestone and Webb produced a magnificent two-door, fixed-head coupé, whilst MPW produced some outstanding convertibles, a feature often favoured by American customers.

In August 1959, some four-and-a-half years after launch, the Silver Cloud and S-Series Bentley gained a significant increase in power with an all-new engine that gave 25 per cent more output. The Silver Cloud II and

The experimental department at Crewe was constantly developing new ideas. Look carefully at the huge tail fins fitted to this S-Series Bentley, which were devised to test for crosswind stability. (Courtesy Rolls-Royce Motor Cars Ltd.)

S2 - the earlier series Bentley now automatically became known as the S1 - achieved extra power from a light alloy V8 engine which replaced the straight 6-cylinder F-Head unit with its overhead inlet and side exhaust valve configuration. The superseded engine had been introduced for postwar cars but the principle had first been used on Rolls-Royce cars in 1904. Plans for the new aluminium V8 were drawn up immediately after the war and development started in 1947.

Exterior styling of the Silver Cloud II and S2 may have remained virtually identical to the first series cars, but interior trim was modified to include facia layout, and a driving position revised in response to the cars' top speed of over 115mph (184kph) and slightly more athletic acceleration. As a Grand Tourer the S2 Bentley Continental boasted unequalled elegance; feature of these cars was the reshaped bonnet which enhanced the car's sporting appearance.

Throughout the forties and fifties, the Silver Wraith was still a true bespoke coachbuilt Rolls-Royce. Whilst the model shared a number of features with the original 1946 car, the new V8 engine eventually led to the vehicle's demise in 1959 in favour of the Phantom V, a variant based upon the Silver Cloud II chassis which offered truly exceptional coachwork styling.

The final phase in Silver Cloud and S-Series model development was the introduction of the Silver Cloud III and Bentley S3 towards the end of 1962. These cars are instantly recognisable by impressive frontal styling which incorporates a twin headlamp system, a styling feature popular at the time and found on a number of cars. Styling differences went a lot deeper than the headlamps, though: front wings were restyled and the radiator profile lowered, along with the bonnet line; combined side lamps and indicators were fitted, as were redesigned front overriders. The interior of the cars also received a face-lift and the specification included separate front seats. Revised mechanical specifications included

Buckingham Palace makes a fine backdrop for this Silver Cloud II on what was a warm summer's day. (Courtesy Rolls-Royce Motor Cars Ltd.)

The S2 was the Bentley equivalent of the Silver Cloud II, and this particular car completes what is quintessentially an English scene. (Courtesy Rolls-Royce Motor Cars Ltd.)

S-Series Bentleys enjoy a particular following; this example of an S1 is ahead of a Silver Cloud of similar vintage. (Author's collection)

Experiments were carried out to find a suitable four-headlamp system for the Silver Cloud and S-Series cars. In this photograph, taken in the styling department, several ideas are being tried in plasticine. Note the differences between the left hand wing line and twin headlamps and the right hand wing, as well as the differing styles of indicator lenses. In the background is stylist Martin Bourne. (Courtesy John Blatchley)

modified power steering and an increase in performance. Interestingly, a Silver Cloud IV and Bentley S4 had been envisaged, and would have been equipped with disc brakes and independent rear suspension. This car did not materialise due to the advanced development of the Silver

The concept of the Silver Shadow was the work of Harry Grylls (without whom it almost certainly would not have existed), here shown standing between Captain Vautier (left), and John Blatchley. The date of the photograph is not known (possibly early 1950s), but there is certainly some interest in the Silver Ghost. (Courtesy Martin Bourne)

Twin headlamps were a feature of the final Silver Cloud series and S-Series Bentleys. The styling treatment is very evident on this Silver Cloud III standing outside the main entrance of the Pyms Lane factory. (Courtesy Rolls-Royce Motor Cars Ltd.)

Shadow which did incorporate these features.

A Shadow on the drawing board

Until the introduction of the Silver Shadow and Bentley T-Series, it was almost inconceivable that cars of such revered marques could be built without a separate chassis. Hardly a new innovation, monocoque construction - which involved building the chassis and body together as a complete unit - was more usually associated with the mass production methods of the more popular type of car. Builders of specialist and luxury cars were normally expected to use what were considered more traditional manufacturing methods.

In designing the new cars' specification, the decision to adopt monocoque construction was taken at an early stage, even before the Silver Cloud had been launched. For traditionalists the Silver Cloud and Bentley S-Series retain the importance of being the last standard production cars from Crewe to utilise a separate chassis, apart from the few Phantom models built to special order. Rolls-Royce's plans were quite specific: the new car had to comply with future trends of an auto industry catering for an ever-increasingly car-conscious society. As traffic volume increased, the design of the motor car would change to meet the need for smaller exterior

dimensions without sacrificing interior space and comfort. If the car was to be shorter in length and width than the Silver Cloud, but roomier inside and with greater luggage capacity, Rolls-Royce would have to accept that a monocoque construction was the only way to do this.

The move towards standardised chassis design, and adoption of standard steel saloon bodies, meant it was a matter of natural evolution for Rolls-Royce to consider integral, or unitary, construction for the new models. This was especially relevant, bearing in mind it was intended that the cars would lead production throughout the second half of the sixties, span a whole decade and more into the eighties. Development costs, which included tooling-up for the new car, were acknowledged to be exceptionally high, and it was therefore expected that the cars would enjoy a long production run. The change to standard steel bodies had proved entirely successful with previous models, and it was anticipated the new generation of cars would receive an enthusiastic reception, especially from America which was seen as possibly the most important export market. The American motor industry had been almost entirely given over to building cars in the unitary style and by the mid-fifties Europe was belatedly following in America's footsteps.

Even if he did not need convincing about unitary construction methods, Ivan Evernden produced, shortly after a visit to Detroit in 1955, an important report on why a monocoque design should be adopted by Rolls-Royce. It was from America that the integral chassis and body had originated in the late 1920s when the Budd Organisation had shown some exciting prototypes to the motor industry. Amongst the manufacturers who took up Budd's ideas was Lancia in Italy, as well as the French manufacturer, André Citroën. It was the latter's celebrated Traction Avant which astonished the motoring world in 1934 with its sleek design. Twenty one years later the same company produced another remarkable car, the DS19 which, together with unitary construction, featured an advanced hydraulic system that controlled not only braking, transmission and steering but also suspension.

First indications of Rolls-Royce's commitment to producing a monocoque-chassied car can be traced to February 1954 when the project of developing such a vehicle was given the code name Tibet. The design engineers at Crewe were already busy perfecting the Siam project, which was the development of the Rolls-Royce Silver Cloud and S-Series Bentley. Only after the launch of the cars had it been possible - apart from the vaguest of outlines - to give proper thought to the proposed car. It was not until 1958, by which time the Silver Cloud and Bentley S-Series had been in full production for three years, that serious consideration was given to the new Rolls-Royce, and the Tibet programme was expanded to include a Bentley version, allocated the code

An historic photograph, the only picture of the members of the Crewe design department. Taken in August 1956 when plans were afoot for the Silver Shadow, the occasion marks the retirement of chief designer, Bill Hardy. From left to right (front row): Agnes, Muriel and Thelma (surnames unknown); Harold Peak; Geo. King; Frank Tarlton; Vivian Stanbury; Bill Hardy; Reg Davies; Jack Phillips; Bert Jeal; Ralph Lever; Mavis Bonsall; Cecily Jenner; Margaret Jones. (Second row): Ted Holland; Reg Spencer; Harry Bamford; Frank Holt; Les Robinson; Eric Langley; Fritz Feller; Bill Allen; Horace Kirby; Eric Howarth; Norman Webster; Geo. Clarke; Harry Taylor; Charlie Monk; Geo. Cooper. (Third row): Cliff Evans; Arthur Horsnall; Reg Swinburne; Jim Burnham; Alan Lord; Jim Edwards; Ron Biggins; Bob Hill; Bill Condliffe; Arnold Turnaley; John Everett; Alan Tomlinson; John Gorman; Peter Pryke; Ralph Allcock. (Fourth row): Ken Trinder; Geo. Tearle; Ernie Knibbs; Brian Carpenter; Alan Jobson; Aubrey Scragg; Gordon Linney; David Mason; Martin Bourne. (Courtesy Martin Bourne)

name Burma. Originally the project was limited to a Rolls-Royce badged car but the huge costs involved encouraged senior management to reconsider their decision. By marketing the Bentley (at the time intended as an altogether smaller vehicle), an opportunity arose to widen the models' appeal. Other variants were also considered and these were given the equally exotic code names Korea, Java, Bengal, Tonga and Rangoon. Development of these projects came about as a result of an odd collaboration between Rolls-Royce and the British Motor Corporation (BMC). Interest in a sports car (again, in collaboration with BMC), which was designed to rekindle the Bentley marque's sporting heritage, brought about a brief interlude with an unlikely model which, had it been developed, would have been known as the Alpha. This, and other experimental cars, are dealt with in more detail later.

Curious code names have typically been allocated to Rolls-Royce experimental projects; throughout much of the early postwar period they were far-eastern countries. Harry Grylls (*Gry*), the car division's engineering director during this period, chose the names, which do not appear to have any particular significance other than to suggest he was a romantic with a sense of humour! Harry Grylls was appointed chief engineer in 1951; he had joined the company 21 years before, in 1930, when aged 21. He was well accustomed to Rolls-Royces, his father having bought one of the first cars the company produced. Always a keen driver, Harry Grylls ensured he regularly tried for himself the company's experimental cars, at every stage of development, and often, after 1953, at Oulton Park. He also made sure he knew what other manufacturers were planning and tried out their cars whenever he could.

Although the Tibet project had been on the minds of Harry Grylls and Ivan Evernden for some time, the first indication the design team had of the new car coincided with the launch of the Silver Cloud. Bill Allen (*JPB/Aln*),

who joined Rolls-Royce as a stylist on August Bank Holiday Monday, 1935, remembers Harry Grylls calling the department together and, in a stunned but excited atmosphere, telling everybody the news that the Silver Cloud's eventual replacement would be an altogether radical new car.

John Blatchley, who was chief stylist under Ivan Evernden, was very enthusiastic at the prospect of designing such a car, even to the extent of losing sleep over it. When asked whether styling the car around a monocoque shell worried him, John was emphatic that the concept allowed him greater freedom from the usual constraints that a separately chassied car imposed. Unitary construction, he added, provided the opportunity of lowering the passenger area to inside of the four wheelarches, so maintaining passenger comfort within a shorter frame.

As to the design of what was ultimately to become the Silver Shadow and T-Series Bentley, stylists such as Bill Allen and Martin Bourne

The code name of the project intended to replace the Silver Cloud was Tibet, and a full-size mock-up is shown here alongside its predecessors. On the left is the Silver Dawn, centre is the Silver Cloud, and Tibet is on the right. It's interesting to see how the designs progressed over the years and that Tibet, even in the early stages of development, is remarkably similar to the definitive Silver Shadow. (Courtesy Jock Knight)

were given a relatively free hand. It was appreciated that a monocoque car would not only be lower in profile than a separately chassied car, but that it could support full-width frontal styling. As well as being more compact, which was considered a necessary styling feature, it had actually been possible to achieve greater cabin space than on previous models. There

were parameters on which the styling team worked, such as a 126 inch (3200mm) wheelbase, which was 3 inches (76.2mm) greater than that of the Silver Cloud, and sub-frames front and rear to support engine, gearbox, rear axle and suspension. The wheelbase of Burma, incidentally, was 119.5 inches (3035mm), 3.5 inches (88.9mm) shorter than the Silver Cloud's. The suspension system was, from the outset, designed to be nothing other than standard, but it was the hydraulic self-levelling - utilised to provide an even keel under all road and load conditions - that made it different. Hydraulic self-levelling was considered a necessity not only because of the car's sheer size and weight, but also to appeal to the American market which was used to cars with extremely soft springing.

Stylist Martin Bourne scrapes away at the modelling clay on a scale model of Tibet II. Note the distance between the wheels and the door leading edge, shorter by 6.5 scale inches (165mm) on Burma and hence Silver Shadow, the shape of which is quite evident, even though there were many changes before the definitive form emerged. (Courtesy Martin Bourne)

28

John Blatchley, seen here on the right, was responsible for the styling of the Silver Shadow. In designing the car he had to come up with a style which would be acceptable for at least 10 years. On the left is Bill Allen with Martin Bourne in the centre. The date is 1969, the year that John Blatchley retired. (Courtesy Martin Bourne)

Two power units were originally proposed for the Silver Shadow: a 6-cylinder, 3990cc, in-line 'F' engine for the Burma project, and the 'L' 6230cc engine for Tibet. The latter was utilised for 'SY', the product which resulted from the merger of the two projects.

John Blatchley, as chief stylist, was ultimately responsible for the new car's definitive outline, and he it was who took the first steps to produce the shape. The body styling evolved firstly from a number of outline sketches and, once these had met with his approval, a model was crafted from wax. Supplied in large blocks, the wax had first to be cut into pieces and warmed gently in an oven before it could be used. It was difficult to control the heat of the oven, and it was something of a relief once the wax achieved the correct consistency and could be applied as a whole to the modelling table. The bulk of the model was a large, empty 1.5 inch (13mm) ply box, padded out by glued-on blocks of balsa wood. The final wax thickness was usually no more than about 0.37 inch (12mm) as it was very expensive.

The working surface of the table, which included a measuring bridge, consisted of a large panel of duralumin approximately 0.25 inch (6mm) thick that had a grid of 2.5 inches (63mm) squares - representing 10 inches (254mm) on the actual car - scribed upon it. The same method of measurement was also applied to the bridge in order to gauge correct vertical levels. The idea of the measuring table was to produce an accurate quarter-size scale model, which was usual in the early planning of a new car. As John Blatchley carefully and painstakingly scraped away at the wax block the design department watched as his styling theme emerged.

The stylists' modelling and measuring table had been devised by Bill Allen in 1951, before the design department was installed at Pyms Lane. The department at the time was situated at Clan Foundry, Belper, one of Rolls-Royce's many sites, and John Blatchley had just been appointed chief stylist with the immediate aim of producing a new standard saloon, the Silver Cloud.

Luckily, wax as a material is extremely forgiving and, when more was needed to fill any hollows or raise the surfaces of the model, it was easy to prepare and apply. Experiments were carried out creating a number of wax models which depicted different styling ideas. The only tools which would work the wax suitably were commercial paint scrapers, and it was by using these that the stylists became skilled craftsmen. Wax is highly vulnerable to changes in temperature and, after the Christmas holiday when the factory heating had been turned off, large cracks had appeared in the model John Blatchley had been working on. Fearing the worst, the stylists were relieved to see the cracks disappear as soon as the central heating was turned on and room temperature began to rise. While the stylists worked at sculpturing the body design, others in the department concentrated on the chassis layout, created the interior design and devised accessories such as bumpers and lamps.

The model was then drawn, quarter-scale, using thousands of spot dimensions from the bridge, and scissor-cut tracing paper and card templates, and the result passed to Bert Jeal, who was in charge of the Body Office, for scaling up to full-size.

Once formed, the fragile nature of the wax made the model susceptible to the most minor knocks and scratches. To prevent damage it was decided to use the example as a pattern for a mould which would allow a permanent model to be made from dental plaster. Although this proved a lot more durable than the wax, it was disadvantaged by being extremely heavy and cumbersome to move. By using fibreglass as an alternative to dental plaster, a satisfactory solution to the problem was eventually found, making presentation of styling proposals to directors and sales staff somewhat easier. Producing quarter-size models was also more cost-effective than embarking upon expensive full-

During his ninetieth birthday celebrations in summer 2003, John Blatchley discusses the styling features of a Derby-built Bentley sedanca coupé with Gurney Nutting coachwork (chassis number B166JD). John styled this particular car when he was chief stylist at Gurney Nutting, before he joined Rolls-Royce.
(Courtesy James Clough/Rolls-Royce Enthusiasts' Club)

size mock-ups before definitive styling had been accepted.

Looking at a scale model and visualising a full-size car was very difficult to do. Dr (*Doc*) Llewellyn-Smith (*LS*), Harry Grylls and Ivan Evernden could do this, and it was Evernden who spent his last few weeks before retirement designing and building an optical viewer which adjusted the perspective of the model to that of a full-sized car. It was only when 'democratic' styling committees came along, consisting of people from other departments, that full-size models were introduced to make visualisation easier.

No attempt was made, as some manufacturers had, to introduce 'see-through' quarter-scale models. The use of perspex for the windows, whilst providing an interesting three-dimensional aspect, would have made any alterations to the roof and glass areas extremely difficult to accomplish, especially as minor detail changes were constantly being tried out.

Considered just as important as external styling was the car's interior arrangement. Rolls-Royce's attention to detail and thoroughness meant that the most minor control or switch had to have the right feel about it, and would operate in a manner commensurate with the quality of the car.

Above all else there remained in the stylists' mind concern about what the customer would make of the design. Monocoque construction meant sacrificing many old ideals, such as a flat floor in the rear compartment and, for the first time, introduction of footwells for the rear passengers. The slab-sided coachwork might have been considered featureless at the time but eventually, of course, the styling became quite acceptable.

Once a design was approved, the quarter-scale drawings were supplied to the Body Design department where the drawings were made full-size. Eric Langley (*EAL*), second in command to departmental head, Bert Jeal (*HPJ*), remembers laying out the body full-size on to 15ft by 5ft (4572mm x 1524mm) sheets of pale green aluminium, marked out with a 10 inch (254mm) grid. These formed the master layouts from which the entire prototype car was constructed. The whole process of styling, designing and building a prototype car was naturally a time-consuming affair, taking approximately two years to complete.

Experiments begin

From the time the Tibet project was first mooted it was something like four-and-a-half years before an experimental car appeared in August 1958. Bearing the registration number

Tibet in the experimental garage at Crewe. Note the high-mounted indicators on the front and rear wings; clearly evident is the length of the wheelbase, especially the distance between the front wheels and the base of the screen. When the Burma project got under way (which had more influence on the ultimate Silver Shadow design), the wheelbase was shortened. (Courtesy Jock Knight)

The first Tibet car, chassis number 41-B, photographed at Crewe in 1958. The car is seen here in a basic state, with a radiator more in the style of Bentley (note the jack under the front of the car; there are also oil drips under the vehicle). On a later occasion it's pictured in Rolls-Royce guise, and furnished with brightwork, hub caps, etc. (Courtesy Rolls-Royce Motor Cars Ltd.)

styling feature later incorporated into the third series of Silver Clouds and S-Series cars which, at the time, was still four years away from production.

Features of 41-B were prominent front indicators, built into the upper leading edge of the wing tips; ultra-slim windscreen pillars, and the oddly-shaped, wide rear quarter panel. Equally prominent were the indicators built into the top edge of the rear wings. For initial testing purposes and in order to prevent the car from being recognised as a Rolls-Royce, the prototype was without the traditional radiator and, instead, was fitted with a plain example which resembled something akin to that found on the Bentley. The car was, however, later

5 ELG, the first Tibet prototype car, built on chassis number 41-B, showed a surprising likeness to the definitive outline of the future Silver Shadow. In evidence was a clean and unfussy straight-through waistline. Not only was the design thoroughly modern but the car had a markedly lower profile in comparison to that of the Silver Cloud. Any link with previous models was incidental, apart from the adoption of a fashionable twin headlamp system, a

photographed with the usual Rolls-Royce radiator in place, probably to test for wind noise. The camouflage went a stage further with concealment of anything that might suggest the car's origin, including all brightwork. Compared with the production Silver Cloud, 41-B appeared very modern with its slab-sided bodywork and immense window area.

The car's first outing on road test revealed much to be done to perfect the prototype: excessive noise was noted coming from the rear axle, and the front brakes had an unacceptable squeal; the steering was too heavy and not nearly flexible enough, and some discomfort was experienced from vibration that stemmed from the transmission system. As for performance, roadholding was reasonably good although spoilt, perhaps, by too much roll on cornering. Overall, road noise was acceptable considering the car's unitary body shell, a feature which often took on the qualitites of a sound-box. A problem that did exist - and about which customers of the standard steel saloons generally complained - was the difficulty of closing the doors, a complication hardly ever experienced with coachbuilt cars.

For all its less favourable aspects 41-B was nevertheless a remarkable achievement, considering that the design department at Crewe had little experience of the engineering concept demanded of it. Martin Bourne, who joined the design team in September 1955, recalls how each stage of Tibet's development was treated with a degree of both excitement and caution, the department as a whole feeling its way in what was essentially unknown territory. An overstatement, probably,

but Martin considered it a wonder that the exercise was made to work as well as it did. In retrospect the project worked due to the care, attention to detail, and sound engineering for which Rolls-Royce was renowned.

Rolls-Royce's chief development engineer, Tony Martindale (*AFM*), whose experience with Rolls-Royce and Bentley cars dated from prewar days, tested 41-B. The car weighed almost 38 hundredweight (4256lbs/1930kg), virtually three hundredweight (336lbs/152kg) less than the kerb weight of the Silver Cloud in its final version (the laden weight of the Silver Cloud III, as tested by *Autocar* in August 1963, had been about 44 hundredweight (4928lbs/224kg)). Considering this, 41-B's weight was little more than that of the experimental Siam project car that pre-dated the production Silver Clouds and S-Series Bentleys.

There is much evidence to suggest that the development of the Tibet project, with its numerous and radical innovations, many of which broke with tradition, placed a heavy strain upon the design team at Crewe. Bert Jeal and his team were clearly worried about dispensing with a separate chassis and building a monocoque shell to the required rigidity. The need for heavy-duty sub-frames fore and aft was recognised, but it was features such as all-round disc braking and the new self-levelling suspension system which caused much of the concern. Rolls-Royce had been working towards perfecting disc braking for some time, and it had been intended that the Silver Cloud III and S3 Series cars, as well as a Series IV version which never materialised, should have been so equipped. In the event, disc brakes

were never used on the Silver Cloud or its Bentley equivalent, and it was left to the tried and tested hydro-mechanical brakes of the Series I and II cars to serve throughout the car's production life.

The suspension for Tibet was initially designed around a compressed air system and, although this worked well enough while the car was in motion, it suffered from a loss of pressure once the vehicle was left standing for any length of time. Invariably the system deflated overnight and required re-pressurising from a compressed air line each morning. Air pressure was used to produce a constant ride height and the system devised was quite unlike that of Citroën's hydropneumatic or BMC's hydrolastic designs. To maintain the correct height, Rolls-Royce's engineers adapted a diesel injection pump which was different to the pully-driven belt operating a high pressure pump as found on the suspension system of Citroën's DS19. Rolls-Royce considered Citroën's method unreliable, possibly leading to suspension failure had the belts broken or suffered extensive wear.

In order to examine Citroën's hydraulic suspension, which had first appeared in 1954 as a self-levelling device on the rear axle of the 6-cylinder Traction Avant, before being developed to control the futuristic D-Series cars, Rolls-Royce purchased a DS19 and progressively dismantled it. This was common practice in the motor industry and research through Rolls-Royce's archives shows that a considerable number of cars were so evaluated, including the rotary-engined NSU RO80 and, in more recent years, the Renault Espace multi-purpose vehicle. Air suspension

The Burma project - a wax model of the car is shown here - was originally intended as a Bentley-badged car. Ultimately, the Tibet and Burma projects were cancelled and the best features of both cars combined in what became the SY. The definitive shape of the Silver Shadow is evident, but look at the ungainly wing line. The frontal styling is unlike any Bentley but note the peak above the windscreen, which is reminiscent of the BMC Farina cars, and which was a popular styling feature of the fifties. John Blatchley, incidentally, was required to keep the windscreen rake at a maximum angle of 32 degrees, a constraint he found particularly irksome. (Courtesy John Blatchley)

was not entirely new to Rolls-Royce, as the company had experimented with it during the war years.

In order to resolve 41-B's vibration problems the car was taken out of the experimental programme and sent to the bump rig for several weeks of severe testing. Work in the meantime was progressing with the second prototype car in the Tibet project, which was delivered to the test department during the first few weeks of 1959. Carrying the registration 835 FLG on chassis 42-B, this prototype was relatively short-lived; it was considerably heavier, by 150lbs (68kg), than the previous car and had been designed to use the same type of suspension layout which had proved so problematic with 41-B. In less than a year 42-B had been withdrawn from the test schedule to allow engineers to completely modify the suspension to a hydropneumatic system.

Testing resumed on the car in October 1960 but it appears that the vehicle remained troublesome as only around 3000 miles (4800km) were recorded before the car was withdrawn less than a year later. Eventually dismantled, the car did not quite achieve 20,000 miles (32,500km) in total.

43-B, a third experimental car, registered 500 GMB, was delivered to the test department during the middle of 1959. This, too, suffered from a number of problems, and, more seriously, a series of under-bonnet fires were recorded. The cause of the fires was ultimately attributed to seizure of the oil pump drive. 43-B was heavier than its two predecessors; half a hundredweight (30kg) more than the second experimental car.

The Burma project
Whilst development of the Tibet project had been a continuous operation, at the same time the design department at Pyms Lane was under some pressure to improve and modify existing models.

The Silver Cloud II and Bentley S2 were due a face-lift and, once this had been achieved and the Series III cars successfully launched, there was more time to meet the demands of the new car.

A couple of months after the first Tibet car was produced, attention was turned towards a Bentley version, intended to be fundamentally different to the Rolls-Royce. This serves to illustrate it had not been Rolls-Royce's intention to allow the Bentley name to lapse, but to develop a sports saloon in the best tradition of the marque. To develop any new car is a truly expensive business, even for a volume car producer, and for Rolls-Royce, building relatively modest numbers of cars annually, the cost of a completely new project was prohibitive. Code named Burma, the design was for an altogether smaller car which, whilst using unitary construction similar to that of Tibet, had a planned wheelbase of a fraction under 10 feet - 119.5

inches (3035mm). Burma was both narrower, by 2 inches (51mm), and lower, by 2.5 inches (63.5mm), than Tibet. In addition it sported 15 inch wheels (381mm) whereas Tibet was fitted with 16 inch (409mm) wheels. The car was also lighter by 781lbs (354kg). The cabin space of Burma remained identical to that of Tibet, and a reduction in the car's overall length was achieved by removing 6.5 inches (165mm) from between the scuttle and the front wheels.

It was originally intended that the Burma car would be equipped with a smaller engine than had been envisaged for Tibet. From the outset the Bentley was designed around a new Rolls-Royce F-series, 6-cylinder, 4-litre engine (3990cc), unlike the Tibet which was always intended to use the L-series 6230cc, V8 unit. Ultimately the Burma project abandoned the 4-litre engine in favour of the V8 as the former was not powerful enough. John Astbury, who worked on engine design at Crewe from August 1959, recalls it was a mammoth task squeezing the V8 into the confines of the Burma bodyshell. He remembers that space was so restricted, it took more time to find a location for the dipstick than to resolve almost any other problem!

When work initially started on Burma there was some question about the design of sub-frame required for the car. Jock Knight, who had been involved with chassis design on Tibet, remembers sitting at the drawing board with John Blatchley and discussing the matter at some length. Eventually they devised a layout that is now familiar on the Silver Shadow.

Before prototype cars could be built, the usual quarter-sized scale models based on outline sketches were produced in wax. Once approved, detailed drawings were created before a full-size model was produced. This was standard procedure throughout the motor industry, and allowed design engineers to make alterations before committing to the building of expensive prototype vehicles (a senior design engineer at Rolls-Royce once calculated that a prototype car cost 17 times more to build than a production car!).

Early scale models show that the Burma styling evolved through a number of ideas. The frontal appearance could, at one time, have been considered somewhat ungainly; front and rear wings changed in shape and, on one model, the car had prominent tail fins! Headlamps were inset into a full-width radiator grille and direction indicators installed into the leading edges of the front wings. As successive design changes occurred there emerged three distinct phases, each aspect of which became ever more dignified until it reached something close to the definitive model.

Burma experimental cars numbered seven in total and were built on chassis numbers 51B-57B inclusive. The first of the cars, which weighed 34.5cwts (1753kg), experienced a number of problems, including poor performance and braking, axle noise, and a general rattle from the door trims, as well as excessive exhaust noise. For a new car, however, there was less fouling and clunking than expected. A particularly impressive feature of 51-B was its stable roadholding, quite unlike that of the early Tibet cars. The feel of the car was made all the better by seats which allowed a high driving position with good visibility.

Although 51-B had a profile not dissimilar to that of the Tibet cars, its frontal styling was not in the least bit pretty. The huge, full-width mesh grille was divided in the centre by a vertical bar, and the headlamps were positioned each side in the upper corners. Indicator and side lamps were built into the leading edge of the wings in similar fashion to the definitive Silver Shadow. The shape of the rear quarter panels meant that it was difficult to see the rear wings from the driving seat so, to redress this situation, the rear was given tail fins which also housed the rear lamp assemblies. Less than 8000 miles (12,800km) were recorded on the car when it was dismantled in January 1964, the reason being that it was used extensively on the bump rig to investigate noise levels. The prolonged testing resulted in some suspension parts cracking and the car was stored from 1961 until it was scrapped in 1964.

The second Burma car, 52-B, had similar styling to 51-B but was 38kg (0.75cwt) lighter. Endurance testing was quite intensive; it was road tested by day and bump rig tested at night. At Oulton Park the car underwent steering and handling tests but, after only 26,000 miles (41,600km), it, too, was scrapped.

53-B, the third Burma car, had a surprisingly short life. Entering

Burma, chassis 54-B, underwent extensive trials in France. The car was also tested at Le Mans, where this picture was taken; test driver John Gaskell takes a welcome break. In 18 months of trials, some 71,000 miles (113,600km) were recorded. (Courtesy John Gaskell)

service in the early months of 1960, it was involved in two accidents and was broken up in August the same year with fewer than 14,000 miles (22,400km) recorded. Accidental damage aside, 53-B was a poor performer and suffered transmission and hydraulic problems.

The fourth Burma car, 54-B, which carried registration number 120 MLG, was taken to France for testing. Test driver, John Gaskell, remembers taking the car around Le Mans where he was photographed taking a break from the arduous test programme. John recalls that the car suffered a

number of problems, especially with the hydraulic throttle, but the main complaint was that the heater failed to work to any extent and test drivers had to continually stop the car to get some exercise to warm themselves. After trials lasting something like 18 months (in which time 71,000 miles (113,600km) were recorded), the car was put into storage and later dismantled.

All the Burma test cars had been fitted with right-hand steering until 55-B, the fifth experimental vehicle. With left-hand steering, the car entered service at the beginning

of 1961, and tests were generally conducted on the M1 motorway. John Gaskell remembers driving at high speed along the motorway and passing another Rolls-Royce or Bentley. The driver of the car recognised that the vehicle which had passed him at such high speed had to be a new model and quickly contacted the factory to see if he could buy one! 55-B was used to test air conditioning equipment and was also subjected to a ferocious spell on the bump rig, so severe that the body had to be rebuilt, although the suspension stood up to the constant battering remarkably well. It is a

Burma 3 experimental car 56-B. Note how the frontal styling has changed from that of 54-B in the previous picture. (Courtesy Rolls-Royce Motor Cars Ltd.)

matter of interest that 55-B was used as part of Rolls-Royce's and BMC's coalition, which is explained in greater detail later.

The two final cars in the Burma project were 56-B and 57-B, both of which underwent some restyling and received a much more attractive frontal appearance. Previous cars had had a pronounced peak above the windscreen which was now removed. The cars also looked better with their wrap-around bumpers and lowered rear wing line. Test driver, John

A coalition existed between Rolls-Royce and BMC during the sixties, but the only model to come out of it was the Vanden Plas Princess 4-litre R. Rolls-Royce's development model was the Java, shown here with its unique frontal styling and Bentley badging. The stacked headlamp arrangement of Java is similar to that of the Alvis TE21, otherwise known as the Three Litre Series III, which was announced at the London Motor Show in the autumn of 1963. (Courtesy Rolls-Royce Motor Cars Ltd.)

Gaskell, was again involved in the trials of 56-B in France and, after some 20,000 miles (32,000km), the car returned to Crewe. Burma cars were, of course, fitted with the 4-litre engine but 56-B was eventually equipped with the 6230cc V8 unit in 1963. Before this, though, tests were carried out using a 6-speed gearbox and revised suspension. 56-B testing continued until the Silver Shadow was being put into production and assisted in that car's familiarisation programme. In January 1966, after completing 60,000 miles (96,000km), the car was withdrawn from service.

57-B was the last of the Burma cars and, although originally fitted with the 4-litre engine, was converted to a V8 between 1962 and 1963. The Burma programme was eventually scrapped, as was this last experimental car, which was used for barrier crash testing.

Whilst the Burma project was progressing, parallel work continued on Tibet. Following trials with 43-B the first Tibet phase came to an end and phase II commenced. Aptly named Tibet II, outline work on the project began as early as the closing months of 1958, but it was more than three years before the first development car made its appearance. 44-B displayed many of the features from Burma and, together with its Rolls-Royce radiator, revealed much of what was to come in the shape of the Silver Shadow.

Tibet II's frontal styling - with its twin headlamp system - was strikingly modern and aesthetically pleasing; front direction indicators were positioned lower on the wing's leading edges than previously, and changes to the bonnet allowed a one-piece design which was hinged at the front. Shortly before this stage in the car's development a centrally hinged bonnet, as found on the Silver Cloud, had been contemplated. Clearly, the Burma development had considerable influence on Tibet II as the car was equipped with doors made from aluminium alloy rather than steel. The Burma project had experimented with aluminium in order to reduce the overall weight of the car, and it also proved more resistant to corrosion. Adversely, aluminium was more expensive and, being a softer metal, was also more prone to damage. Rover, incidentally, used a similar material, known as Birmabright, on the P4 range of cars (60, 75, 90 and 100 models, etc.) before reverting to steel shortly before production of the series ended. The reason for the move away from Birmabright was financial, with aluminium costing much more than steel.

Much experience was gained from 44-B; the suspension system was modified so that the hydropneumatic system operated as a self-levelling device on the rear axle only, while coil springs were substituted at the front. The car, however, completed only a nominal mileage; fewer than 3500 miles were recorded before it was withdrawn and eventually dismantled.

Alongside Burma, essentially a Bentley-inspired project, a Rolls-Royce version of the same car had the code name Tonga. Eventually, the separate projects were cancelled and development continued in one direction. A further reason for doing this was the huge cost of developing two quite different models. It became clear that the Bentley would not be anything other than a badge-engineered alternative to the Rolls-Royce.

For Bentley enthusiasts, notwithstanding the best of intentions at Crewe, the onset of badge-engineering spelt oblivion for the marque which had achieved so much in motor sport. Had events at Rolls-Royce offered a new direction for Bentley during the gestation period of the Silver Shadow, the history of the Bentley motorcar might have been very different. Throughout the ensuing years there has been much criticism of Rolls-Royce for allowing Bentley development to be stifled to the extent that the T-Series cars were nothing more than Silver Shadows carrying the Bentley emblem.

An odd coalition

As Tibet and Burma became obsolete, a search for replacements to the Silver Cloud and Bentley S-Series, which combined each car's best features, was conducted. The new project received the code name SY. This notation came about due to Rolls-Royce's engineering department's identification codes, and was retained throughout the remainder of the car's development.

During the development period of Tibet and Burma, Rolls-Royce had almost succumbed to a strange courtship with the British Motor Corporation (BMC). Had the relationship evolved fully, this could have had a devastating affect on the Crewe company and the cars it produced. BMC was looking for a place in the luxury car market, certainly with something of greater appeal than already existed in its top-of-the-range models, and Rolls-Royce appeared an attractive means of achieving this. The collaboration between the two companies began in 1962 and, whilst several themes were thought of and

The only product of the Rolls-Royce and BMC coalition was the Vanden Plas Princess 4-litre R. The engine used for the car was the F-60, 6-cylinder unit designed by Jack Phillips. (Author's collection)

design exercises carried out, there was only one model which came to fruition as a production vehicle - the Vanden Plas Princess R.

A hybrid of the Austin Westminster 110, the car was of handsome appearance and its features - though restyled - had origins as a Rolls-Royce project, code named Java. In place of BMC's 3-litre engine was the 4-litre, F60, 6-cylinder Rolls-Royce engine which, it will be remembered, had been originally developed to power the Burma car. Had the project evolved as intended when collaboration between the two concerns began, Java could have become a mass-produced 'small' Bentley. First appearing at the 1964 Motor Show, the 4-litre R enjoyed only limited success, probably because the exterior of the car suggested an Austin rather than a Rolls-Royce. The car's price was also a disadvantage;

at £1995 it was more expensive than the Rover 3-litre coupé and the Jaguar S-Type and only fractionally cheaper than the Jaguar Mark 10. Within three years the car had been discontinued.

BMC had supplied to Rolls-Royce the front-wheel-drive 1100 and 1800 full-size mock-ups for evaluation, and Martin Bourne can remember being sent along to a disused test bed to carry out detail measurements of both cars, which were still very secret. What was of interest were the dimensions of the 1100's cabin which, surprisingly, offered just as much space as the Silver Cloud's! Styling exercises were carried out upon what was known as the Bengal theme, and quarter-scale models show a car which shared identifying features with the 1800, and which at the time was being quite seriously considered as a future Bentley. Possibly the oddest creation

was a variation coded the Rangoon which had the Rolls-Royce radiator; on a relatively small car this feature was totally out of place. When collaboration with Rolls-Royce ended it's apparent that the design eventually progressed from the BMC 1800-derived car to a stretched version to form the basis of the Austin 3-litre. Close examination of the 3-litre Austin reveals it has the same central body section as the Austin 1800.

As the BMC and Rolls-Royce collaboration developed there appeared a number of interesting designs, some of which were intended as aspiring sports cars. Some of the drawings and illustrations penned at the time display a distinct leaning towards Italian design style. Included in these is Alpha, a finely proportioned two-door sports coupé and the only existing quarter-scale model of this

Bentley prototypes pictured within the Experimental Garage at Pyms Lane. From left to right: Siam, Burma 3, and Korea. (Courtesy Ian Rimmer)

A further styling theme was a proposed Continental version of Burma, known as Korea. The wax model pictured here shows the car's sporting attitude and remarkably contemporary frontal appearance. (Courtesy Rolls-Royce Motor Cars Ltd.)

project, built in fibreglass, which now enjoys an elegant location in its stylist's office. Quaintly, the design of Alpha, which is over 40 years old, has more than a suggestion of current styling trends, especially with its tear-drop-shaped headlamp lenses. Martin Bourne remembers with pleasure that the car was the winning entry in a competition for a design based upon BMC's 1800 chassis.

Martin is reluctant to take full credit for Alpha, however. The basic car was designed on a Healey chassis by two German design students, and, in that form, won a Farina-sponsored

This Korea prototype car (61-B) had a Park Ward body. Note the sleek styling and Bentley wheeltrims. (Courtesy Rolls-Royce Motor Cars Ltd.)

The interior of Korea prototype 61-B which would, had the car materialised, have been marketed as a Bentley sports coupé. Note the Bentley monogram on the steering wheel hub. (Courtesy Rolls-Royce Motor Cars Ltd.)

design competition. Farina built one and displayed it at various shows; when BMC turned down the project it was left to Martin to redesign the front end.

BMC's interest in Rolls-Royce waned once it had negotiated the takeover of Jaguar and found for itself a niche in the luxury car market. The irony of the whole affair is that it mirrored in many ways exactly what W. A. Robotham had envisaged before the war.

Final developments and the SY project

As SY development continued from the remains of Burma and Tibet, so most of the road testing was carried out using the Bentley style of radiator, in order not to draw too much attention. While workshop tests were being conducted it was usual for a Rolls-Royce radiator to be substituted, especially when air flow was being measured. By this time the new car's specification had been carefully defined: it would have Burma's 119.5 inch (3035mm) wheelbase and the V8, 6.230-litre engine.

Five SY experimental cars were built before the Silver Shadow and T-Series Bentley went into production. A change was made to the project numbering system so that the experimental car's registration number corresponded with the chassis number. This allowed easier identification and was made possible by the introduction of a change in Britain's car registering system which, from 1963, employed a suffix letter following the index letters and numbers to denote the year of registration. As chassis numbers were suffixed 'B,' so an arrangement was made with the licensing authority to supply Rolls-Royce with a corresponding set of numbers. The first three SY experimental cars, bearing the chassis numbers 45-B, 46-B and 47-B, bore the corresponding registration numbers ALD 45B, 46B and 47B, and were hand-built in the experimental

A number of clay scale models were made in order to perfect the styling. Here, ideas (code named Tibet and Burma 3) have been sculpted for both Rolls-Royce and Bentley versions of what eventually became the Silver Shadow and T-Series. (Courtesy John Blatchley)

department. Instead of the bodies being prepared by Pressed Steel or Park Ward, the panels were supplied by Airflow Streamline of Coventry. Successive test cars were built using bodies supplied by Pressed Steel, so were therefore more representative of the production models.

Road testing 45-B revealed the now familiar problem of excessive vibration and noise from the suspension system. In an attempt to cure the fault the car was subjected to the torturous bump rig, which simulated conditions with varying degrees of violence far in

The SY project evolved from the Tibet and Burma projects, which were cancelled. The outcome was the Silver Shadow, seen here alongside a Silver Cloud III. 100 LG was a registration used for publicity cars. (Courtesy Martin Bourne)

excess of what the vehicle was likely to actually encounter on the road. Testing continued until engineers were satisfied with the results. 46-B was also subjected to the tortures of the bump rig and suffered substantial damage to the body as a result.

The third SY experimental car, 47-B, was considered developmentally advanced enough to endure long-distance road-testing, and was dispatched to France where road surfaces were considered especially poor. Test drivers in charge of the car managed to achieve remarkably high mileages and, when the vehicle returned to Crewe, it had covered over 21,000 miles (33,600km) without serious problem. Continuous testing did, naturally, reveal minor faults and weaknesses, which were dealt with as they arose. There is evidence that road noise and vibration was still of some concern, as noted when Dr Llewellyn-Smith and Harry Grylls tested the car.

The last two pre-production experimental cars were made available, as tooling for the new car was being arranged. 48-B, which was constructed with a Pressed Steel body, featured left-hand steering and was built to export specification. After a brief test period in France, the car was taken to America and did not return until two weeks before the launch of the Silver Shadow and T-Series to Bentley and Rolls-Royce agents at Crewe. A period of endurance testing in America was obviously considered of great importance, especially as this promised to be one of the cars' strongest markets.

Despite attempts to keep the identity of the Silver Shadow a secret, rumours of its existence began as test cars were seen in the area around Crewe. The tests were under the direction of the chief test driver, Tony Martindale, who was well qualified for the job. As well as being a test pilot he had a formidable reputation for handling a motor car, and could often be seen putting Silver Clouds and S-Series Bentleys through their paces on narrow Cheshire lanes.

Crash testing was all part of the experimental programme and, whilst costly, was nevertheless a very important part of the Silver Shadow's development. It was mostly possible to treat the exercise with some economy by using the same vehicle up to four times for crash purposes. Once a rear end and side-impact crash had been staged, the car could be subjected to a front end collision before being dismantled. Trials were also carried out at MIRA, the motor industry's proving ground at Nuneaton, where tests were conducted on exhaust emissions, stability under tyre deflation, and crash resistance.

As road testing progressed, so pressure was put on the experimental department to eliminate the problems that arose. One considerable difficulty had been to find a solution to the sometimes excessive road noise and vibration, problems far easier to cure when designing a car with a separate chassis. A monocoque shell, by virtue of its fundamental engineering, acts something like a drum; what was needed was a suitable cushion between the bodyshell and the sub-frames. Other manufacturers would often use rubber blocks for this but, for a vehicle the size and weight of the Silver Shadow, this was insufficient. Instead of rubber mountings Rolls-Royce used cylindrical pads of stainless steel wire mesh which, due to their density, acted like variable-rate springs. Developed by Delaney Gallay, it was not the first time Rolls-Royce had used 'Vibrashock' mountings and had enough experience with them to insulate the exhaust system on the Silver Cloud III.

The Silver Shadow's exhaust system proved problematic in its installation and a solution to how to fit all four required boxes was difficult to find. Harry Grylls was eventually consulted and Jock Knight spent several hours with him deciding which way the installation should be tackled.

Ride comfort was all-important and many hours went into perfecting the self-levelling arrangement associated with the suspension which provided unique stability. Not to be confused with the hydraulic suspension used by Citroën, Rolls-Royce utilised a completely conventional system of coil springs with double wishbones, and anti-roll bar at the front and semi-trailing arms at the rear. Unlike Citroën's hydropneumatics which allowed the car to settle an inch or so from the ground when idle, the Rolls-Royce rested quite normally upon its coil springs. Neither was the self-levelling system inter-connected between front and rear. When driven, the car was kept at an even keel by hydraulic rams which operated very slowly; when the car was stationary the system worked ten times as quickly, instantly adjusting to changes in weight distribution as passengers got in and out, the petrol tank was filled, or luggage loaded.

Interior styling was just as important as it had to reflect the sumptuousness of the luxury carriage,

Part of any car's development programme is crash testing and, as far as the Silver Shadow was concerned, this was under the direction of Jock Knight. This particular photograph was taken in 1968. (Courtesy Rolls-Royce Motor Cars Ltd.)

part of the Rolls-Royce and Bentley hallmark and superior reputation. When it came to the coachwork, modern techniques may have been acceptable, but the cosseting of passengers was a different matter. The same attention to detail was carefully applied, and Martin Bourne can remember spending many hours ensuring perfection. Harry Grylls was anxious to test every stage of development, and if the engineering

Barrier crash tests were an essential part of the Silver Shadow's development programme. The deformation of this experimental vehicle, as it hit the barrier, was filmed and carefully studied.

SILVER SHADOW
SALOON
COACHWORK BY ROLLS ROYCE LTD.

director found the seats comfortable for his 6ft.3in. (1.95m) height, this was acceptable.

The specification of the Silver Shadow was enticing: electric windows and seat adjustment, finest leather and veneer combined with the softest cloth. Driver satisfaction could not be ignored and close attention was paid to the attractiveness of the instrumentation and facia. Added to this exquisite comfort was the pleasure of driving a car with power steering and an effortless gearbox. Safety was always at the forefront: stopping power was provided by all-round disc braking, the system tested, improved and tested again until it surpassed even Rolls-Royce's own high standard.

An unfortunate design of the handbrake assembly, which protruded in a somewhat ungainly manner from under the dashboard, went unnoticed for a long time. When Bill Allen was allowed to use a test car for a weekend, a relation's wife climbed into the driving seat only to find the position of the parking brake highly inconvenient for feminine attire. This was not an

There were smiles all round when the Silver Shadow was presented to Rolls-Royce dealers at Crewe. The identity of the gentleman standing alongside the car is unknown, but Dave Tod (Scottish sales representative) can be seen standing beneath the porch and, in front of him, is Ian Vetch. (Courtesy Martin Bourne)

isolated complaint about the car's handbrake, and is best left to Martin Bourne to describe the problem the styling and design departments were faced with:

"We did not want a great long lever with a noisy ratchet between the front seats (not R-R!), or even outboard as in the days of yore. The only alternative was an exquisite variation on the Ford Popular umbrella handle theme, a beautifully styled and engineered pull-out job under the facia - just above the outboard knee. It worked beautifully but, due to the weight of the car and the leverage required, handle travel had to be quite long. It was a relief when the foot-operated parking brake came along!"

By the summer of 1965 Rolls-Royce was ready to put the Silver Shadow and T-Series Bentley into production at Crewe. Changes were made at the factory to accommodate the new manufacturing process, which included inspection and rectification, where necessary, of bodyshells received from Pressed Steel. Upheaval at Crewe during this period was understandable and production was severely affected by the tooling process. Final testing of the prototype cars was carried out even while arrangements were being made to equip the production areas. Although it would have been legally inadvisable, the M6 motorway was used to conduct speed trials, during which, on occasion, it had been possible to achieve more than 120mph (192kph).

The Silver Shadow and the T-Series Bentley were scheduled for presentation to Rolls-Royce agents at Crewe at the end of September. Due to the number of invitations it was necessary to extend the event to two days, and it was held on Thursday 30th September and Friday 1st October. During the two days 120 representatives of the home sales organisation were able to visit the factory and try for themselves the two demonstration cars made available for the occasion. At least three cars were on show but it was a Regal Red Silver Shadow, carrying the registration number 100 LG, and a T-Series Bentley, 1900 TU, that were used for testing purposes. These registration numbers, incidentally, were retained by Rolls-Royce for use on publicity cars. Though reaction to the cars was undoubtedly mixed, the agents were, without doubt, of the opinion that the models lived up to everything expected from a Rolls-Royce or Bentley.

Although the new car had now been launched there was no time to waste as constant improvement was

an essential facet of manufacturing. It was business as usual in the design department as plans were under way to announce a two-door version of the Silver Shadow and T-Series. In addition, MPW was also preparing a spectacular drophead version.

All smiles for the T-Series Bentley, too. Standing by the driver's door is David Buckle. (Courtesy Martin Bourne)

2

Without a Shadow of doubt

Relieved at the Silver Shadow's successful launch to its agents, Rolls-Royce got on with the task of building cars for sale. The design and test departments, instead of being able to relax their work schedule, were immediately subjected to further pressure. Solutions had to be found to the many problems encountered by the engineering department, service section and, ultimately, the customer.

Testing the Silver Shadow and Bentley was, therefore, all the more important once the car was in production and, to this end, experimental cars were put through their paces with a great sense of purpose and urgency.

Derek Coulson (*DC*) and J. (Mac) Macraith-Fisher (*McF*) were responsible for development, and well remember the many hours spent trying to find solutions to particular problems, some

Last of the original SY experimental cars, 50-B, was built in October 1966 and used for testing purposes. Wearing registration ALD 50B, the vehicle had coachwork built by Pressed Steel and was painted Astral Blue. Under the bonnet was a 7 litre engine, which was replaced with a 6¼ litre unit soon after testing at MIRA began. 50-B served a number of purposes, not least in connection with the MPW two-door models and, later, with the Delta project, which materialised as the Camargue. (Courtesy Rolls-Royce Motor Cars Ltd.)

Harry Grylls standing alongside an early Silver Shadow, the car he developed. (Courtesy Rolls-Royce Motor Cars Ltd.)

of which, at the time, seemed almost insurmountable. Their first impression of the initial prototype car left them with a feeling of dismay: in their own words it was "... almost appalling by Rolls-Royce standards." The most striking feature about the original Tibet car had been its sheer size, but when Burma came along it was an altogether better car, apart from being grossly underpowered. Performance was improved tremendously when the V8 engine was substituted for the 6-cylinder power unit under the bonnet.

Road testing the cars had produced some nerve-wracking experiences, especially when it came to stopping. A favourite venue of the test team for brake tests was Hopton Hill, near Belper in Derbyshire, where the gradient was so steep that, if the car reached the bottom without incident, it could be reasonably assumed the brakes were without fault. On a particular occasion Dr Llewellyn-Smith, who was managing director at the time, experienced complete brake failure while trying out one of the experimental cars for

a few days on extended trial. Mac Fisher remembers the incident well, especially following the telephone call from a very distressed Mrs Llewellyn Smith who had been in the car with her husband!

There's no denying that the design and development departments at Rolls-Royce did encounter some quite extraordinary difficulties which often took a long time to resolve. It could reasonably be assumed that a car with the reputation of being "The Best In The World" would be devoid of teething troubles but, logically, it is the thorough way in which the cars were evaluated that earned them this epitaph.

Derek Coulson had the task of taking experimental car 48B to the American continent where he subjected it to a gruelling two month endurance ordeal. Wherever the car went, from Mexico to Arizona, it never failed to attract attention. Of course, the car was disguised, the Rolls-Royce radiator having been replaced with something more like the Bentley's, and anything to suggest the car's origin was removed. Even so, the vehicle's identity was guessed by some, whilst others were sure it was the latest Jaguar. From Arizona the car was driven north to Canada and in total covered some 10,000 miles (16,000km) before returning to Britain.

On an another occasion a test car was being taken to France when it disgraced itself mid-Channel. When Derek Coulson, who again had the job of conducting the test, went to the car which he had left with the other cars on the ferry, he found that all the hydraulic fluid had leaked from the self-levelling system onto the deck.

Everything on a Rolls-Royce and Bentley - and the Silver Shadow and T-Series were no exception - was designed to be reliable. Should failure occur, it would usually happen at a slow rate, usually allowing the driver time to take compensating action or to rectify the fault. An indication of Rolls-Royce engineering thoroughness was that every 100th engine was taken off the test bench, dismantled and checked for wear. The engines were never reassembled for use in a production car.

The meticulous way in which the experimental cars were tested is evident from the trials each component underwent. If it failed, the item was carefully examined to discover exactly why and how it had failed; the remedy was to have the item redesigned to prevent future failure. Tyres were a point in question: Rolls-Royce took products from three manufacturers, Avon, Dunlop and Firestone, and tested them for safety beyond any reasonable level at establishments such as MIRA. In order for Rolls-Royce to accept the tyres, the manufacturers had to ensure even higher than usual tolerance levels.

For all its diligence the development team was economical in its costs and overheads, but never frugal when ensuring quality and safety. In February 1966, a period when the department was at its busiest, the year's budget of £485,000 was underspent by £50,000.

The successful presentation of the Silver Shadow and T-Series to agents and journalists was, in effect, the pinnacle of achievement for one man, Harry Grylls, whose drive and determination had assured the project of success. Grylls foresaw that, should Rolls-Royce remain a mainstream producer of luxury cars, there would be no alternative but to change the company's manufacturing traditions. From the outset he had full belief in electing the change to unitary construction and, in so doing, fully understood that a long and difficult passage lay ahead. He recognised there would be many problems but, nevertheless, was confident in the knowledge that his engineers had the ability and resources to overcome them all.

The cars displayed at the agent and press launch may have seemed to untrained eyes to resemble those early Burma and Tibet prototypes, but were, in effect, very different. Certainly, some similarity in outward style and shape remained, even though the only parts of the car that did not undergo any alteration were the doors. In retrospect both Mac Fisher and Derek Coulson were adamant about the cars' development: there was just one way to evaluate a car and that was by sitting in it and driving it. It had taken a little over two years to perfect the cars to where they could go into production: Rolls-Royce's board of directors had given their approval to the definitive car on 9th July 1963.

First reactions

Just what did motoring journalists think of the Silver Shadow when it was presented to them at Crewe in 1965, a few days before the London Motor Show? The late John Bolster, a Rolls-Royce enthusiast, if ever there was one, tried the Bentley T-Series after having driven to Crewe in his 1911 Silver Ghost. The difference between the two cars is hardly comparable, apart, that is, from the remarkable build quality applied individually to each car. The Silver Ghost had been advertised in 1907 as 'the most graceful, the most attractive, the most silent, the most reliable, the most flexible, the most smooth running six-cylinder car yet produced.' How the motor car had progressed!

About the Silver Shadow, John Bolster was emphatic in his report for *Autosport*: 'A remarkably comfortable ride' he noted; further comments indicated that it '... felt astonishingly small being a car of reasonable size' but as he got more accustomed to it he clearly admired the car and liked

Apart from its radiator and dedicated badging, the T-Series Bentley was virtually identical to its Rolls-Royce counterpart. (Courtesy Rolls-Royce Motor Cars Ltd.)

its style. Summing up in a simple statement he claimed it to be '... a new car for modern conditions.' That, of course, was exactly what it was: the car-owning population was increasing rapidly - in 1959 there had been one car for every ten people; by 1969 the figure had doubled to one car for every five. The rapid increase in popularity of the motor car did not, however, mean that Britain was doubling its output of cars, rather that there was a large increase in sales of foreign produced vehicles imported into Britain.

'New look for The Best Car In The World, now with a lower, wider radiator shell and less flamboyant body contours.' was *Autocar*'s caption to one of Rolls-Royce's publicity photographs. A Rolls-Royce or Bentley is usually associated with grace and good taste but hardly flamboyancy, which has a suggestion of vulgarity about it. It's true the Rolls-Royce and Bentley driver no longer sat head and shoulders above most other motorists

and, compared to the Silver Cloud, the Silver Shadow did appear somewhat smaller. Yet there was no mistaking the sheer elegance and finely sculptured features that made the Silver Shadow and T-Series Bentley a car totally superior to any other.

The Australian journal *Modern Motor*, in a report by Harold Dvoretsky, sought to impress its readers by suggesting that something of a revolution at Rolls-Royce had made the company face up to the '... hard, cold economic and competitive facts of life,' and go the way of most other popular manufacturers. Intended, perhaps, as a slight dig at the luxury car maker, to make amends the article concluded: '... when Rolls decide to change, they change in typical Rolls-Royce style - perfection personified.' The Silver Shadow was so unlike anything else Rolls-Royce had ever produced, it was only natural it should make an impact at Earls Court in 1965. It was quite usual for manufacturers of some of the

more popular makes to parade their cars in 'cutaway' style to show how every part of the car fitted together, but never Rolls-Royce - until the Silver Shadow, that is. Prominently displayed, but well protected from those eager to try out a Rolls-Royce for size, a Silver Shadow with doors removed demonstrated just how accessible the new model was. It was not simply a question of accessibility but more to do with comfort and sophistication, the sumptuous luxury of burr walnut and finest hide, deep pile Wilton carpets and superlatively soft West of England cloth.

Unfortunately, displaying a car in this way rather spoilt its smooth styling line so, instead, the emphasis was on door hinge brackets and lock mechanisms which were normally out of sight. This may have seemed a little distasteful to some devotees of the marque, who considered it quite unnecessary to denude the car of its fine lines (bare chassis of Rolls-Royce

From the outset, the Silver Shadow was intended to appeal to the owner/driver and therefore have a wider market.
(Courtesy Rolls-Royce Motor Cars Ltd.)

John Blatchley envisaged that the Silver Shadow would stay in production for a number of years, and created a shape that would seem as fresh after 10 years as when the car was launched. In saloon form it continued for 15 years and in Convertible guise for 30 years, such was the foresight of Rolls-Royce's chief stylist.
(Courtesy Rolls-Royce Motor Cars Ltd.)

This artwork of the Silver Shadow depicts the car's clean styling lines. John Blatchley, by utilising the monocoque shell to its full extent, managed to produce a car with as much interior space as the Silver Cloud, but of a more compact design. This is, in fact, a wash drawing of a long wheelbase car, prepared by Peter Wharton. Originally the long wheelbase cars were to be known as Touring Limousines. (Courtesy Rolls-Royce Enthusiasts' Club)

and Bentley cars had, after all, once been a feature at some motor shows) but, in defence, the display was impressive. What is more, it attracted unprecedented attention and interest. (Around 1963/4, Rolls-Royce put a Silver Cloud III chassis - which is now at the R-REC Headquarters at Paulerspury - on the stand, which had never been done before. 'Very nice,' said one journalist, 'but rather like seeing royalty in the nude ...')

At £6556 the Silver Shadow cost almost as much as four Rover 3-litre coupés and nearly two of Daimler's impressive Limousines. Those motor show visitors who were happily considering the purchase of a new car such as the Ford Anglia or Austin or Morris 1100, might have been wryly amused by the thought that they could have bought a whole fleet of ten of these cars, and still had a pocket-full of change, for the price of a single Silver Shadow!

Displaying the Silver Shadow without its doors was Crewe's way of showing how the marque had adapted to the motor industry's advancing technology. This Rolls-Royce was no longer a carriage with its separate chassis, the motor car for aristocracy, but a car for those who, quite simply, wanted the best that money could buy. It was a town car, a vehicle to be enjoyed, to sit in and be surrounded by the monocoque bodyshell, itself the result of mass-production methods. The finery was also there to relish, of course: fold-down picnic tables, centre arm rests, electric windows, and even powered front seat adjustment. Above all, the car had that unmistakable aura of opulence. In many ways the Silver Shadow and Bentley T were responsible for taking some of the mystique out of

Rolls-Royce ownership; in the eyes of some the car had been brought down to earth which, in a way, was only to be expected as Rolls-Royce was in the market to sell cars profitably.

There was no mystery at all about the fact that, whilst the Silver Shadow was being presented around Europe at all the major shows, Rolls-Royce did not have any examples to sell. This was particularly unfortunate as the car had been so well received that a healthy demand existed. Understandably, the company's agents and sales representatives were besieged by customers and dealers clamouring to get their hands on the new car. The board of directors at Rolls-Royce had been anxious to launch the Silver Shadow at the 1965 Paris Motor Show, and not wait until the car was safely in production. The latter would certainly have meant postponing until 1966 an announcement of the new model, meaning that the first occasion

the cars could have been seen publicly in Britain would have been the London Motor Show.

There were a several reasons for the delay in having cars to distribute to agents: firstly, Rolls-Royce had to be sure the cars were ready for production with as many teething problems as possible rectified; secondly, Pressed Steel had to be able to supply the bodyshells to the strict requirements of Crewe's engineering division.

The arrangement was that Rolls-Royce would supply Pressed Steel with a hardwood model of the Silver Shadow/T-Series to formulate blueprints. Once this process was completed the design had then to be 'detailed' in order that the bodyshell could be built as an entire unit at Cowley. Rolls-Royce and Bentley customers might have experienced grave concern on learning that the Silver Shadow and T bodyshells were produced alongside - and by virtually

the same process - many of Britain's most popular cars. They need not have worried, however, as Pressed Steel not only produced the bodies for Morris and Austin, and other cars in BMC such as Riley and MG, but was also a major supplier to the Rootes Group, responsible for famous names like Humber. As a company, Pressed Steel was quite accustomed to the demands made by Rolls-Royce, and had been its major supplier of body components from the immediate postwar period, when the Mk VI Bentley - and later the Silver Dawn - were introduced, through to the late fifties and the Silver Cloud III. Moreover, body production of quintessentially British car makers, Jaguar and Rover, was also undertaken by Pressed Steel.

The cars which had been made available to agents and motoring journalists for the models' launch at the end of September and beginning of October 1965, were quickly prepared

once the events were over and shipped to France in time to make an appearance at the Paris Motor Show. A couple of weeks later they arrived back in Britain and made ready for display at the London Motor Show at Earls Court.

David Tod, Rolls-Royce's sales representative for Scotland, remembers potential customers offering amounts well over and above the car's selling price in order to jump to the top of the waiting list, to no avail, of course, as Rolls-Royce certainly did not operate in this way. As sales representative, David was allocated a demonstration vehicle, and had the privilege of receiving the first production T-Series Bentley, which was built on chassis number SBH1010. Those customers lucky enough to get hold of one of the early cars were in the fortunate position of being able to re-sell it, should they so wish, at considerable profit.

In recalling the initial effect the Silver Shadow and T-Series Bentley had on his customers, David Tod remembers some were a little apprehensive about the car. More used to being chauffeur-driven in the expansive style of the Silver Cloud and Silver Wraith, the Silver Shadow appeared, by contrast, rather confined. Some even found it impersonal. The Silver Shadow and T-Series Bentley were designed for a different generation; owner-drivers who did not employ chauffeurs. In recalling those early days with his Bentley, David recalls the reactions of prospective customers when he demonstrated the car to them. Any suggestion that it, or the Silver Shadow, was a lesser vehicle than previous cars was quickly dismissed. The car handled surprisingly well, much better than most thought it would, as long as, David recollects, performance was kept within the car's limits. There's no denying that the handling had shortcomings, as was recognised by John Hollings (*Hgs*) who, as chief engineer of the company after 1968, revealed Rolls-Royce's engineering practice during the 1970s at the 1982 Sir Henry Royce Memorial Foundation Spring Lecture.

With the Silver Shadow, Rolls-Royce was confident it could build upon the successes previously enjoyed in America with the Silver Cloud. Actively courting the American customer, production at Crewe was so geared that the first 249 cars were allocated to the home market and the 250th car was destined for the USA, leaving Liverpool on 1st March 1966. To please American customers Rolls-Royce had to tread a careful path and, whilst it was important the car retained its very unique 'British feel,' it also had to have a ride commensurate with that of the Cadillac. In contrast to European motorists, who generally favoured cars with firmer suspension, American drivers preferred the ride to be wallowing and relaxed. The Silver Shadow's hydraulic self-levelling was, therefore, considered a very important feature.

Coming after the Silver Cloud there was a danger that the Silver Shadow might have seemed rather small, compared to some of the huge American machines with their vast bonnets (hoods) and massive boots (trunks). In the event, America welcomed the car with open arms. (Rolls-Royce, incidentally, had taken the precaution of obtaining a Pontiac which was sent to Crewe to allow the development team to examine just what American customers liked.) Some commentators have since suggested that the Silver Shadow was a car expressly designed for the American market, built for America and sold to America ...

The first detailed information about the Silver Shadow appeared in America early in 1966, courtesy of *Road & Track* magazine where, immediately - and still, some four years later - comparisons with Buick and Lincoln were made, not to mention Mercedes. The Rolls-Royce did have a 50,000 mile warranty, it stopped quicker than the American machines and was more manoeuvrable in traffic. As to the bottom line, some jealousy is evident and the following comment made by the journal almost certainly would not have pleased the directors at Crewe: '... a small manufacturer, is hard-pressed these days to match the standards set forth by the giant automakers - American or otherwise - and that Rolls-Royce can no longer be considered the completely magical motoring experience it had the reputation for in the past.'

America has always been an important market for Rolls-Royce, not only its cars but aero engines, too. During the Second World War Rolls-Royce Merlin engines were produced in America by Packard. Rolls-Royce, Inc. was established in Detroit where it manufactured the 'Rotol' blade rotator, a major component of a propeller hub assembly. In postwar years the car business moved away from being a distributor-based operation to one where Rolls-Royce, through Rolls-Royce Inc., became the direct distributor, so retaining for itself the distributor's profit margin.

Direct distribution began from 1st October 1964, and in charge of the operation was John Simonson and George Lewis. Simonson was appointed wholesale manager, the position he had held with the major Rolls-Royce distributor, J.S. Inskip Inc., of New York. It was whilst employed by Inskip that Simonson had been particularly successful in building up a Rolls-Royce dealer network, acquiring invaluable experience in the process. Lewis was hired as sales manager, the position he had held with Ford of America, as well as being one of that company's executives.

As in Britain, arrival of the Silver Shadow in America was watched with some concern: the Silver Cloud had been immensely popular and its replacement at first appeared very much less imposing. Marketing of the Silver Shadow took a different theme: it was aimed at a much younger owner-driver. To a large degree the new marketing ploy was successful and demand quickly outstripped supply.

More than just a new car from Rolls-Royce, the Silver Shadow was part of the era popularly termed the 'Swinging Sixties,' characterised by the Beatles and the Mersey Sound, flower power, Britain's love affair with the Mini, and the mini skirt, which symbolised the generation gap. There was social change, too: a Labour government had been elected under Harold Wilson after years of Conservative rule; dedicated followers of fashion shopped in Carnaby Street, and John Lennon shocked society with his psychedelic Phantom V. James Bond became an international hero and drove an Aston Martin, while Boeing 707 airliners flew millions of jet-set holidaymakers around the world to previously unknown resorts. On the motor racing circuit the world cheered on Graham Hill and Jackie Stewart; John Surtees was champion on two wheels as well as four, and Britain mourned the death of Jim Clark in 1968 when his Formula Two Lotus crashed at the Hockenheim circuit in Germany. The decade was also one of great technological advances: the QE2 was launched, Concorde made its debut, and man walked on the moon.

The monocoque

In fundamental engineering terms the monocoque structure of a car is all about frequency and torsional stiffness, and motor engineers had to achieve a frequency equal to that of the wheel rotation of the car when at full speed. In the case of the Bentley T and Silver Shadow, this represented something above 1200 cycles, the speed of rotation of the road wheels at maximum revs. Suffice to say, the design team achieved over and above what was required.

The bodyshells were delivered to Crewe from Pressed Steel by road transport where they were immediately subjected to what was known by the Rolls-Royce engineering department as 'white lining.' The bare unpainted shell was referred to as 'body-in-white' and the department through which it passed prior to painting was known as the White Line, under the control of its foremen, Fred Molyneux and Stan Burrell. Having had its protective wax coating - which had been applied before leaving the Pressed Steel plant at Cowley - removed, each bodyshell was given a rigorous inspection to check for imperfections, which were carefully noted. Correcting blemishes, lead filling any inconsistencies in the bodywork, and repairs to accidental damage sustained in transit were then carried out. All panel work was painstakingly examined and meticulously measured, and every

aperture carefully checked for accuracy.

Each bodyshell received from Pressed Steel was made to the same precise specification. The adaption to either left- or right-hand steering was carried out at Crewe where, at the same time, all necessary drilling of holes in the panels to accommodate instruments, wiring and mechanical equipment, was completed. On average it took a total of two days to perform these initial tasks.

Where imperfections were found in the bodyshells rectification was always carried out in-house at Pyms Lane. The extensive reorganisation necessary at Crewe to facilitate production of the Silver Shadow allowed for the installation of a completely new manufacturing process. Included was an up-to-date preparation plant which enabled complete bodyshells and panels to be finished to the highest standard. Alterations to the Crewe factory were made throughout the summer of 1965, the pinnacle to events which had been planned, it seemed to Macraith Fisher, for a very long time.

At first glance the bodyshell of the Bentley T seemed indistinguishable from that of the Silver Shadow, which resulted in a dramatic downturn in Bentley sales as most customers opted for the prestige of a Rolls-Royce. On closer inspection, however, it was evident that the bonnet panels had a slightly different pressing which allowed for each marque's shape and style of radiator. Although the main frame of the monocoque was constructed from steel, the doors, bonnet and boot lid were formed from aluminium, representing a substantial weight saving.

The build process of the Silver Shadow and T-Series cars included protection against corrosion. Water traps, as far as possible, were eliminated and vulnerable areas underneath the cars either galvanised or stove enamelled. Something like 400 parts were so treated, on top of which approximately 70lbs (32kg) of under sealant was applied in two stages. Stainless steel was used for many of the components, replacing chromium plating where possible.

A new paint shop, which facilitated total immersion of the bodyshell to apply the primer and protect against corrosion, was all part of the new manufacturing plant. Fifteen coats of paint were applied to each bodyshell and the whole process included numerous inspections, washing down and degreasing. After each session in the drying ovens the surface of each car was meticulously examined for any blemishes which were marked by pieces of white tape. Only when the finish was perfect could the final painting operation be carried out - the steady and painstaking application by hand of the coach lines.

The average time taken to build a car was 12 weeks and, depending on whether the customer required any special features, could take longer. The whole process for each vehicle was fastidiously recorded in a log file containing anything up to 40 pages. Details of each car are, incidentally, kept as a permanent record and these are currently available at the Rolls-Royce Enthusiasts' Club headquarters at The Hunt House at Paulerspury in Northamptonshire. As the car passed through each section, defects were noted and put right before the car was allowed to continue. As the vehicle

Bodyshells were delivered to Pyms Lane direct from Pressed Steel at Cowley. In its unpainted state, the shell was referred to as 'body-in-white' and given a thorough inspection for imperfections. It took two days for all the initial checks to be carried out, which included adaptation to left or right hand steering and drilling of all necessary apertures for instruments, etc. Here, a bodyshell is being prepared for the fitting of window frames.
(Courtesy Rolls-Royce Motor Cars Ltd.)

had to be signed off at each stage, any flaws or imperfections could be immediately traced to a department or individual. Quality control was the domain of Frank Dodd, whilst Doug Fox was in charge of testing. Doug's son, John, incidentally, spent a number of years as manager of the experimental department. The assembly hall was divided into three areas: pre-mount, mount and post-mount. As the bodyshell and sub-frame assemblies (built on their own assembly lines) progressed along the route upon specially designed trolleys, so the components were fitted at pre-arranged stations. It was at the

mounting stage that the bodyshell and front and rear sub-frame assemblies met with each other and were made to resemble a motor car. The jig that was used to knit the car together was known affectionately as the 'Queen Mary,' no doubt due to its impressive structure. It was at the post-mount stage that items such as wheels, tyres and exhausts were fitted to the car before being sent to the finishing shop for fitting out.

All cars were road tested minus the radiator shells, bumpers and trim items such as hub caps, sometimes for as much as 150 miles (240km) but usually a lot less, which allowed a

close watch to be kept on the vehicle, and gave an opportunity to make any necessary adjustments. Only when the test drivers were sure the cars performed as they should, and were without squeaks or rattles, were they dispatched to be valeted, cleaned and waxed.

Most evident about the 'platform' of the Silver Shadow were the car's two massive subframes, each appearing more like a chassis structure. The front sub-assembly consisted of forward and rear pick-up points, which supported the main structure and were connected just ahead of the A-post rear of the wheelarch,

To accommodate Silver Shadow production, extensive reorganisation was necessary at Crewe and included establishment of a body preparation plant. Rubbing down the bodywork was only a part of the process which culminated in 15 coats of paint. (Courtesy Rolls-Royce Motor Cars Ltd.)

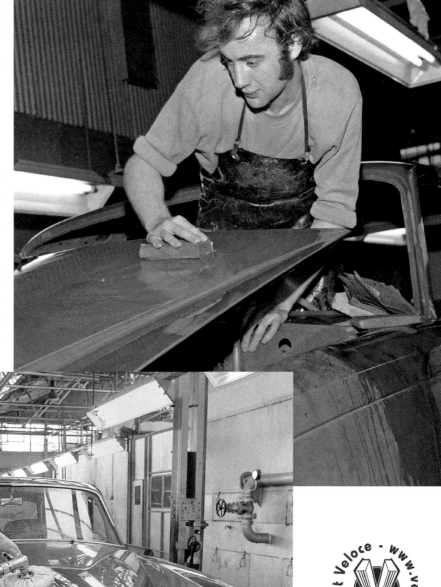

immediately ahead of the front wheel assemblies. The rear subframe was similarly constructed and connected to the body on each side of the car both ahead and behind the D-post.

Supported upon the front subframe was the engine and gearbox, steering assembly, front suspension, and braking system. At the rear of the car, the sub-frame supported the rear axle and final drive, suspension and brakes. Forming a means of insulation between the sub-assemblies and the bodyshell, Vibrashock mountings

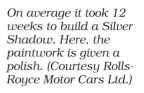

On average it took 12 weeks to build a Silver Shadow. Here, the paintwork is given a polish. (Courtesy Rolls-Royce Motor Cars Ltd.)

Destined for export, this car receives attention in car assembly at Crewe. The assembly hall was divided into three areas: pre-mount, mount, and post-mount. (Courtesy Rolls-Royce Motor Cars Ltd.)

(universally known as 'pan scrubbers' as they were made of stainless steel wire), which had been developed by Delaney Gallay, prevented, to a large degree, road noise and vibration from being transmitted to the car's interior via the suspension system. Incorporated as part of the car's suspension, the self-levelling device compensated for changes in vehicle load and also allowed a certain freedom of fore and aft movement. Whilst providing a stable ride, the horizontal compliance also induced

a degree of vagueness about the car's steering which provoked a considerable amount of controversy and criticism. Ultimately, of course, this was rectified.

Motoring journals considered the hydraulic system - and suspension layout - to be probably the most innovative of all the car's features. Motoring correspondents paralleled it, rather erroneously, with that of the hydropneumatic self-levelling system adopted by Citroën for the large D-series cars, but closer examination

reveals distinct differences. There were similarities, inasmuch that Rolls-Royce used high pressure accumulators and pressure regulating valves built under licence from Citroën, but it's here that any fundamental likeness ended. Whereas the system employed on the DS was totally hydraulic - no other form of springing was used - and height settings were selected by the driver, that used by Rolls-Royce and Bentley merely kept the car at a specific level and was supplementary to a conventional system.

The main car assembly shop. In the foreground engines await installation. (Courtesy Rolls-Royce Motor Cars Ltd.)

Lowering a V8 engine onto a sub-frame assembly. This photograph was taken in 1967. (Courtesy Rolls-Royce Motor Cars Ltd.)

Hydraulic system

To explain the Silver Shadow's suspension it is necessary to first examine the car's hydraulic system which controlled three distinct functions: pressure generation, braking, and height control. Each function had its own circuit which, in turn, was made up of a number of components.

Taking each function separately, each pressure generation circuit comprised a fluid reservoir, brake pump and two accumulators, the latter incorporating a valve and sphere assembly. The reservoir, which enabled a head of hydraulic fluid to be maintained, as well as allowing the fluid to expand as it heated, was, in fact, two units, front (number one system) and rear (number two), supported by a single housing. The fluid passed to the brake pump where it was contained between the outer casing and the body of the pump. The pump unit, which

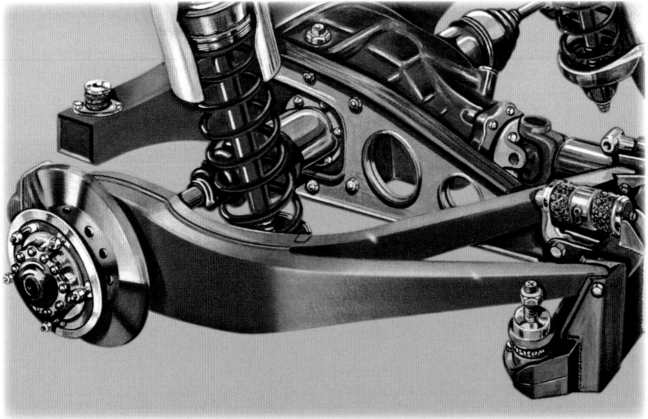

Top left: The front sub-frame assembly. (Courtesy Rolls-Royce Motor Cars Ltd.)

Bottom left: Rear sub-frame assembly. (Courtesy Rolls-Royce Motor Cars Ltd.)

Work in progress in car assembly, Crewe. In this busy scene, cars are having trim items fitted. (Courtesy Rolls-Royce Motor Cars Ltd.)

Awaiting body furniture, the car in the foreground has left hand steering. Most of the cars in the assembly shop seem intended for export. (Courtesy Rolls-Royce Motor Cars Ltd.)

was bolted to the engine tappet cover, took its drive from a pushrod operated from the camshaft and displaced the fluid, so forcing open a non-return valve. The fluid was then passed to the accumulator which stored and regulated the pressure. After use the fluid returned to the reservoir. Originally both accumulators were located at the rear of the engine on the left- hand side of the car, but, after 1975, the forward accumulator was moved to the front right-hand side of the engine. The accumulator

comprised a sphere charged with nitrogen at 1000psi and incorporated a diaphragm which allowed fluid to be contained in the upper segment. As the pressure of the fluid rose and equalled the pressure of the nitrogen, so the diaphragm dropped, letting the sphere fill with fluid. Pressure was allowed to reach 2500psi before fluid was returned to the reservoir.

The braking system of the Silver Shadow was a sophisticated affair which incorporated all-round disc brakes (Rolls-Royce, incidentally, was

the last of the major car manufacturers to adopt disc braking). Not only had drum brakes proved extraordinarily efficient, but the company needed to be sure that the system it had decided upon was without problems and did not suffer the inherent brake squeal that had so often plagued other car makers. Understandably, a lot of time and effort was spent by the development department which had worked alongside component suppliers to establish a suitable design. The front brakes comprised two calipers

Getting to grips with the job: adjustments are being made while a car is on the overhead ramp.
(Courtesy Rolls-Royce Motor Cars Ltd.)

on each wheel and the rear brakes a single caliper on each wheel, all brakes utilising two sets of pads, with those on the rear wheels being larger than those on the front.

The braking system, which was activated by two distribution valves and operated by pressure on the brake pedal, supplied hydraulic fluid under pressure at 2500psi via two independent circuits, each with identical components. In addition, a pressure limiting valve was fitted to the rear brakes which prevented the rear wheels from skidding under emergency stop conditions. As if this was not enough, a third circuit was provided which took the form of a conventional system and utilised a master cylinder in the usual manner that operated on the rear wheels only. Had the conventional circuit not been added, the braking system would have had very little 'feel' to it and the driver would have been subjected to the 'full-on' effect so often experienced with Citroën's hydropneumatic system.

The ratio at which the braking system operated was 47 per cent from the forward accumulators, which divided the effort between front and rear at a ratio of 31 to 16 respectively, a further 31 per cent of the total for the front only, and 22 per cent in respect of the conventional system. The handbrake (in America the parking brake), which provided, in effect, a fourth braking circuit, worked in a quite conventional manner, operating mechanically on the rear brakes which were also served by the master cylinder. For the American

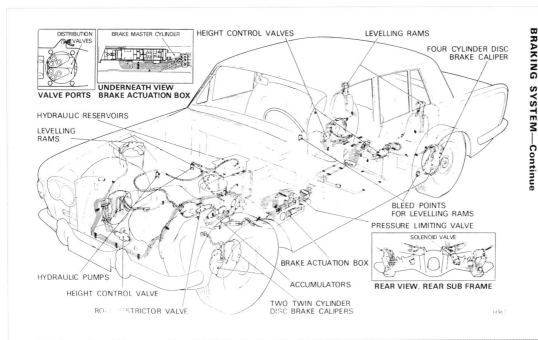

Diagram labels:

DISTRIBUTION VALVES

VALVE PORTS

BRAKE MASTER CYLINDER

UNDERNEATH VIEW
BRAKE ACTUATION BOX

HEIGHT CONTROL VALVES

LEVELLING RAMS

FOUR CYLINDER DISC
BRAKE CALIPER

HYDRAULIC RESERVOIRS

LEVELLING
RAMS

BLEED POINTS
FOR LEVELLING RAMS

PRESSURE LIMITING VALVE

SOLENOID VALVE

REAR VIEW, REAR SUB FRAME

HYDRAULIC PUMPS

HEIGHT CONTROL VALVE

RO... ...STRICTOR VALVE

BRAKE ACTUATION BOX

ACCUMULATORS

TWO TWIN CYLINDER
DISC BRAKE CALIPERS

The Silver Shadow's hydraulic system was necessarily complex, as shown here. (Courtesy Rolls-Royce Motor Cars Ltd.)

market a foot-operated parking brake eventually replaced the more usual umbrella-type handle specified for British and European production, and was positioned under the facia ahead of the driver. In Britain anything other than a hand-operated lever for the parking brake caused a great deal of confusion: the hydropneumatic DS and XM Citroëns similarly employed a foot-operated system which, whilst appreciated by the French, seemed to provoke endless criticism elsewhere.

Rolls-Royce specified Girling calipers with 11 inch (280mm) discs which incorporated in their peripheries a band of stainless steel wire. This was designed to dampen brake squeal, a problem which had troubled the development team for a long time and had prevented earlier adoption of disc brakes. A safety feature later built into the system was the provision of facia-mounted warning lamps which indicated either a loss of hydraulic pressure, or that the brake pads were worn to the extent that they required changing.

The height control system consisted essentially of four major components: height control solenoid, solenoid restrictors, height control valves and levelling rams. The function

of the system was to keep the car at a constant level whatever load was carried and however distributed, and had nothing to do with wheel movement or road surface. Had the Silver Shadow - a particularly heavy car at 40.6 hundredweight (4546lbs/2062kg) - been designed to have conventional springing which still gave the soft ride required, there would have been the need to compensate for those occasions when extra loads were carried. Had, however, the conventional springing been able to carry all the weight asked of it, it would by necessity have been very firm. The quality of the ride under these circumstances would have suffered, unless the load had been evenly distributed. Since it was not feasible to satisfy both conditions, the self-levelling device offered suitable automatic adjustment at all times, whether the car was on the move or stationary.

The height control valves operated at two speeds and, under all driving conditions, did no more than compensate as the fuel level dropped in

*This colour cutaway illustrates some of the Silver Shadow's complicated engineering.
Courtesy Rolls-Royce Motor Cars Ltd.)*

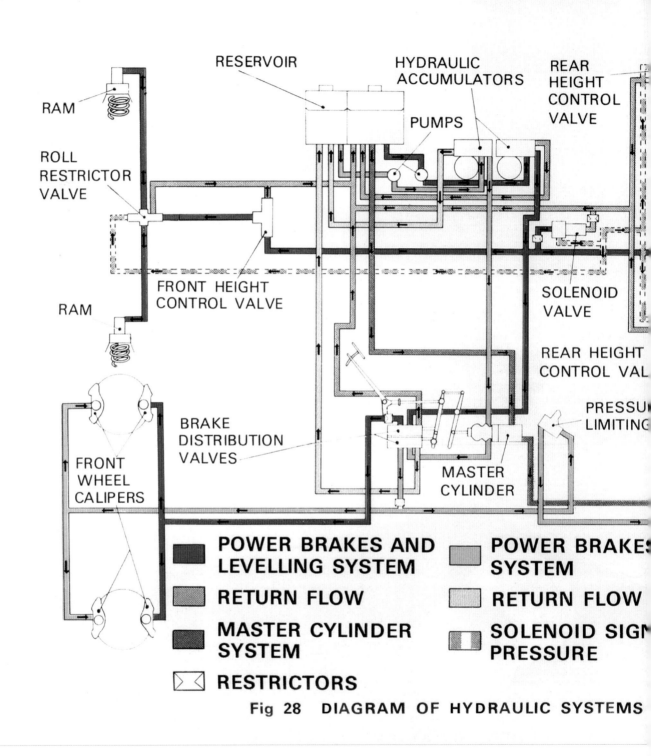

RESERVOIR

HYDRAULIC ACCUMULATORS

REAR HEIGHT CONTROL VALVE

RAM

PUMPS

ROLL RESTRICTOR VALVE

REAR HEIGHT CONTROL VAL...

RAM

FRONT HEIGHT CONTROL VALVE

SOLENOID VALVE

PRESSU... LIMITING

BRAKE DISTRIBUTION VALVES

MASTER CYLINDER

FRONT WHEEL CALIPERS

POWER BRAKES AND LEVELLING SYSTEM

POWER BRAKE... SYSTEM

RETURN FLOW

RETURN FLOW

MASTER CYLINDER SYSTEM

SOLENOID SIG... PRESSURE

RESTRICTORS

Fig 28   DIAGRAM OF HYDRAULIC SYSTEMS

The hydraulic system of the Shadow and T-Series cars could reasonably be described as a plumber's nightmare!
(Courtesy Rolls-Royce Motor Cars Ltd.)

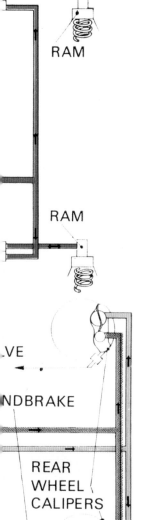

RAM

RAM

VE

NDBRAKE

REAR
WHEEL
CALIPERS

H 965

the fuel tank. Once the car was at a standstill and weight distribution rapidly changed due to passengers getting in or out, or the fuel tank was refilled, the valves operated ten times faster. Three height control valves operated the four hydraulic rams at the front and rear of the car. A single valve, which was bolted to the front sub-frame just under the radiator, responded to rotary movements of an anti-roll bar. The two were connected by a linkage which adjusted the two

forward levelling rams. Built into the hydraulic circuit was a roll restriction valve which, as well as dividing fluid between the two rams, restricted any crossflow between them. Without the restrictor, fluid would have drained to either side of the car, causing it to roll alarmingly. Two separate valves, bolted on to the forward assembly of the rear sub-frame and linked to the trailing arms, operated the rams on the rear axle. It may have seemed simpler to install a height correction valve on

Mechanical brake linkages. (Courtesy Rolls-Royce Motor Cars Ltd.)

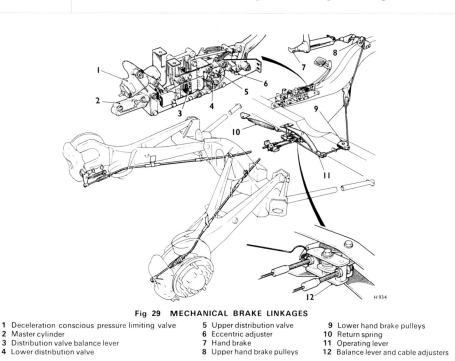

Fig 29 MECHANICAL BRAKE LINKAGES

1 Deceleration conscious pressure limiting valve
2 Master cylinder
3 Distribution valve balance lever
4 Lower distribution valve
5 Upper distribution valve
6 Eccentric adjuster
7 Hand brake
8 Upper hand brake pulleys
9 Lower hand brake pulleys
10 Return spring
11 Operating lever
12 Balance lever and cable adjusters

K 36

Fig 30   REAR DISC BRAKE

1 Power brake circuit bleed screw
2 Master cylinder circuit bleed screw
3 Disconnecting point
4 Securing clip
5 Locating pin
6 Hand brake pads
7 Adjusting ratchet seal

Rear disc brake assembly. (Courtesy Rolls-Royce Motor Cars Ltd.)

each wheel but, with this method, it would have been virtually impossible to achieve the correct balance. In the event of rapid redistribution of weight - such as passengers getting in or out - the solenoid valve was activated to provide almost instant levelling, made possible by sensors located in the gearshift, when neutral was selected, and on the courtesy lights, which denoted a door opening.

The rams which operated the rear

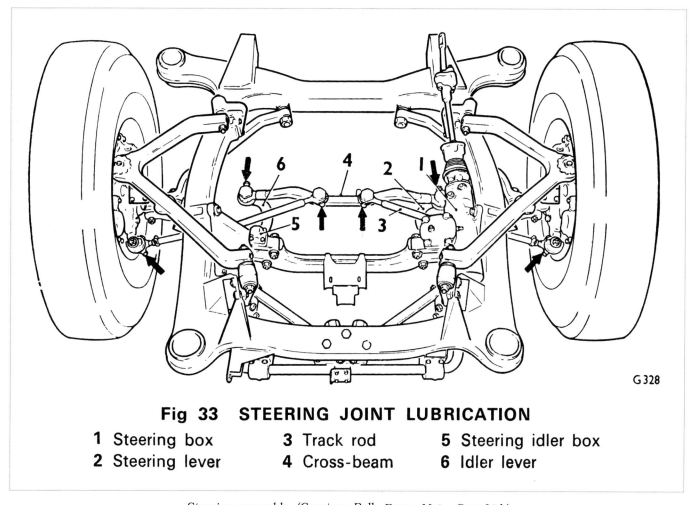

Fig 33 STEERING JOINT LUBRICATION

1 Steering box **3** Track rod **5** Steering idler box
2 Steering lever **4** Cross-beam **6** Idler lever

G 328

Steering assembly. (Courtesy Rolls-Royce Motor Cars Ltd.)

levelling device had a 3 inch (75mm) stroke, whilst those located on the front suspension had a movement of just 1 inch (25mm). This meant that the more weight the car carried the further the rams had to extend and, conversely, when the car was unladen travel was reduced. Nothing more than a piston inside a cylinder with a seal, the rear rams were bolted on to the body of the car at the top of the coil springs, and connected to the isolating cones which supported the rear shock absorbers and springs.

To ensure that the self-levelling system worked efficiently, and the valves were prevented from working quickly when they should be operating slowly, solenoid restrictors constantly checked the hydraulic pressure. The

levelling device, whilst functioning perfectly well at the rear of the car, did experience some early problems on the front axle and it was this which led to claims of steering vagueness. Compared to the rear levelling, the front device had very little work to do and it was decided to dispense with it. An official modification kit was eventually supplied by the factory, and with it were full instructions on how to disconnect the front system. It's unlikely many cars still exist which have not had this modification.

Compared to the hydraulic self-levelling, the car's mechanical suspension layout appeared quite conventional: independent, with double wishbone geometry at the front, together with coil springs

and Girling telescopic dampers; at the rear, independent suspension again but with single trailing arms, coil springs and Girling telescopic dampers. It's no wonder that the series of hydraulic pipes required to disperse the suspension fluid quickly were described as a plumber's nightmare!

When introduced, the Bentley T and Rolls-Royce Silver Shadow models were specified with three levels of suspension. The American market demanded cars with a much softer suspension than would normally be required in Britain and Europe. As a result, cars exported to the USA had relatively soft springing, more in the style of American produced vehicles. For the home market and Europe, the springing was firmer, a benefit of which

Apprentices fitting the V8 engine to a sub-frame. The picture was taken in 1965. (Courtesy Rolls-Royce Motor Cars Ltd.)

was markedly improved handling. The third suspension level was somewhat obscure and was reserved for those cars whose destinations were known to have the worst possible road surfaces. In such circumstances where it might have been possible to cause serious damage to a normal suspension, the springing was made considerably stiffer to withstand violent shocks. Cars with this 'colonial suspension' were usually destined for Australia and African countries.

Another feature new to the Silver Shadow and Bentley T was the steering mechanism. Instead of using its own powered steering, Rolls-Royce bought in the American Saginaw system which used a recirculating ball steering box instead of the Marles type of cam and roller specified for the Silver Cloud. As with the Silver Cloud, hydraulic pressure was obtained from a belt-driven Hobourn-Eaton pump in conjunction with a Saginaw steering box with integral ram. As well as being lighter than that of the Silver Cloud or S-Series Bentley, the Silver Shadow had a tighter turning circle of 4 turns lock-to-lock. Even so, Harry Grylls' 'sneeze factor' was still evident - this was a safety margin in the event of

the driver's attention being distracted (such as whilst sneezing), or in case of slight error when a twitch of the wheel might have caused other cars to veer off course. Ironically, soon after Harry's retirement the turning circle was reduced even further.

With safety as the main concern a collapsible steering column was designed, the first time such a device had been used on either a Rolls-Royce or a Bentley. The column was kinked at its division which made it all the easier to install. For the first time also the steering wheel, which was 17 inches (432mm) in diameter, had

Extensive testing was all part of Rolls-Royce's commitment to engineering excellence. (Courtesy Rolls-Royce Motor Cars Ltd.)

just two spokes, instead of three as previously, although the rim retained the same dimensions as that fitted to the Silver Cloud. A central horn push was provided, but *Autocar*'s test driver was clearly not impressed with the two-spoke wheel, much preferring the previous three-spoke version.

Engine and transmission
Under the bonnet of the Silver Shadow and Bentley T was the familiar 6230cc V8 engine developed in 1959 which first saw service on the second series Silver Cloud and the Bentley S2. A V8 configuration had been decided upon quite early when choosing a replacement for the faithful 4887cc straight six; the straight eight B80 engine had been a contender but was considered far too bulky. Apart from being fitted to the few Phantom IVs which had been produced, the B80's role had previously been to power commercial and military vehicles, and it was used for industrial purposes. Again, Harry Grylls looked across the Atlantic to Detroit to see what the Americans were doing: he saw and appreciated the lightweight V8s being fitted by Cadillac and Chrysler and acknowledged this to be the route Rolls-Royce should take.

Before committing to the V8 layout, some consideration was given to alternative configurations. Rolls-Royce had previously developed a V12, which had been used in the Phantom III in the late thirties, and it was this principle that manufacturers such as Ferrari and Jaguar adopted. Daimler chose the V8 route for its Majestic Major and DR450 limousine, the 250 saloon (the Jaguar MKII lookalike), as well as the desirable SP250 sports car. The V8 was specified for the big Fords also, and used by some specialist car makers such as Jensen, which opted for the Chrysler unit.

It should be appreciated that, when development of the Silver

Shadow first began, it was the 6-cylinder engine which was considered. In adopting the Silver Cloud's V8 the opportunity was taken to implement a number of changes to the engine which suited the design of the new car. A new combustion chamber shape, made possible by redesigning the cylinder heads, proved more efficient and, as a result, improved maximum output by something like 2 per cent. At the time, Rolls-Royce never revealed the bhp rating of its engines, choosing instead to describe it merely as 'adequate.' Sparkplugs - which previously had been almost inaccessible beneath the exhaust manifolds - were made more readily available.

In its previous form, engine accessibility was so dire that panels had to be provided in the inner wheelarches of the Silver Cloud just to allow sparkplug removal. Even with the engine modifications, underbonnet space in the Silver Shadow was extremely tight. Maintenance and servicing was decidedly easier, but few owners concerned themselves with such detail ...

The increase in power was, to a great extent, needed to drive the car's sophisticated hydraulic system as well as the plethora of ancillary components. Torque also improved and a maximum speed of somewhere between 115mph (184kph) and 118mph (189kph) was possible. Incidentally, the best the Silver Cloud III could manage was 117mph (188.3kph), impressive in view of it's size.

Aluminium alloy was used to form the crankcase, cylinder heads, timing covers, and inlet manifolds. The 'wet' liner principle was used, which meant that the cast iron cylinder liners were in direct contact with the coolant. Rolls-Royce had no concerns about the engine's specification: the valve gear was of the overhead in-line type with pushrods and rockers, and hydraulic tappets completed the package. Two levels of compression ratio were offered: 9.0 to 1 for 100 octane fuel and, optionally, 8.0 to 1, for less refined fuels. Carburation was provided by two diaphragm-type SU HD8 carburettors, whilst two electric SU pumps fed the fuel supply. In order for the car to have a low bonnet line it had been necessary to modify the radiator header tank and, for the same reason, the air cleaner was relocated to inside the right-hand front underwing. Flexible trunking from the air cleaner led to the carburettors.

To those who appreciate and understand Rolls-Royce's commitment to engineering, the V8 engine is a work of art. Weighing something like 30lbs (14kg) less than the 6-cylinder it replaced, it featured almost 30 per cent more in the way of swept volume. The design of the engine was conventional enough as a V8: it had a five bearing crankshaft and the camshaft was positioned neatly between the two cylinder heads, within the vee. Totally refined, as was to be expected, the unit promised a lifetime of smooth running as long as it was respected and carefully maintained.

In deciding the type of gearbox for the Silver Shadow, Rolls-Royce faced something of a dilemma. The automatic gearbox used in the Silver Cloud and S-Series Bentley had proved itself beyond all measure but, in the light of competition from new designs emanating from America, was showing its age. Although the gearbox, with a certain amount of modification, was acceptable to the British market, it had less chance of being appreciated in America. The costs in developing an all-new gearbox would have been prohibitive in terms of both time and money, so it was decided that right-hand drive cars would have a refined version of the existing General Motors Hydramatic box.

Whilst of American design, the GM four-speed gearbox for Rolls-Royce and Bentley cars was actually assembled by Rolls-Royce at Crewe. For left-hand drive cars, and principally the American market, Rolls-Royce undertook to fit a completely new gearbox to the Silver Shadow and Bentley T. In seeking a suitable unit Ivan Evernden did not have to look further than Detroit and the new GM400, again from General Motors. The gearbox, which was a very refined unit and totally smooth in operation, proved fully up-to-date in specification. Acknowledged as being just about the best available, it had already been chosen by Buick and Cadillac for their 1963 models. The first experience Rolls-Royce had of the GM400 box was when it had been installed in an experimental car as early as November 1964. It was fitted to 48B, at that time undergoing trials. Torque was increased so much that, under tests requiring full-throttle starts, a halfshaft was snapped.

The new GM400 gearbox, known as the TurboHydramatic, had a number of modifications compared to the old four-speed type. It was fitted with a torque converter and three forward speeds, which did away with the previous fluid coupling, and second gear had just about the same ratio as the old unit's third. Performance was definitely better than that of the four-speed box, with first gear being a little quicker. Overall speed through

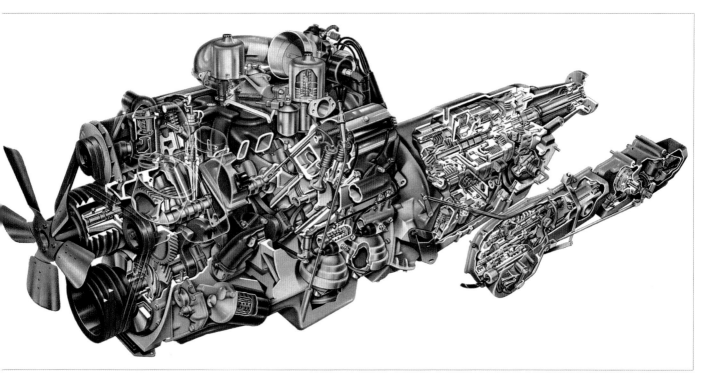

The 6.230-litre V8 engine as originally used in production Shadows and Bentley Ts.
(Courtesy Rolls-Royce Motor Cars Ltd.)

the gears was superior. The absence of the low-ratio bottom gear ensured an absolutely smooth operation, which was mirrored throughout the gear range. Of interest is the fact that Rolls-Royce decided against building the GM400 at Crewe and, instead, bought in the gearbox as a complete entity, modifying it to accept electric actuation.

As for the faithful old four-speed gearbox specified for right-hand drive cars (it was intended that all Silver Shadow and Bentley T models would eventually receive the new GM400 box), some quite serious modifications were made. The main casing, instead of being formed from cast iron, was made from aluminium alloy, as were many of the internal castings. To enhance smoothness, a freewheel device was incorporated with first and second gear ratios, but it remained possible, by selecting the hold on second gear, thereby making the freewheel inoperative, to obtain engine braking if required. A further refinement was the ability to change gear electrically, instead of having direct linkage, and a finger-light lever

positioned on the steering column actuated a motor bolted to the rear of the transmission casing. Mechanical links were, of course, provided to the selector levers in the usual manner, but the refinement meant that physical gear selection was eliminated.

The reason for electric actuation extends back to the fifties when the Silver Shadow was conceived. In that period it was fashionable to allow front seat occupants to leave the car from either side, which was especially useful if the driver had parked against the nearside kerb and, not wanting to step out into the traffic flow, could simply slide across the front seat and leave by the passenger's door. As centrally-mounted gearchange levers presented an obstruction, a popular solution was to place the gear selector on the steering column. A number of snags were associated with column change such as rattles and difficulty of operation, but, by placing a selector switch at the top of the column and connecting it to the actuator on the gearbox casing by nothing more complicated than an electrical cable, these problems could be eliminated.

Jock Knight, who was involved in developing a suitable electrically-actuated gearchange for the Silver Shadow, was aware that great care had to be taken with the design and choice of materials for the electrical contacts of both switch and actuator. It was important that effective sealing of the actuator was achieved to protect against corrosion from water and road salt ingress; also that it was properly ventilated. Several mechanisms were mounted on experimental cars undergoing endurance testing and, in addition, switches and actuators were tested on specially prepared rigs. One particular mechanism was installed in an environmental test chamber, where it completed several million gearchange cycles whilst exposed to extremes of temperature and humidity, including submersion in brine.

In the case of electrical failure it was still possible to get the car home. Rolls-Royce engineers had thought of everything as, included in the car's tool kit, was a specially-designed tommy bar which, when inserted into a hole in the top of the gearbox, allowed direct manual changes to be made.

Fig 8   MANUAL SELECTION OF GEAR RANGES

1 Tommy bar   2 Sealing cover

All Silver Shadows and T-Series Bentleys had gearboxes with electric actuation. On early cars a 'get-you-home' device allowed manual selection of the gears in the event of electrical failure. (Courtesy Rolls-Royce Motor Cars Ltd.)

Needless to say the carpet over the gearbox housing had to be removed first. As a matter of interest it had been necessary to use the emergency tommy bar early on while testing experimental car 49B in France. The electrical gearchange had failed and the test team happily continued using the direct manual change until replacement parts were delivered from Crewe. After a few years' production with virtually no failures, the 'get you home' device was abandoned.

Instead of the two-piece propeller shaft which had been fitted to the Silver Shadow's predecessors, a one-piece affair was now specified. Not only did this add to the car's overall handling (the shaft connected with the differential which was fixed to the bodyshell, increasing the stiffness of the chassis) but also enabled a reduction in body length. The hypoid-beval final drive unit was supported upon one of the two vertical crossmembers which basically made up the rear subframe, the other crossmember supporting the suspension trailing arms. On the driveshafts could be found constant velocity universals of the ball and trunion Detroit type; on the outer shafts the usual Hooke-type Hardy-Spicers were specified.

Under the bonnet and out of sight (out of mind also for a great many owners!) was a plethora of ancillary equipment which included the cooling system comprising two thermostats and 28 pints (16 litres) of coolant, an oil filter - which had to be changed every 6000 miles (9600kms) - and hydraulic pumps, as well as all the associated belts, hoses and electrical wiring. The battery, a 12 volt, 64 ampere model, was positioned in the boot on the nearside between the wheelarch and rear panel, while the alternator was a 35 amp Lucas unit. The engine sump held 14.5 pints of oil (8 litres) and the gearbox 24 pints (13.6 litres). The final drive held 4 pints (2.3 litres) of oil and the fuel tank had a capacity of 24 gallons (28.8 US gallons, 109 litres) of fuel. When just 3 gallons (3.60 US gallons, 13.64 litres) remained in the tank a warning light illuminated on the facia. Greasing of six grease points had to be attended to every 12,000 miles (19,200 kms).

Both inside and outside the Bentley and Rolls-Royce a most notable feature was the car's quietness. Excellent sound-proofing ensured occupants were spared mechanical and traffic noise, and the finely engineered exhaust boasted no fewer than four silencers, and stainless steel ones, at that.

An example of absolute sophistication was the electrical system which, on many more humble cars, would have seemed beyond all imagination. Not only the window lifts were electrically powered but also the seat adjustment. Should a headlamp fail, a secondary circuit automatically and instantly illuminated the stand-by filament, and red lamps were installed in the rear doors to provide warning to following traffic. The headlamp safety

An air conditioning unit being assembled at Crewe. (Courtesy Rolls-Royce Motor Cars Ltd.)

adjusted warm air into the car's interior, one for each side of the car, and the airflow could be directed either upwards, to demist the windscreen, or downwards, for cabin warmth. Heating ducts were also positioned in the rear compartment for the comfort of passengers but, surprisingly, these could not be regulated or closed i n d e p e n d e n t l y and were, in fact, controlled to provide the same output as the lower front heater outlets.

circuit was introduced after Harry Grylls, driving an experimental car, experienced a floor-mounted headlamp dipswitch explode, leaving its entrails lying on the floor and Harry with no headlamps, a frightening experience he did not want a customer to suffer. The solution was to provide the headlamps with an auxiliary circuit, in addition to the normal one, whereby in the event of an open circuit failure, a relay switched in a second circuit. In the event of a short circuit failure, a relay operated the headlamps intermittently, thus allowing the driver to bring the car to a halt with some semblance of lighting.

Today, it's taken for granted that a rear windscreen de-mister will be fitted as standard equipment in almost every car, and electrically-operated aerials are commonplace, as is remote control opening of the fuel filler cap. In 1965 such features were luxuries, however, and certainly air conditioning in a car was almost unheard of. The heating and ventilation system proved an elaborate affair and *sundym* tinted glass was a standard feature when air conditioning was specified. The main heating and ventilation air intake was positioned on the scuttle, immediately in front of the windscreen: in addition, two supplementary air intakes were placed at the front of the car, directly under each of the double headlamp units. The slim rectangular grilles positioned each side of the radiator provided cool air for the cabin, which was fed to outlets on the side scuttle panels (generally known as 'ankle freezers') alongside the front occupants' legs. These were deleted one by one during the early life of the car, although the grilles remained at the front for some time.

For the heating system, two four-speed blowers forced temperature-

In its appraisal of the Silver Shadow, *Autocar*, in the autumn of 1965, was critical of the overall heating system inasmuch that it lacked any thermostatic device by which to control the temperature. The report also considered that, had extractor vents been provided, these would have allowed a through-flow of air. It seemed a pity to have to open windows in an attempt to aid ventilation and heating efficiency. Much modified to that which had been specified for the Silver Cloud and S-Series Bentley, the air conditioning system was controlled by an evaporator unit and heater matrices positioned behind the facia. On the previous model these main components were housed in the valence of the front right-hand wing. The compressor was belt-driven from the crankshaft, and the condenser located immediately ahead of the radiator.

A youthful Martin Bourne takes a break from putting an early Silver Shadow through its paces in Switzerland.
(Courtesy Martin Bourne)

Craftsmanship and excellence

Without doubt the single most recognisable hallmark of any Rolls-Royce is its radiator and, in this respect, the Silver Shadow was certainly no exception. To untrained eyes the imposing radiator shell appeared quite flat and vertical when, in fact, it was neither. It took twelve highly-skilled metal workers, all of whom had at least 25 years' experience in serving the marque (the company's own publicity material referred to them as acolytes), to make the hallowed radiators, and Rolls-Royce rightly believed that no-one outside the factory could do the job as well. Looking more like silver or silver plate than the stainless steel it was, the perfect finish was the result of hours of polishing. The shell may have seemed composed of a single piece but, in fact, comprised no fewer than eleven separate items of steel, all of which were approximately 0.062 inches (2.5mm) thick, and worked until the edges were perfectly mitred.

Such precision may seem

excessive; to other manufacturers, perhaps, but not Rolls-Royce, where only the best was good enough. Traditional methods and tools of metal working were employed, such as age-old soldering irons heated over an open flame. The same applied to the Spirit of Ecstasy, possibly the best-known car mascot in the world. In 1911 Charles Sykes ARBS created the emblem for Rolls-Royce as a commission, and thereafter, for a number of years, cast each figure - the base metal was an alloy of copper, either brass or bronze - himself. The model for the emblem was Eleanor Thornton, secretary to the first Baron Montagu of Beaulieu. Surprisingly, this prestigious item was not standard equipment until after the Second World War; before then it was supplied as an optional extra. For many years the mascot was crafted at Crewe by Rolls-Royce's own engineers, but, following the sale of Rolls-Royce to BMW, and Bentley to Volkswagen, the Spirit of Ecstasy in its latest form is produced by a specialist firm in Southampton using the 'lost wax' process. Standing proudly on the radiator shell top tank, the figure conformed to then-current safety regulations and is spring-loaded so as not to cause injury. As part of the

company's quality control measures even the spring-loading mechanism of the mascot was checked by being struck by a wooden ball, encased in rubber, measuring 6.5 inches in diameter (165mm) and weighing 15lbs (6.8kg). Understandably, the Spirit of Ecstasy became one of the most desirable items for trophy hunters. Many mascots were lost, which resulted in Rolls-Royce owners having to alarm them or remove them altogether when parking the car.

In order to appear perfectly rectilinear, each surface and component that made up the radiator shell had to have a slight curve; a practice appreciated by the Greeks who knew it as entasis. Look very carefully at the radiator and it can be seen that it's not entirely vertical but has the slightest forward inclination. Notice the vertical bars on the radiator - these should never be referred to as vanes but shutters. No longer do these open and close to control the flow of air; technology has come up with far more sophisticated ways to control cooling.

Care and fastidious attention to detail did not begin and end with the radiator. On every wheel fitted to the Silver Shadow there could be

found a white spot which showed that particular wheel had been carefully checked to ensure proper welding, finish and accuracy. Production checks as stringent as this were not good enough, however; one in every 1500 wheels was subjected to close examination and had a section cut out of it. The weld structure was inspected under a microscope and, if the wheel had a fault, the whole batch was rejected.

Underneath a new Silver Shadow or T-Series Bentley it would have been possible to see 86 yellow-painted nuts (in fact, there were 91 but 5 were out of sight). Only when the torque of each nut had been checked, and every component examined as far as was humanly possible, was the dab of paint applied.

The same exacting tests were also applied to engine building. Cast iron cylinder liners were honed to an almost perfect roundness of within 0.0005 inches (0.0127mm). Crankshafts were machined to a tolerance of 0.0001 inches (0.00254mm), and connecting rods were weighed, matched and tested for any imperfection. Pistons, too, were selected in pairs and carefully checked for weight before being matched to make a complete set. All engines were run-in using gas on the test bench to the equivalent of 150 miles (240kms); in addition one in every 100 was run for eight hours on petrol, after which it was dismantled and minutely examined. As if this were not enough, test cars were subjected to gruelling 50,000 mile (80,000kms) ordeals; the only time the cars were allowed to stop was for a change of driver and to refuel.

Low profile tubeless crossply tyres, 8.45 x15, on 6 inch (152mm)

Rolls-Royce went to great lengths to ensure hide and veneer quality. Each car was equipped with eight perfectly matched hides, and each year a visit was made to Italy to buy only the best veneers. Here, veneer expert Micky Glynn can be seen preparing veneers for use in Rolls-Royce and Bentley motor cars. (Courtesy Rolls-Royce Motor Cars Ltd.)

The facia panel and door garnish rails of the Mulliner, Park Ward two-door saloon and drophead coupé are veneered in the finest, specially selected walnut. (Courtesy Rolls-Royce Motor Cars Ltd.)

rim pressed steel disc wheels with five studs were initially fitted to the Silver Shadow and T-Series cars. Tyres by three manufacturers were specified: Avon, Firestone and Dunlop. Radial tyres were quite commonplace at the time, Michelin having introduced its 'X' tyre in the early fifties, but the common feature of this type of tyre as opposed to crossplys was increased road noise. The first British car designed to use radial tyres, incidentally, was the Rover 2000, which made its debut in 1963. Although radial tyres were not adopted by Rolls-Royce until the early seventies, owners of earlier Silver Shadows and Bentleys have now fitted them quite happily and without detriment.

As can be expected, Silver Shadows and Bentleys were supplied with an impressive array of features, such as two-speed, self-parking

windscreen wipers, screen washers, an alternator instead of a dynamo, laminated screen, and reversing lamps, most of which would have been optional extras or, more likely, quite unobtainable on more modest cars. These features were in addition to the electrically-operated front seats, with their eight-way adjustment controlled by switches positioned centrally on the transmission tunnel. Along with the electric windows, there was a facia panel rheostat, hazard warning lamps, and a four-speaker radio (usually a Motorola).

Even for a standard car as well-equipped as this there were optional extras such as seat belts. Safety harness anchorages were provided as standard but, at the time, the compulsory wearing of seat belts was a long way off.

The facia and instrument panel

was a model of design ingenuity. Through the two-spoke steering wheel the driver had an excellent view of the main controls, traditional in appearance and neatly positioned. The instrument layout included speedometer, fuel gauge, ammeter and temperature gauge. Every eventuality had been thought of: the engine could not be started if either of the parking lamps was lit; warning indicators showed whether the hydraulic system was operating at the correct pressure, and the driver could check the engine oil level without even having to leave his seat by pressing a button inside the car. In the event of a stop lamp failing a light on the facia indicated as much and, for convenience, the fuse box was positioned under the facia instead of being buried in the engine compartment. A later innovation, around the early to mid-1970s, was that the 'park' position was automatically selected if the ignition key was removed from its Yale-type lock without the parking brake first being applied.

One criticism did exist, though, which concerned the design and location of the electric gear selector switch on the right-hand side of the steering column. As it was identical to the turn indicator, which was similarly positioned on the opposite side of the steering wheel, confusion between the two was inevitable with the possibility of disastrous results. The problem was quickly dealt with, before any cars found their way into customer's hands, and the gear selector stalk replaced by a much larger lever with a positive, upward-facing position.

Luxury and elegance

The interior appointment of the Silver Shadow was without compromise, and the same careful attention to detail was applied to the Bentley T version. From the durable and washable headlining - Rolls-Royce publicists thought this important enough for customers to be made aware of it - to the Wilton carpet on the floor, the finish was the ultimate in good taste. It goes without saying that only specially selected, top grade English hides were used for the upholstery and that each veneer for the facia and other areas where burr walnut was used, such as garnish rails, was the finest that could be found.

Front and rear seats were provided with centrally-positioned folding arm rests, the top of the rear rest lifting up to reveal a trinket box. For rear passengers there were wedge-shaped foot rests; cigar lighters were installed in each of the rear doors as well as on the facia and, built into the roof of the cabin, were four courtesy lights, the two at the rear incorporating reading lamps. Rear seat passengers were cossetted and for their convenience each had a map pocket and mirror. The luxurious interior would not have been complete without the usual folding picnic tables, finished in the same burr walnut veneer.

Leather for the upholstery, padded capping rails, and carpet bindings was supplied by Connolly Brothers, which selected only the finest hides. In its raw state the material arrived at Connolly's premises in stiff bales, having been preserved in salt, but it was slender, finely grained and supple consignments of eight perfectly matched hides that eventually were supplied to Rolls-Royce. Available in eight colours - Beige, Tan, Grey, Blue, Red, Green, Scarlet and Black - each consignment was enough to upholster a complete car. In the trimming department skilled hands deftly cut and sewed the hides, forming them carefully over the seat frames to produce the ultimate armchair comfort. Good taste extended to the Wilton carpets, which matched the colour of the hide upholstery, and West of England cloth headlining which was optional to Ambla, a PVC material normally used; even lambswool rugs were laid in the rear passenger compartment.

The use of burr walnut in a Rolls-Royce and Bentley may be rather taken for granted but its selection and application was a highly-skilled process; a work of art, in fact. Each year Micky Glynn, Rolls-Royce veneer expert, made an annual pilgrimage to Milan in Italy to select the veneer. The amount of veneer required by Rolls-Royce each year was huge - enough to cover two football pitches - and it was not from a single supplier that the material was purchased. Visits were made to countless dank and dimly lit storerooms, often subterranean, where the veneers were closely examined. As the walnut tree grows, so the grain of the wood around the foot of some of the trees is broken by a growth of warts, and it is these imperfections, when the timber is sliced into wafer-thin sections, that produce the fine patterns.

When the veneers arrived at Crewe the material was stored in an old air raid shelter, chosen because the underground conditions exactly matched those of the supplier. The art in preparing the burr walnut is the careful cutting and matching of each sheet so that a veneer on one side of the car has a perfect mirror-finish on the opposite side. Up to eight veneers, all skilfully and invisibly joined, formed the facia panel alone and no two cars shared the same grain pattern. The glass-like finish on the veneers was the result of hours of painstaking polishing and lacquering of the wood to bring out the full beauty of the grain. Surprisingly, approximately 60 per cent of each veneer was discarded during preparation, and a further 10 per cent kept back for future use, should it be required, for example, to repair damage. The section of veneer that was retained was numbered and catalogued with the car's chassis details and carefully stored away in the dank conditions of the air raid shelter.

Performance - how it compared

The Silver Shadow - or any other Rolls-Royce or Bentley for that matter - certainly wasn't purchased because it had excellent fuel consumption. Initial tests showed that fast continental touring could consume petrol at the rate of 11 miles per gallon (25.7 lts/100km), although a lighter touch on the accelerator could improve this figure to 15mpg (19lts/100km). Overall, the Silver Shadow owner had to be content with something like 12mpg (23lts/100km).

Most owners were happy to believe their cars were without rival - but what of other large luxury cars available then? Certainly, large American machines such as the Buick Riviera and Cadillac Fleetwood were slightly less economical, but who in the US worried about fuel consumption at that time? The huge Mercedes 600, with its 6.3-litre V8 engine, had tantalising features, including pneumatic suspension and compressed air braking that was almost as impressive as that of the Rolls-Royce. It matched the Silver Shadow's fuel consumption but appalling handling let the car down badly. The clear winner in the fuel league was the Daimler Majestic Major, which was not superior to a Rolls-Royce or Bentley, claiming an overall consumption of 15mpg (19lts/100km).

Of the four contemporaries the Rolls-Royce and Bentley were the slowest: as a maximum even the Daimler achieved a mean top speed of 120mph (192kph) compared to 115mph (184kph) for the Silver Shadow; the Mercedes outshone everything else with 125mph (200kph) whilst the Buick and Cadillac settled for a more conservative 123mph (197kph) and 118mph (189kph) respectively.

A closer rival, perhaps, was the Jaguar Mark X which, by the mid-sixties, was powered by a 4.2-litre version of the trusty XK engine. This was a car much appreciated by customers seeking the opulence of hand-crafted veneers and leather, mated with refined engineering. At £2200, the big Jaguar offered good value for money with performance to match: maximum speed was 118mph (189kph), but the trade-off was fuel consumption of 14mpg (20lts/100km). The Daimler Sovereign, too, eventually became a contender in the rival stakes, especially in Double-Six vogue. The new generation Daimler Limousine, which was based upon the floorpan of the Mark 10 Jaguar, and powered initially by the 4.2-litre XK engine, might have been a more serious rival. In the event its role was more that of courtesy car, offering comfortable travel to and from airports, and the like.

Through the gears and from standing starts the Bentley T and Silver Shadow were never clear winners, but, after all, who bought the cars for sheer performance? As far as devotees were concerned, the vehicles offered superlative comfort with more than enough speed, and prices were academic. The Daimler cost a mere £2749 but failed to command the same level of respect; the price tag of the Mercedes was a massive £9000, less a few pennies, and the American offerings could be bought for between £4400 and £5200. At around £6500 the Silver Shadow and Bentley T oozed quality and refinement, dignity and sophistication. These cars were not merely assembled, but created, products of dedicated engineering and skilful hands. Perhaps more importantly than anything else, they epitomised a deep-seated loyalty to the company and its traditions.

Not just new models from the most respected car manufacturer in the world, the Silver Shadow and Bentley T were also the beginning of a new era. The cars that followed included a second series Silver Shadow, the Shadow II and, alongside it, the Bentley T2; coachbuilt versions were offered and these included the now rare James Young-bodied two-door saloon and the delightful Corniche from MPW. The Corniche, incidentally, remained in production long after the Silver Shadow had been superseded by the Silver Spirit, and it was almost thirty years after the announcement of the Silver Shadow that the last car was built. Long wheelbase models, which eventually evolved as the Silver Wraith II, and the controversial Pininfarina Camargue, made their debut within the lifetime of the Silver Shadow and are examined later in this book.

Whispering power

The mid-sixties was a time of reward and disappointment at Rolls-Royce: reward because of the achievements that culminated in production of a car which, for Rolls-Royce, was quite new in its engineering concept, and disappointment at the level of losses in the motor car division. Losses had been expected during this period because of the enormous cost of development of the Silver Shadow, and the board of directors, which had been kept fully informed at all times, had given its approval.

As the Silver Shadow and its Bentley equivalent went into production, the cars' futures were overseen by the company's general manager, Ray Dorey OBE (*Dor*). Dorey had accepted the position of GM at Crewe in the early fifties, rather than head the company's interests in Canada, a position he had also been offered. His career with Rolls-Royce began in the late twenties after he graduated from university. Dorey was invited to join the experimental division at Derby, working on aero engines, and immediately made a name for himself testing engines on the run-up to the 1929 Schneider Trophy Race. Cars and motoring were amongst his keener interests and, during those early years at Derby, he owned a Bugatti. (As a point of interest it was Ettore Bugatti who had referred to W.O. Bentley's cars as the fastest lorries on earth!)

During his term as general manager, Roy Dorey witnessed a frustrating period in Rolls-Royce's finances. Just as the motor industry recovered from shortages caused by the aftermath of war, and began to look forward to a new decade - the sixties - with confidence, severe restrictions were placed upon the industry by the then chancellor of the exchequer, Selwyn Lloyd. In his budget, the chancellor created taxes that would deter potential customers from buying expensive motor cars. Dorey had no option but to cancel orders with Rolls-Royce suppliers in order to reduce the effect of a sudden down-turn in sales.

The motor industry suffered as a whole, of course; Rolls-Royce was not the only company manufacturing highly-priced cars. Public perception of large-engined cars, such as the Silver Cloud and Bentley S-Series, was badly affected by the chancellor's tax burden, and it was upon a campaign of damage-limitation that the general manager embarked. It was to this end that two interesting managerial decisions were taken at Rolls-Royce: firstly, the ultimately abortive discussions with BMC took place and, secondly, a radically different Silver Cloud and Bentley were unveiled - the Series III and S3 models.

Although potentially a successful venture, the collaboration with BMC turned out to be a dismal failure. There were few customers for the Vanden Plas Princess R, and a Rolls-Royce-engined Austin Healey never materialised. Rolls-Royce was left with two engines which Jack Phillips, who had been responsible for development of the V8, had purposely designed: the 3.9-litre F60, which produced 178hp at 4850rpm and was fitted to the Princess 4-litre R, and the G60 of the same capacity which produced 268hp at 6000rpm. It was the latter engine which was proposed for the Big Healey. With sales of the Princess R at a disappointingly low level, the F60's production line at Crewe remained idle for much of the time before being

dismantled. Luckily, both engines have been saved for posterity at the Rolls-Royce Enthusiasts' Club headquarters at Paulerspury.

Losses in the motor car division escalated rapidly: a deficit of £300,000 was recorded in 1963 and, within two years, this amount had trebled. A year later, 1966, the loss increased further to over £1 million, and it was not until two years later that a profit - albeit a small one - was made.

Ray Dorey had foreseen, in the mid-fifties, that developing a car as complex and innovative as the Silver

Shadow would result in a difficult period for Rolls-Royce and, as a precaution, had strengthened the design department with some very able stylists and engineers. His philosophy worked and, as has been revealed in earlier chapters, the department produced some outstanding results. Having successfully overseen the launch of the Silver Shadow and Bentley T-Series, Dorey decided to retire in 1968. As he had predicted, the gestation period of the models had proved very challenging and, what was worse, he had found himself caught in

the crossfire between some very strong personalities.

Harry Grylls, who had engineered the Silver Shadow concept virtually single handed, appreciated the importance of such an innovative design, while Geoffrey Fawn (*GF*), who had joined the aero engine division of Rolls-Royce at Derby from the nuclear experimental establishment at Harwell, was critical of a car that incorporated so many new ideas at one time. The friction between Dorey and Fawn was often very evident and the final two years of Dorey's career

were somewhat turbulent ...

Geoffrey Fawn succeeded Ray Dorey and, at about the same time, Harry Grylls also took retirement. The position of chief engineer was taken by John Hollings who remained in that post until 1981 when he was appointed technical director. Hollings was no stranger to Rolls-Royce, having joined the company in 1948 as an aero engine designer. In 1957 he was appointed chief designer on nuclear reactors for submarines and, in 1962, moved to Dounreary in Scotland as manager and chief engineer at Admiralty Reactor Test Establishment. A further move, in 1965, to take up the post of chief quality engineer at the car division of Rolls-Royce, took John Hollings to Crewe.

Taking over from Harry Grylls would have been a difficult task for any successor to the post of chief engineer, but Hollings, having acknowledged his predecessor's enormous contribution to both the auto industry and the motor division of Rolls-Royce, set about building upon the legacy he had been left. When talking to John Hollings about his early days as chief engineer, he recalled he knew less about motor cars than the engineers under his control. Valuing them greatly, he therefore concentrated upon managing his team effectively, and leading it in the right direction.

John Hollings accepted that his task was one of continuation and improvement of the Silver Shadow throughout the remainder of the car's production period, which he understood needed to be somewhat longer than previous models due to the car's extraordinarily high development cost. Nevertheless, there had to be a plan for the car's eventual replacement

which, as history has shown, evolved as the Silver Spirit. Initial work on the car, designated SZ, began in 1969.

The period throughout the late sixties and the seventies, however, was particularly testing for the new chief engineer, who had to oversee a number of important events. Firstly, the American motor industry was in a state of upheaval as a result of US safety and emission control regulations. As a company that relied heavily on selling cars into America, Rolls-Royce was forced to comply with the legislative changes, or risk losing this lucrative market. Secondly, there was the fuel crisis which erupted in the early seventies, the shock waves of which were felt worldwide.

While this was happening continual progression and development of the Silver Shadow and T-Series Bentley led towards the introduction of the second series models in 1977. A third development was the introduction of a special-bodied derivative of the Silver Shadow, the Camargue coupé. This was intended as the marque's flagship and an alternative to the already prestigious two-door saloon which was renamed the Corniche (the car proved somewhat controversial, but more of this later). The most devastating event of the period was undoubtedly the financial collapse of Rolls-Royce on February 4th, 1971. On what became known within the company

as Black Thursday, Rolls-Royce - national institution and possibly the most marketable name in the world - teetered on the edge of disaster.

The seventies: a decade of engineering changes

One of the first engineering policy decisions made under John Hollings' control was that concerning the coachbuilt cars produced by MPW. Although the coachbuilt models based upon the Silver Shadow and T-Series Bentley are described in greater detail in a separate chapter, it is necessary to emphasise it was intended that these cars should pioneer any engineering modifications before they were applied to the usual production, or 'Crewe,' cars. In addition to the very elite two-door model - later known as the Corniche - it was decided to produce a wholly new coupé which supported styling from outside the company, rather than from within Crewe's own styling department. Italy had a reputation for producing some of the world's most beautiful cars, and it was the stylist, Pininfarina, whom Rolls-Royce approached.

Pininfarina had been responsible for a number of designs, including a fastback version of the Silver Dawn which had been exhibited at the 1951 Turin Motor Show. The company had also produced five cars based upon the Bentley Mk VI chassis, as

well as a single example of the R-Type Continental. Pininfarina also produced for Lord Hanson a single coupé based on the T-Series Bentley, and it is generally considered that it was this car which led to the Italian styling house being commissioned to design the Camargue. Nearly thirty years later enthusiasts may wonder why Rolls-Royce decided not to entrust the coupé to its own stylists, especially when considering that the department had produced such exciting machines as the Bentley R-Type and S-Type Continentals under the direction of Ivan Evernden and John Blatchley. It has to be said that, within Rolls-Royce circles, the decision to place the Camargue - as the coupé eventually became known - outside the company met with some misgiving ... The idea of a car such as the Camargue had originally been proposed by Geoffrey Fawn, who had the notion that Rolls-Royce needed an exclusive model with an exotic-sounding name.

In accordance with the policy of modifying the Rolls-Royce 'Crewe' cars, changes were specified for the Camargue a year before featuring on the Corniche. A year after that, revisions were finally applied to the production models, the Silver Shadow and T-Series saloons. The reason for this tiered system was so that new features would initially appear on the most expensive cars to satisfy first the company's wealthiest and most discerning customers.

Of strong influence during the seventies was the need to meet the stringent US regulations aimed at improving safety and control of exhaust emissions. One of the first tasks that the development department had to attend to was head impact, which meant conducting tests using a 6.5 inch (165mm) diameter sphere to simulate a driver's or passenger's head striking the facia. Similarly, tests were carried out imitating a rear passenger's head hitting the top of the rear section of the front seats. Some of the modifications which resulted affected the Silver Shadow facia, which was redesigned to incorporate a thickly padded surround to prevent a human head striking any of the control knobs or switches on the instrument board.

In some cases, where the roof had to provide enough strength to absorb sudden impact, the design of the Silver Shadow exceeded all requirements, and no modifications were needed. This ably demonstrated the safety margins built into the car, especially as the roof was required to withstand 5000lbs (2273kg) without deflecting more than 5 inches (127mm).

British or European car manufacturers like Rolls-Royce, who relied on American sales, could not afford to be complacent when complying with Federal Motor Vehicle Safety Standards. While having to conform to regulations was obviously very expensive and time-consuming, there were important benefits, and it was these that helped put Rolls-Royce safety specifications far ahead of most other car makers. In general terms, US safety legislation was ten years ahead of Britain's and, allowing for some flexibility on America's part, it enabled Rolls-Royce to keep something like seven years ahead of other British car manufacturers. An example of this is that, whilst airbags became available on most British and European cars in the early nineties, Rolls-Royce had this technology by 1984.

Side impact protection was an important issue for Rolls-Royce in the seventies when American standards required an intrusion test on each door. The aim was to deflect two cars meeting at an angle and prevent them interlocking and spinning round, thereby reducing the risk of injury. The tests that the development department had to instigate were, by necessity, complex, but it did mean that special bars were fitted to the insides of the doors, forming a barrier between the locks and hinges. An outcome of the tests was a modification which actually weakened the wooden waist-rail finishers in each car so that, in the event of an accident, they would not splinter and spear the occupants.

Front and rear impact tests - as previously described - were a necessity and these, generally, were carried out under the supervision of Jock Knight, who usually managed to 'crash' each test car at least four times before it had to be scrapped. An important modification was a new type of bumper required by US regulations which came into force in September 1972. The bumper, in situ on the car, had to withstand two tests, the first of which involved the car being crashed into a solid wall at 5mph (8kph). To meet this requirement the bumpers were mounted upon specially designed shock absorbers filled with silicone rubber, which gave a better

Rarely have so many Silver Shadows been seen together. (Courtesy Rolls-Royce Motor Cars Ltd.)

performance than an oil-filled damper. After impact, the energy absorbing bumpers had to return slowly to their original positions without any damage or deformation. The second test involved the bumper being hit at an angle at 3mph (5kph) by a weight equivalent to that of the car to which it was fitted. This ensured the bumper beam had adequate built-in strength to withstand minor impacts.

Along with meeting the stream of safety demands which emanated from America, Rolls-Royce had to conform to exhaust emission controls which were being instigated by a number of countries in addition to the state of California in the US, which was the most stringent. To satisfy the regulations, progressive changes to the Silver Shadow were necessary at the rate of two year intervals. Not

Photographed in Warsaw, the Silver Shadow has restyled wheelarches which allow larger section, radial tyres to be fitted. (Courtesy Rolls-Royce Enthusiasts' Club)

90

Bentley badged cars were built in remarkably low numbers in comparison to the Silver Shadow. The difference in cost between the two models was so little that most customers opted for the prestige of a Rolls-Royce radiator. There was always some demand for the Bentley T-Series cars, however, especially from committed Bentley enthusiasts, for whom nothing other than the famous winged B emblem would do. The car nearest the camera is a Corniche. (Courtesy Rolls-Royce Motor Cars Ltd.)

Within six months of the Silver Shadow's launch, the two-door saloon was announced and built in conjunction with MPW, in-house coachbuilder to Rolls-Royce. (Courtesy Rolls-Royce Motor Cars Ltd.)

only did Rolls-Royce cars suffer from reduced fuel economy as a result of these regulations, but performance was also affected. The need to run engines on leaner fuel mixtures resulted in an overall loss of power, and this was a major contributing factor in the development of a new V8 engine in 1970.

By lengthening the stroke and increasing capacity of the existing V8 engine from 6230cc to 6750cc, Rolls-Royce effectively overcame the power loss problem. Needless to say, the company declined, as usual, to announce its bhp rating, although estimates calculated it at approximately 220bhp, a possible 20bhp increase over that of the 6.23-litre engine. Further controls followed which curbed the use of 5-star, 99 octane fuel in favour of 4-star, 97 octane fuel, and thereafter work was carried out in preparation of 91 octane lead-free fuel. In America during the mid-seventies, serious efforts were being made to reduce pollution levels, which resulted in the introduction of catalytic converters.

Following the fuel crisis of the early seventies, when petrol rationing in the UK was all but a reality, Rolls-Royce, together with the motor industry as a whole, treated the question of fuel economy with some priority. John Hollings acknowledged the importance of the issue when he presented the 1982 autumn lecture on the engineering of Rolls-Royce cars. Hollings told his audience: "The two most important factors are vehicle weight and engine efficiency. We are working on the reduction of vehicle weight by painstaking attention to detail, and we are working on improvements to the engine which will increase efficiency by allowing higher compression ratios without detonation. We shall also reduce the engine capacity and improve breathing to restore power. In this way we expect to provide a significant improvement in fuel economy in a few years' time using our present V8 engine with some significant changes."

American car manufacturers were given very precise time limits in which to comply with US Federal safety and emission control regulations. Luckily, Rolls-Royce, as a foreign producer, was allowed some leeway by the American government in implementing the requirements; had this not been the case Rolls-Royce would have lost important export orders, resulting in almost certain disaster.

Throughout the Silver Shadow's era it is now evident that the Bentley marque was allowed to decline to such an extent that it almost disappeared. In comparison to Silver Shadow production, that of the T-series was abysmally small, at one time accounting for a mere five per cent of production. At its nadir, the Bentley influence amounted to the radiator design, with its familiar Flying B mascot together with the famous winged-B emblem that had been designed by Freddie Gordon Crosby for W. O. Bentley. As if to add insult to injury, the Rolls-Royce emblem appeared on the Bentley's instrumentation, and even the owner's handbook said it was a Rolls-Royce. Happily, Bentley was saved from oblivion, though customers were surprised - but relieved - to see the marque represented when the Silver Spirit was unveiled. Alongside the Silver Shadow's successor, the Mulsanne rekindled memories of Bentley's racing era at Le Mans.

The importance of the Bentley name was acknowledged when the new generation of models included such cars as the Mulsanne Turbo, Eight, Brooklands, and Continental. The success of the mighty Turbo models secured the future for Bentley, and during the ensuing years the emergence of the Java concept car in the mid-nineties, followed by the Continental R, T and SC (Sedanca Coupé), bolstered the marque's profile. With the introduction of the Arnage in 1998, a divergence of Bentley from Rolls-Royce was apparent, and today the future of Bentley under Volkswagen ownership is secure.

In what was recognised as the ultimate in badge engineering, the T-series Bentley was completely overshadowed by its Rolls-Royce counterpart and, in some of the company's publicity brochures, received hardly a mention.

Rolls-Royce management considered, at that time, that the Bentley's role was subordinate; although the T-Series cars were Silver Shadows in all but name, badge and radiator shell, they were denied that special reverence. In certain companies a Rolls-Royce might be awarded to the chairman, while the deputy chairman would have the Bentley, which was regarded as not having quite the same status. In one instance of price structuring, the Bentley version was forgotten altogether, hence the nominal difference of just a few pounds when the error was realised! The fact that the Rolls-Royce-badged car was just £64.00 more than the T-Series Bentley obviously decided which would be the more popular buy.

Describing his involvement with the Silver Shadow, John Hollings

recalled some of the early problems experienced with the car. The ride and handling did have some shortcomings which, to a great extent, were rectified when self-levelling was removed from the front axle; fitting compliant suspension to the front wheels, which enabled the use of radial tyres, helped even further. The car's electrical system was often a cause for concern and, more often than not, troubles were traced to loose connections. The wiring loom which - on a car of such complexity - was, in essence, a complicated affair: behind the facia alone there were something like 300 cables. Close collaboration was essential with manufacturers such as Lucas, but this was not always entirely satisfactory. Noise from the differential was often the cause of complaint, and hundreds of hours

were spent trying to cure the problem. Ultimately, a dampening device was installed between the propeller shaft and flange on the differential casing.

There were fewer problems with the saloons, once the Camargue and Corniche variants were introduced, for the simple reason that any irregularities had mostly been eliminated on the coachbuilt cars within the two years it had taken to apply the same modifications to production models. It was for this reason that John Hollings regarded the Series II cars, which were introduced for 1977, as very satisfactory and, from his point of view, the late seventies and early eighties were a period of fulfilment and reward.

Silver Shadow chronology
Before reviewing the changes made

to the Bentley T and Silver Shadow during production, it's important to explain the notation system used to denote chassis identification.

A typical chassis number would consist of three prefix letters, followed by up to five digits, such as SRX 12345 or LBH 23456. The first letter establishes the exact body style: S - standard saloon; L - long wheelbase saloon; C - two-door saloon and convertible up to chassis number 6632; D - convertible from chassis 6646; J - Camargue. The second letter confirms whether the car is a Bentley (B) or Rolls-Royce (R). Thirdly, the prefix determines right hand drive (H) or left hand drive (X) and, in the case of the latter, should the car be destined for North America, the X will be replaced by a letter: A-G or J-L dependent upon model year as

The Convertible had to undergo major chassis reinforcement in order to compensate for lost torsional stiffness when the roof was removed. The sills were strengthened and a cruciform added to the floorpan, a feature deleted around 1976 except in certain countries, such as South Africa, when, after 1978, the mounting brackets were deleted.
(Courtesy Rolls-Royce Motor Cars Ltd.)

A=1972, B=1973, C=1974, D=1975, E=1976, F=1977, G=1978, J=1979, K=1980 and L=1981. The digits that followed the letters simply verified the chassis numbers which were in batches: 1001-4548; 5001-5603; 6001-8861; 9001-26708 and 30001-41648 (Series II models). 00000

Rolls-Royce adopted a policy of continual improvement throughout the entire lifespan of the Silver Shadow and Bentley T-Series cars and, by studying the list of specification changes that were applied to these models, it can be appreciated just how much development work was carried out. Many of the changes, however, while important in maintaining the company's upgrading policy, were, to a major extent, quite insignificant to the owner. Within a few months of its launch, the first derivatives of the Silver Shadow appeared: the two-door saloon by James Young in January 1966 and, two months later, the MPW two-door saloon. These and other variants are described in-depth in the next chapter.

Amongst the first changes to the saloon cars, from chassis number 1467, was the provision of a lighter brake pedal movement at the end of 1965. From October 1967, and chassis number 3000, a Saginaw power

James Young built fifty two-door saloons based on the Silver Shadow. The car illustrated is one of only fifteen Bentley versions. (Courtesy Rolls-Royce Motor Cars Ltd.)

anti-roll bar as well as fitment of an anti-roll bar at the rear.

All cars, left- and right hand drive, were fitted with General Motors GM400 transmission from chassis 4483. Although the GM400 gearbox was bought-in direct from America, the electric selector actuation was not part of its specification and this, therefore, was added at Crewe. Rolls-Royce was the only manufacturer to fit electric actuation to this type of gearbox - which allowed the lightest finger-tip control - and whilst such cars as the Cadillac were fitted with the same unit, ratio selection was operated manually. Originally fitted to left hand drive cars only, the GM400 gearbox, when fitted to home market cars, had the following ratios: 1:1 (top), 1.5:1 (intermediate), 2.5:1 (first) and 2:1 (reverse).

Changes to the suspension, which include a strengthened front anti-roll bar and the addition of an anti-roll device at the rear, apply from chassis 4528. Importantly, this modification applied to British and European market models only which demanded a firmer ride. For the American market, which preferred a softer, more wallowing ride, these changes were not implemented.

Between August and December 1969 several specification changes were announced: longer bonnet locating dowels were fitted from 7209; alternators (C.A.V. type) were made standard from chassis 7500 and from 7620 stainless steel exhausts were fitted. It was found necessary to strengthen the handbrake calipers and modify the design of the hazard warning switch from chassis numbers 7650 and 7904 respectively. A major revision to the suspension system, at

steering pump replaced the Hobourn Eaton type, therefore complementing Saginaw's own recirculating ball steering system. A new type of boot lid seal was fitted from chassis number 3367 and the opening quarter light fitted to the front doors was replaced by a fixed type. During 1968 there were a number of important changes: a revised handbrake was fitted from chassis 4469 and from chassis 6300 new windscreen washers were

specified. A higher steering ratio applied from chassis 6429 and road wheels were provided with a flat ledge rim from 6771. A further change to the steering was made from the end of 1969 when a smaller steering wheel, 16 inch (410mm), was fitted from chassis 8222.

By far the most important specification changes during 1968 were those concerning the automatic gearbox and modification of the front

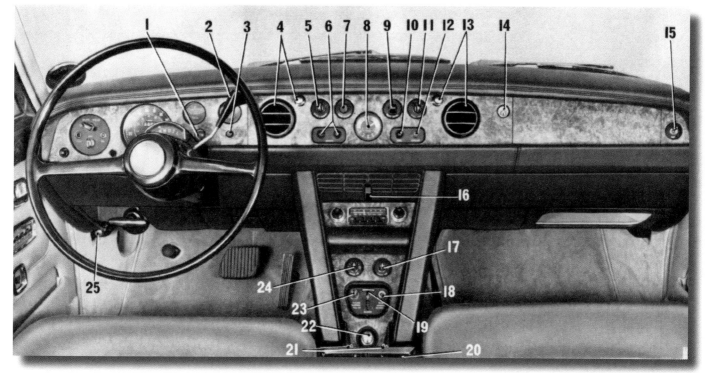

The facia depicted here was designed to comply with American safety legislation. Note the thickly padded edges which protruded sufficiently to prevent injury through body contact with the switches and instruments in the event of an accident. Stylist Martin Bourne remembers using a wooden ball, the size of a baby's head, to ensure that switches and instruments did not protrude too far. (Courtesy Rolls-Royce Motor Cars Ltd.)

1	Hand brake/stop lamp bulb failure warning lamp
2	Gearchange selector lever
3	Fuel/oil level indicator and warning lamps test switch
4	Adjustable outlet and control for fresh or cold air
5	Windscreen wiper/washer switch
6	Accumulator warning lamps
7	Loudspeaker balance control
8	Adjustment knob for hands
9	Aerial switch
10	Fuel level warning lamp
11	Instrument lamps switch
12	Coolant level warning lamp
13	Adjustable outlet and control for fresh or cold air
14	Cubby box lock
15	Map lamp switch
16	Air conditioning outlet
17	Lower heating and ventilation switch
18	Rear window demister switch
19	Blower motors switch
20	Ashtray
21	Front seat switches
22	Cigar lighter
23	Hazard warning switch
24	Upper heating, ventilation and refrigeration switch
25	Control for side scuttle wall outlet

chassis 7404, was implemented when the forward height control was deleted. The reason for this was twofold: firstly, the front self-levelling device had little or no work to do and, secondly, its removal improved the handling and reduced some of the vagueness in the steering which had become a matter of criticism.

As well as alternators being standardised throughout all model production, chassis number 7500 marks the point where air conditioning was specified for all cars. Before this, air conditioning had been an optional extra and only about half the cars sold had it fitted.

A combination of continual specification improvements and tight controls from the USA concerning exhaust emissions were having a serious draining effect upon engine power. This situation, however, helped influence one of the most important engineering decisions in the history of the Silver Shadow and its derivatives. In order to correct the situation with particular emphasis on improving torque, introduction of the 6.75-litre engine occurred at the end of 1969 in readiness for the 1970 model year. America, in fact, was not the only country concerned about pollution issues as Japan and, perhaps surprisingly, Australia were also legislating to fight the problem.

John Bolster, testing the 6.75-litre-engined Silver Shadow for *Autosport* in December 1970, was impressed at how much low-speed torque had been improved. Overall speed also increased and he found the car easily achieved 118mph (189kph). Taking advantage of a long straight stretch of road he was able to better that by at least another couple of miles per hour. As has already been discussed, the extra cubic centimetres were derived from a redesigned crankshaft which produced a lengthened stroke. 6230cc was stretched to 6750cc and the power output, not disclosed, of course, increased to somewhere around 220bhp. Rolls-Royce, incidentally, was carrying out a lot of experimental work on engines at this time and was even considering a power unit of over 7 litres. By increasing the stroke to 4.2 inches (103mm) it had been possible to enlarge the existing V8 to 7269cc and a prototype engine was fitted to the last purpose-built experimental car. Registered XMA 66M, the car was extensively tested in Europe and, on one occasion, with John Gaskell at the wheel, it achieved 127mph (203kph). Although performance would have been greatly improved, fuel consumption would not necessarily have suffered as a result, although this fact was not appreciated at the time by a motor industry preoccupied with the world fuel crisis. Ultimately, it was found that a similar performance could be achieved by restricting the engine size to 6.75 litres.

During 1970 the engine underwent further modification from chassis 9900, when a redesigned camshaft was fitted. This was introduced to amend the valve timing on the Corniche to give increased power output. The modification was not applied to the Silver Shadow saloon, however, until a couple of years later. There were a number of other modifications during the year, too: new brake calipers were specified at chassis 9380 and the suspension height control sensitivity mechanism was adjusted from 9393. Centralised door locking became a feature of the cars and was fitted from chassis 9658. The front seat mechanism received attention for the 1971 model year (at chassis 9630) and a Trico windscreen wash system was specified at 9898.

American safety legislation was responsible for a new-look facia which was also redesigned to incorporate a central console. All edges were softened by the application of thick padding, which gave the facia a narrower appearance. To comply with US regulations it had been necessary to restyle the facia and this was achieved in a most bizarre way. Martin Bourne recalls having to check the distances between the upper and lower padded surfaces with a wooden ball - intended to represent a baby's head - to ensure protection from protruding switches.

The earlier facia, affectionately known by company employees as the Chippendale, gave way to a new design. Instrument layout was changed, the clock being installed in the centre of the facia with switches and controls grouped together, and warning lamps installed in separate panels. The central console, as well as housing the air conditioning outlet and heating and ventilation controls, also accommodated the radio, seat adjustment switches, hazard warning switch, cigar lighter and ashtray.

Even as late as 1970, Rolls-Royce was still experimenting with different types of self-adjusting suspension. Tests were carried out using both Citroën and Rolls-Royce accumulators and, talking with John Hollings, it appears the French product was substantially more reliable. Use was also made of a Telegas self-levelling system devised by Alex Moulton, inventor of the bicycle of the same name, but this proved unsuccessful. The design was something of a hybrid and employed a hydrolastic layout similar to that devised for the British Motor Corporation but including Citroën type spheres. Although experiments lasted for some months, it was eventually discarded and the car to which it was fitted was converted back to the usual suspension.

From chassis number 10,000, the approximate delivery date being January 1971, speed control became an optional feature - at chassis 10322 - and a windscreen wash-wipe system was introduced from 10400; ventilated front wheel discs, to improve overall braking performance and avoid fading, were fitted from chassis 10500 and by the middle of the year there was improved radio suppression and modification to the ignition system.

The speed control, otherwise known as cruise control, enabled the driver to keep the car at a predetermined speed, whatever the road incline. On experimental and early production cars, the control device was operated from the facia but some years later was moved to the end of the gear selector lever. A safety device was built into the control which made it non-operational at speeds under 30mph (48kph) or over 80mph (128kph). In addition, it

A proud owner (whose identity, unfortunately, is unknown) pictured with his Rolls-Royce, the 10,000th Silver Shadow built. (Courtesy Rolls-Royce Motor Cars Ltd.)

would instantly disengage as soon as the brake pedal was depressed.

After June 1971, Rolls-Royce gave further attention to the Silver Shadow's self-levelling system from chassis 11130 and changed the type of hydraulic fluid used. All Silver Shadows use a synthetic brake fluid of various specification, culminating in RR363, which, as well as being hygroscopic, attacks paintwork if allowed to come into contact with it. At about the same time, from chassis 11155, cars destined for the USA and Canada were fitted with modified brakes, which resulted in a slightly lighter pedal action, and, applying to all cars, the steering ratio was altered to 17.5:1 at chassis number 11501.

Another revision to the self-levelling suspension was made at chassis number 11970, this being the installation of a modified height control valve from approximately the end of the year. Further improvements followed in quick succession: a slightly redesigned rear seat was specified

and Kangol seat belts were fitted as standard to all cars being exported to the USA; modified striker plates were fitted to the doors, and a new type of expansion tank was fitted to the car's cooling system. A different type of piston ring was fitted to the engine, from chassis 12657, and minor alterations - such as modification to the windscreen wiper and facia panel light switches - were also introduced.

Of significance were the modifications made to the chassis dimensions introduced from 1971. Although the changes were minimal they were nonetheless of extreme importance, being necessary for improved road holding and handling. An increase in the length of the wheelbase, from 119.5 inches (3035.3mm) to 120.062 inches (3049.6mm), and the track - from 57.5 inches (1460.5mm) to 59.5 inches (1511.3mm) at the front and 57.75 inches (1466.9mm) at the rear - was made in order that compliant suspension and, later, during 1972,

radial ply tyres of 205VR x 15, could be accommodated.

Compliant suspension, the term used by Rolls-Royce for the revised suspension layout, involved the design of a new system of subframe mounting. The stainless-steel, wire-mesh type of dampers - more commonly referred to as pot scrapers or 'pan scrubbers' - were eliminated and in their place were fitted specially designed rubber bushes. A cranked-arm top link replaced the upper triangle levers fitted originally and a measure of fore and aft movement (graphically described as 'rock and roll') was obtained from a compression strut linked between the top link and the subframe. It has to be added that compliant suspension - fitted to all cars from chassis number 13485 - was first introduced on the Corniche models from chassis number 12734 with delivery of these cars being effected from the end of 1971 and beginning of 1972.

Black Thursday

Without any doubt whatsoever, 1971 was a devastating year, not only for the car division of Rolls-Royce, but the company as a whole. The aero division of Rolls-Royce, as well as the motor car division, had established itself as a national institution and the R-R monogram on the casing of the world's most respected engines instilled unparalleled pride.

Alas, the company had become embroiled in a costly issue over its new aircraft engine, the RB211, and for 1970 recorded a deficit of £3 million. The engine was being developed for the new generation of wide-bodied jets; in particular the Lockheed Tristar. Difficulty had been experienced with construction of the fan blades which,

during testing, were found to be susceptible to bird strikes and it was necessary to form the 25 huge blades from titanium instead of the carbon fibre material originally specified. Not only was titanium very much more expensive, but development costs soared out of control as the engines failed to perform as well as expected, due to the increased weight of the blade material. (Titanium, incidentally, was also used to manufacture the turbine blades of Rover's gas turbine car JET 1, a project in which Rolls-Royce had once shared an interest).

Acknowledging the difficulties which faced the company, Rolls-Royce management took two courses of action. Firstly, Sir Stanley Hooker, the former chief engineer of the company's jet engine division, was consulted and agreed to return to Rolls-Royce from retirement to undertake the redesigning of the RB211, which he successfully accomplished. Secondly, the British government was approached for help; assistance was not forthcoming which

left Rolls-Royce no alternative but to appoint a Receiver to take over the company's affairs.

John Hollings remembers clearly the 4th February 1971, which became known at Rolls-Royce as Black Thursday. It was appreciated by the car division, which was operating at a profit, that the aero division was in trouble but it was not known to what extent. At 9am John Hollings was called to the boardroom at Pyms Lane and given the news that Rupert E. Nicholson had been appointed Receiver. Hollings was devastated. (An interesting point is that Rolls-Royce was never declared 'bankrupt' as assets far exceeded debts or potential debts). Martin Bourne recalls the air of disbelief in the styling department when, shortly after 9am, Fritz Feller - who had taken over from John Blatchley as chief stylist - announced the news. Everybody was stunned: throughout Rolls-Royce there had always existed a unique sense of loyalty - that feeling is evident to this

day, now that the factory is home to Bentley Motors and under Volkswagen ownership - and it was felt that a tragedy had befallen the whole family that was Crewe.

Trading ceased at that moment; no deliveries could be made and supplier's lorries were turned away at the gate - including the brewer's dray with the beer for Saturday night's dance in the ballroom. That really brought home the gravity of the situation! Leaving the boardroom a few minutes after being told of the bankruptcy, John Hollings' task was one of reassurance; he realised it was essential not to allow staff morale to suffer any more than it had already and therefore, as chief engineer, he toured all departments in order to try and defuse the situation. After that, as far as he was concerned, it was a matter of 'business as usual'.

Within a matter of weeks of Rolls-Royce going into receivership the company announced a new model. The Corniche, built as a Bentley (shown here), and a Rolls-Royce, was a development of the two-door car, and did much to restore confidence in what was considered to be a national institution. (Courtesy Rolls-Royce Motor Cars Ltd.)

And business as usual it was. The Receiver, fortunately for the car division, was sympathetic and gave specific instructions that car output was not to be affected. In addition, accepting that the company was within five weeks of launching a new model, the Corniche - a modified version of the existing two-door saloons and convertibles, he agreed this should go ahead as planned. Geoffrey Fawn had already been recalled to Derby in January and David Plastow (DP) was appointed managing director, a promotion from the post of marketing director which he had held since 1967. These were challenging times for both Rolls-Royce and the new MD, and David Plastow worked in close association with Rupert Nicholson.

The collapse of the company also affected Rolls-Royce in America. Rolls-Royce Inc. became Rolls-Royce Motors Inc. and, because the new company was interested in motor vehicles only, instead of aero engines primarily and cars as an off-shoot, sales of vehicles increased dramatically. From 700 cars a year, sales increased to over 1000 cars per annum. As for the aero division of Rolls-Royce, this was nationalised and effectively separated from the car making business. Rolls-Royce Motors Ltd. was formed and, eventually, floated on the British stock market as a public company; David Plastow retained his position as managing director of the newly created concern and Ian Fraser was nominated chairman.

The launch of the Corniche went ahead as scheduled and, as it happened, the new car acted as something of a fillip to company morale. Unveiled at a special celebration in Nice on the French Riviera, the party of motoring journalists invited to the ceremony might have wondered at the seemingly incongruous timing for such a spectacular occasion. Any such thoughts soon evaporated, however,

Cars specified for the American market were equipped with special impact absorbing bumpers, as shown here. The car in the photograph is actually a Silver Shadow II. (Courtesy Rolls-Royce Motor Cars Ltd.)

when David Plastow explained that the entire event had been staged for less than half the cost of a Corniche. Had the model not been launched with such high profile there could have been at risk not only the status of Rolls-Royce Motors, but also the confidence of the motor industry in general - especially that of Rolls-Royce's component manufacturers and suppliers.

Car production throughout this turbulent period in Rolls-Royce history actually increased: in 1970 2009 cars of all types were built and by 1971 the figure had risen to 2280; 2470 cars sold were recorded for 1972 and, for 1973, 2760 orders had been fulfilled. Rolls-Royce order books were full and the future looked promising.

With Rolls-Royce cars re-established, work on progressive development continued: from chassis 13051 modifications to the distributor advance were made in respect of those engines with emission controls and the sound system was improved with Philips double-cone speakers from chassis 13178. The American

emission control requirements were becoming very effective and to comply with the 1973 Detox regulations, the cars specified for the USA received specially modified engines from chassis number 14954. All cars received a modified hydraulic fluid reservoir at chassis 14980 and for the 1973 model year cars exported to the USA had to be fitted with larger 'brakes on' stop lights. Another modification to the hydraulic system was the specification of Castrol fluid, RR363, effective from chassis 15638. The brakes received further attention later in 1973 when the pedal was given an even lighter feel (from chassis 15854) and all cars were fitted with a new type of disc brake pad, referred to as type M170, at chassis 15950.

For the Swedish market, cars from 1973 - at chassis 15855 - were fitted with a headlamp wash and wipe system. During the same year, USA and Canada-destined cars were supplied with energy absorbing bumpers at the front and rear; additionally, head restraints were incorporated into the rear seats and a remote control device

fitted to enable the external mirrors on these cars to be adjusted from inside the car. As has already been described, the bumpers had specially designed shock absorbers built behind the stainless steel frames and were designed to return to their original shape after minor impact. The styling department at first was not impressed at the appearance of the US regulation bumper but, in time, not only came to appreciate it but actually advocated it for the Second Series cars. Marque enthusiasts had not been happy about them either, many complaining that the car's appearance was adversely affected. As it happened, similar styles of bumper were subsequently fitted to the majority of cars and the issue was quickly forgotten. Look closely, however, at two cars, one with traditional bumpers, the other with energy-absorbent type, and it will be seen that the car with safety bumpers has a slightly restyled radiator shell, the bottom of which is shortened to accommodate the 2.5 inch (57mm) fore and aft movement of the bumper insert. Further observation will reveal

that a shroud exists around the base of the bumper assembly extending upwards which led to the rectangular air intakes being deleted.

Along with the provision of radial tyres in 1972, some attention was given to facia design. Where there had been separate gauges for oil pressure and water temperature, warning lamps and buzzers were fitted instead. The switch box was moved from the middle of the instrument board to either the left hand or right hand side, depending on whether the car had left- or right hand steering. The windscreen wash-wipe switch which, by this stage, had an intermittent wipe setting, was also relocated to the direction indicator

The events of 1971 put Rolls-Royce at the forefront of media attention; the prospect that one of the most well-known radiators might cease to exist was unthinkable. In fact, the car division of Rolls-Royce remained profitable, and orders for the Silver Shadow actually increased. (Author's collection)

Silver Shadows were exported all around the world, as this Saudi Arabian-registered car proves.
(Courtesy Rolls-Royce Motor Cars Ltd.)

stalk on the steering column and, in its place in the centre of the facia, were a cluster of warning lamps for low fuel, brake pressure and partial failure and hydraulic fluid level. The positioning of the switch previously had given rise to a number of complaints as, to reach and operate it, meant quite a stretch for most drivers. Overall, a considerable amount of attention had been given to the minor controls: while there were individual switches on all doors for the window lifts, on the driver's door a four-in-one switch operated all windows. Additionally, a master switch could disengage those at the rear to prevent children from playing with them.

A further change, whilst slight, was made to the car's dimensions for 1974 and was effective from chassis 18269. The wheelbase was lengthened by a fraction over 6mm to 3049.6mm (120.062 inches) and the front track to 1524mm (60 inches) - an increase of 0.5 inch (13mm). The rear track was also increased, from 1466.9mm (57.75 inches) to 1513.8mm (59.6 inches),

the modifications being necessary for adoption of larger section radial ply tyres. In addition, again to suit the new tyres - 235/70HR 15s - wheelarches were flared to prevent fouling, so giving rise to the term 'eyebrows'.

The specification of cars intended for other than the home market underwent some changes in 1974: Sundym glass became standard on all models from chassis 18340, with the exception of those destined for West Germany and Australia. Australian cars were fitted with speedometers

In 1977 a revised version of the Silver Shadow was introduced. Designated Silver Shadow II, the styling incorporated plastic-faced bumpers and an air dam beneath the radiator (not on American cars, though). Specification also included rack and pinion steering and automatic air conditioning. (Courtesy Rolls-Royce Motor Cars Ltd.)

calibrated in kilometres per hour instead of miles per hour to comply with local legislation (chassis 18865) but long wheelbase cars destined for the same country did not receive the modification until later. (Long wheelbase cars, incidentally, are discussed in more detail in the next chapter).

Several important modifications were introduced for the 1975 model year. They included a change to halogen headlamp bulbs for all left hand drive cars with the exception of those specified for the USA and Sweden (from chassis 21104); a seat

belt warning indicator was fitted to American market standard saloons at chassis 21177. For all cars, rear fog lamps became a feature from chassis 22118, as did a breakerless electronic ignition by Lucas known as OPUS. A vacuum advance distributor was fitted to UK cars from 22572 and for the USA, Japan and Australia from 22600. All North American, Japanese and Australian cars were modified with a lower compression rate of 7.3:1 instead of 8:1, whilst the compression ratio of other cars changed from 9:1 to 8:1.

October 1975 is significant as

it marks the 10th anniversary of the Silver Shadow and T-Series Bentley. When originally designed, the plan was that the car should have a ten-year production run but, in the event, it was to carry on for much longer. Series II cars were not introduced until 1977, continuing until 1980 in saloon form. The Corniche, however, remained in production for another fifteen years after that. There were a number of reasons for extending the life of the Silver Shadow, not least there being no shortage of orders. Financially, the Silver Shadow had been costed on a decade's production but certain factors

The Bentley was similarly modified and classified as T2. In this instance, the location is London, outside the Lobb company, famous for its shoes. (Courtesy Rolls-Royce Motor Cars Ltd.)

had not been allowed for. The collapse of Rolls-Royce had delayed planning of a replacement model and the design department was forced to spend long, and sometimes frustrating, periods complying with US Federal safety and emission regulations.

1976 saw a general phasing out of what has unofficially become known as Series I cars in favour of a revamped model, the Series II Silver Shadow and Bentley T2 announced in 1977. Along with the Series II saloons,

both coachbuilt and long wheelbase cars were similarly upgraded. Series II designation was warranted because of the extent of redesign; far more than a 'face-lift' entailed. The last of the Series I cars, a coachbuilt model, was built on chassis 26708; the final Series 1 saloon, however, a walnut with beige Silver Shadow, chassis number SRE 26700, was delivered to its owner, Delta Leasing Corp., Stamford, Connecticut, on 25th March 1977. By the time the last of the Series I cars

had been built, production of Silver Shadow saloons numbered 16,717; in contrast, only 1712 Bentley T-Series saloons had been produced, a fraction over 10 per cent of Shadow output. When including the number of Silver Shadow and T-Series coachbuilt cars that were made, the total number of first series vehicles rises to 22,457.

Silver Shadow II and Bentley T2
As previously mentioned, the production life of the first series

Silver Shadow and Bentley T models was extended from that originally intended, due mainly to two factors: the regulations emanating from the USA and the aftermath of internal disturbances within Rolls-Royce. If original plans had been allowed to materialise, the second series cars might have entered service as early as 1970, initial trials having been conducted at least a year before on an experimental car. No sooner had Silver Shadow production got under way satisfactorily (it was actually 4 years) when thoughts were directed towards its eventual successor. As with all Rolls-Royces the development period was naturally going to be a prolonged affair but on this occasion it was even more drawn out because of the problems already described.

The main feature proposed for Series II cars was an automatic air conditioning system and this had first been fitted to a vehicle specially built as chassis 63-B within the factory and registered JTU 63G. As did the majority of experimental vehicles, 63-B wore a disguised radiator shell which was Bentley-inspired. This, incidentally, was the same car which tested the Moulton Telegas suspension and, after less than 30,000 miles (48,000km) the vehicle was taken out of service.

John Gaskell recalls the testing of prototype Series II cars and the difficulties experienced in trying to perfect the air conditioning system. Most of the problems were connected with temperature control and the rate at which the air flowed from the outlets inside the cabin. After several trials with a later experimental vehicle, 64-B, the car was taken for a 25,000 mile (40,000km) endurance exercise which involved spending some time in France. The test was not without its problems as the car not only suffered a serious leak from the cooling system - the problem was so bad that at one time the car had to be driven with a plastic tank on the roof with a hose feeding into the radiator - but damage was caused to the exhaust system when a clamp broke free.

64-B was taken out of service between 1972 and 1973 in order for modifications to be made to the fuel tank, air conditioning system and engine. Returning to service in the spring of 1973, the car's first test was suspension compliancy as well as the use of HR70 tyres. These tests ultimately resulted in wheelarch flares. In 1974, extensive modifications were carried out which complied with US emission requirements and, later, the car was further modified after having spent some time in the USA. John Gaskell was involved in a mammoth endurance run with the car as soon as it returned from America: 50,000 miles (80,000km) were completed over a period of 18 weeks when the car was driven on a prepared route around Cheshire and Staffordshire. John claims this was amongst the most tedious test driving he had ever carried out with the course having to be driven to a tight schedule. At intervals of 5000 miles (8000km) the car was taken off the routine for servicing and tests to check emission control. The car was kept going continuously, day and night, apart from when changing drivers, refuelling and pre-arranged service stops.

It was about this time that the experimental department was trying out another test car which, on this occasion, used the Citroën-designed brake pedal - the infamous 'mushroom-shaped' device fitted to that company's idiosyncratic DS model. An unnamed test driver, having taken over the particular vehicle from John Gaskell, was unused to this system and while reversing felt in vain for the familiar pedal. Unable to locate the 'mushroom', he pushed hard against the accelerator by mistake with disastrous consequences: extensive damage to the car.

A test driver's life is rarely boring. When recounting his days behind the wheel of experimental - and production - Rolls-Royces and

Only 558 Bentley T2s were built, which gives the model a rarity factor over and above that of its relative, the Silver Shadow II. (Author's collection)

Bentleys, John Gaskell told of trials using six-speed gearboxes; by putting intermediate ratios into a conventional box it was possible to step-up the gear arrangement to six speeds. The system was too complicated and was therefore abandoned. Before the days of motorway speed limits, a favourite route for test drivers was from Crewe to the junction of the M1 at the Blue Boar Services near Crich, where the cars were filled with fuel. It was then a case of thundering down to the southern end of the motorway which, at that time, was near St. Albans. The cars then turned round and headed north, back to the Blue Boar Services where they were again refuelled. The best time recorded for the round trip of 120 miles (192km) was an amazing 63 minutes but the goal of completing it on the hour was

never achieved. This was before the days of self-service filling stations and speed limits and the attendant at the Blue Boar always refused to believe the journey possible. This, of course, was understandable considering the average speed necessary to do it would have been a little over 116mph (186kph).

In 1977, John Gaskell was involved in evaluating the last experimental Silver Shadow, a dark blue car, 66-B. The car, which had been running by early 1974, was fitted with a 7269cc engine and was used to test new designs of tyres currently being developed by Dunlop and Avon. Trials using Dunlop's Denovo tyres were disappointing with excessive road noise and a loss in ride comfort. Later, the car was used with steel-braced radial tyres to test the rack

and pinion steering which Rolls-Royce intended using. On one occasion, while trials were being carried out in Italy, John was able to attain a maximum speed of 127mph (203.2kph). The car remained with the experimental department until 1981 and was used to assess the reliability of digital instrumentation and effectiveness of the air conditioning system. When it had fulfilled its duties, 66-B was dismantled and crushed, having completed a total of 166,000 miles (265,600km).

The Series II models were launched to the press in February 1977 but not announced to the public until March. Chassis numbers commenced at 30001 for Rolls-Royce-badged cars, and 30046 for the Bentley version. A cursory glance might not have revealed a great deal of difference

Serious styling changes for a Series II car were, at one time, considered. A full-size model is shown here: note the plastic-faced overriders, redesigned rear quarter panel, and lower boot line. (Courtesy John Blatchley)

Viewed from the rear, the styling modifications are quite startling. The project was eventually abandoned. (Courtesy John Blatchley)

This is an interesting picture as it shows not only a Standard Saloon on the left, but also the ill-fated Series II prototype next to it. On the far right is a Silver Cloud III, but look closely at the American car; it's a front wheel drive Oldsmobile Toronado, which Rolls-Royce was evaluating. (Courtesy John Blatchley)

between the first and second series cars but, on closer examination, several important modifications were evident. Most apparent was the adoption of plastic-faced bumpers, complete with polyurethane sides, which looked similar to those specified for the American market cars. It has to be emphasised that the true 'energy absorbing' bumpers were those fitted to US specification models, all the other markets had solidly mounted bumpers. The American type, therefore, protruded two inches (50.8mm) further out than normal to allow for retraction. Consequently the fairings above the bumpers varied in width.

Fitted beneath the bumper, an air spoiler - or dam - was designed to improve stability and road-holding. This feature, along with the headlamp wash and wipe system later introduced for the home market cars, did not apply to US specification models. The design of the radiator shell was also changed so that it became marginally deeper to correspond with that of the Corniche. Due to the design of the bumpers, which were greater in section than before, the grilles beneath the headlamps were deleted, matching the American export cars. From the rear, the cars could very easily be identified by their Series II badging but less obvious changes were the provision of discreet fog lamps mounted beneath the front bumper, side repeater indicators at the rear of the car

and redesigned door handles which incorporated more deeply recessed buttons. This latter modification was made to prevent the buttons being accidentally depressed should the car roll over in an accident. It is important to stress that whilst some cosmetic restyling had taken place, there were no changes to the Pressed Steel body panels, which remained exactly the same as on the original cars. At one time, however, changes to the Silver Shadow's styling for Series II cars had been contemplated. An attempt at what was considered a more modern appearance had been made when an experimental vehicle was substantially restyled from the D-post rearwards. The car was given a lower wing line to present a sleeker look, the D-post itself was elongated and the boot lid allowed to sweep downwards. The tail, instead of the usual upright stance, was angled to almost 45 degrees and looked neat, especially with the early series bumper. Although the styling was quite attractive, the project was nevertheless abandoned.

It was under the bonnet and inside the cars that most of the differences existed. A new facia with revised instrumentation gave the cabin a completely fresh look and the wholly new split-level air conditioning system, which had taken an enormous amount of development, provided extra comfort by supplying different temperatures within the interior. The facia, however, had already been a

feature of the Corniche since June 1975, and the air conditioning was derived from that fitted originally to the Camargue but subsequently improved and updated. It should be added that the Silver Shadow was not unique in having a good quality air conditioning system as many American motorists took it for granted that their cars would be so equipped. What was different about Rolls-Royce's system, though, was that the occupants did not have to have the same temperature throughout the cabin.

The facia on Series II cars received less padding than that of the first series which had to meet US Federal safety regulations. With an expanse of walnut the facia represented something of a return in design to that fitted to the cars from 1965, before implementation of the Federal Safety Standards, but styling and positioning of the instruments was much more selective. Whereas the safety regulations had meant less space for instrumentation - some were deleted in favour of warning lamps to conserve space - a welcome return was made to earlier styling ideas, especially those of pre-T Series Bentleys. Modern in its appearance, the Series II facia adopted a raised cowling ahead of the steering wheel, which itself was reduced in size from 16 inches (407mm) to 15 inches (381mm). Two large dials ahead of the driver housed an electronic speedometer, which replaced a cable-operated

Late Shadow IIs were fitted with headlamp wiper systems. The other cars in the picture are a Phantom 1, first-series Silver Shadow, 20-25, and a Bentley Continental. (Courtesy Rolls-Royce Enthusiasts' Club)

type, together with odometers and separate gauges for oil pressure, fuel, temperature and an ammeter. To the right of the speedometer a rectangular panel housed no fewer than 10 warning lamps which registered everything from freezing external conditions to brake failure and low water in the screenwash bottle. Next to it was the ignition lock - Yale, of course - and lamp switches which were contained within the familiar circular switch box. Positioned in the centre of the instrument board was the clock and an ambient temperature gauge, the main beam indicator being placed between them. On either side of the gauges were the circular upper level air conditioning vents, which were always referred to as 'bulls-eyes.' The sensor

for the ambient temperature gauge was mounted immediately below the Spirit of Ecstasy mascot and was often affected by the heat from the bonnet when the car was standing for any length of time with its engine idling. Once the car was running normally, however, it operated quite efficiently.

The Spirit of Ecstasy, incidentally, was known within Rolls-Royce circles as The Flying Lady. To those who worked at Rolls-Royce for any length of time, she was referred to as 'Phyllis.' Rover's Viking mascot was similarly treated in an affectionate manner and acquired the name of 'George.'

Facia equipment was impressive: ahead of the front passenger seat was a lockable glovebox and, to the side of it, a map reading lamp switch.

Beneath the clock, a radio, tape player, seat belt warning light and cigar lighter were all contained within a rectangular housing. To the left of the steering column were switches to control the air conditioning, aerial lift and hazard warning lights and, to the right, were the controls for fuel filler cap release, panel rheostat, fog light switch and oil level indicator.

The air conditioning system fitted as standard to Series II cars was a highly complicated affair and acknowledged as the best of its type, which accounts for its protracted development. The system allowed air to be introduced into the car at two levels and maintained at two different temperatures. Air, as it entered the conditioning unit, was cooled or

A feature of the Silver Shadow II and T2 was automatic air conditioning. Once set to the required temperature, it needed no alteration, regardless of external conditions. The car pictured in this press photograph is a late model, identified as such by its headlamp wipers. (Courtesy Rolls-Royce Enthusiasts' Club)

heated, depending upon the ambient temperature, to 0 degrees C before being heated or cooled further. The air was also dehumidified, so preventing the windows from misting. A device in the air conditioning system also prevented the lower outlets from emitting cold air onto the occupants' feet before the engine had sufficiently warmed up. Operation of the heated rear window was also fully automatic

and a switch to turn it on and off was not necessary. Describing how the air conditioning system worked, John Hollings explained the objective was to make it as unobtrusive as possible. Particular care was taken in its design and the intention was to allow gradual changes in fan speed and air temperature. When the interior of the car was either too hot or too cold, the air conditioning fan operated at

maximum speed, reducing gradually when the ideal temperature had been reached. When the engine was started in cold weather, the fan switched itself off, closing at the same time the lower air quantity flap to prevent air circulating at foot level. As soon as the coolant reached 44 degrees C, the flap opened. In hot weather, the fan would start immediately to provide cool air.

During development work a

Late Bentley T2s were given the same modifications as the Silver Shadow, as illustrated by this majestic example pictured at an R-REC rally at Harewood House, Yorkshire. (Author's collection)

problem was discovered when an already warm engine was started in cold weather. Warm, moist air trapped within the evaporator unit and the trunking surrounding it was blown directly onto the windows where it condensed within seconds and completely obscured vision. To prevent such a situation from re-occurring, fan operation was delayed for 12 seconds, which allowed enough time for removal of the moisture from the air entering the system.

Unseen, but much appreciated by those who drove Series II cars, was the Burman rack and pinion steering, which made the car much lighter and more positive to handle, even with power assistance. As well as the smaller steering wheel, lock-to-lock was reduced to only 3.5 turns. This was

the first time rack and pinion steering had been used on a Rolls-Royce car and it was used in association with a redesigned front suspension. Having greater swing-axle effect, the geometry of the suspension increased resistance to roll by keeping the wheels more upright when cornering which, apart from improving the car's handling, reduced tyre wear.

With emission controls very much in mind, Series II cars were fitted with two SU HIF7 carburettors. These had 1.87 inch (48mm) chokes which complied with regulations in a number of countries in addition to America. The design of the carburettors, which were tuned for economy, not only very efficiently controlled mixture levels but, adversely, affected engine output. The situation was redressed,

however, by the fitment of a stainless steel twin exhaust system which imposed less back pressure. In an attempt to conserve fuel, the engine-driven cooling fan was augmented by an electric fan. An added advantage - the point was made by motoring journalists at the time - was that it made the car a little quieter. Gone, it seemed, was the era when all that could be heard while travelling at 60mph (96kph) was the clock ticking! The sound of the ticking clock was the subject of an interesting, successful publicity campaign for Rolls-Royce, though it's doubtful that the claims could be substantiated.

The American state of California was so obsessed with emission controls that even Rolls-Royce's efforts to reduce pollution were not good

To improve ride and handling, Rolls-Royce and Harvey Bailey Engineering each produce suspension kits. Andrew Morris, who owns this beautiful T2, has fitted a handling kit to his car: the car's performance has been transformed. (Courtesy Andrew Morris)

enough. For Californian cars only, therefore, carburettored engines were replaced by those fitted with Bosch K-Jetronic fuel injection which ensured

the metering of precise levels of fuel. Eventually this system was widely used by other manufacturers.

The Bentley, now designated T2, received the same modifications as the Silver Shadow. In essence, though, any distinction between the two cars was virtually imperceptible: the engine rocker covers were marked Rolls-Royce, as was the maker's plate showing the chassis number. Even the R-R monogram appeared on the facia instrumentation. On introduction of the new models, both the Silver Shadow II and the T2 were identically priced which effectively removed any distinction between the cars. Obviously the prestige associated with the radiator and badging was the deciding factor but, oddly -and thankfully - there still existed a demand for Bentleys - but only just.

Long wheelbase cars continued in production with the Bentley being known simply as the T2 Long Wheelbase. The Rolls-Royce badged car, however, was renamed Silver Wraith II, evoking the immediate post-Second World War period of the company's history. Described in more detail in the next chapter, these cars benefited by having a further 4 inches (102mm) added to the wheelbase.

Series II cars went on sale at £22, 809, an increase of £3147 on the price of the car it replaced. It can be argued that the increase was due to an upgrading of specification, especially the superb air conditioning. Prices of Silver Shadows and Bentley T had consistently increased from the original £6556 and £6496 respectively; by 1967 the price had risen to £6670 for the Rolls-Royce and £9272 in 1970. The basic price in 1973 was £10,403, which did not include the tape player,

and three years later, in 1976, it had jumped to £17,898.

For those motorists who were not convinced that the Silver Shadow or its Bentley sister car had no rival, there was a choice of exotic cars. Mercedes' 450SEL, with its 6.834 litre engine and at a fraction more in price at £22, 999, was certainly a quicker car with a 131mph (210kph) top speed. The Vanden Plas Daimler, Jaguar's up-market flagship, was nearly half the price but what it gained in performance (136mph/ 218kph) was lost in craftsmanship and finish. Capable of 140mph (224kph) and oozing with sporting traditions of wood and leather was the Bristol 412, and at a shade under £20,000 at that. Aston Martin's V8 saloon was astonishingly fast, over 160mph (256kph) was possible and, at the other end of the scale, Cadillac's Seville was superbly comfortable when driven in a straight line and on smooth road surfaces. The Silver Shadow II was expensive and handling and performance, although dramatically improved, could not be considered sporting. It was, however, totally different to any other car in terms of thoroughness in design, build and finish. In a word, it was quality.

The refinement embodied by the Series II Silver Shadow and Bentley was as expected. The owner was cosseted in the best quality Connolly hide and surrounded by expertly chosen burr walnut veneer. Handling - far different to that of earlier cars - was more positive and the car rolled a lot less, also helped by the provision of a slimmer rear anti-roll bar which compensated for the lowering of the front roll centre, a modification that made the car much more pleasurable to drive. These revisions

Successors to the Silver Shadow II and Bentley T2 were the Silver Spirit and Bentley Mulsanne. Design work was started in 1969 and the project was known as SZ. Seen here at the Geneva Motor Show in 1980, the Silver Spirit shares the spotlight with the front sub-frame assembly that it used. (Courtesy Rolls-Royce Enthusiasts' Club)

The appearance, in 1980, of the Bentley Mulsanne signalled a revival of the Bentley marque. (Courtesy Rolls-Royce Motor Cars Ltd.)

had other advantages: tyre wear was considerably reduced, an important factor given the cost of replacement. Although not obtrusive, the air dam did have a noticeable stabilising effect, especially in crosswinds. The development department paid a lot of attention to the results of tests using the wind tunnel and its efforts had been rewarded.

Maximum speed of the Silver Shadow II and T2 was claimed as 120mph (193kph) and for those owners who were interested, the engine would be working at something like 4600rpm. Overall fuel consumption in the region of 13-14mpg (20lts/100km) could be expected, hence the need for a 23.5 gallon (107 litre) fuel tank which would allow a little over 300 miles (480km) between visits to a fuel pump.

During its production life, specification changes were made to the Series II car, but not nearly as many as for the first series which amounted to something like 2000, including those which had seemed almost insignificant. The last major styling modification occurred at chassis 34573 when the headlamp wash-wipe system, initially installed on Swedish export cars, was fitted to all vehicles except those bound for the USA. Not so much a blade, the headlamp wiper was a nylon brush which was far more successful in sweeping the convex shape of the headlamp lenses.

Mechanical specification changes, too, were kept to a minimum: the final modification note was the introduction, at chassis 40194, of Bosch fuel injection for Californian cars.

Prices continued to rise and in 1979 the cost of a Silver Shadow II and Bentley T2 was £36,652, more expensive than most cars considered

anywhere near comparable. BMW's 733i was well under half the price and by 1979 the Mercedes 450SEL 6.9 attracted a price tag of just under £30,500. In the supercar league, the Rolls-Royce and Bentley were the most sedate and the Daimler Vanden Plas 5.3 and Ferrari 4001, two high performers capable of virtually 150mph (240kph).

Some revisions (to the suspension,

for example), were made to the Silver Shadow range of cars, but were not applied to the standard saloons. Instead, modifications such as the use of gas struts, which supplemented the coil springs, appeared on the Corniche and Camargue and were effective on the Silver Shadow's and Bentley's replacements, the Silver Spirit, Silver Spur and Bentley Mulsanne. The Series II saloons, although very successful

The Rolls-Royce Silver Spur II. (Courtesy Rolls-Royce Motor Cars Ltd.)

Styling of the Silver Spirit facia was not unlike that of the Silver Shadow II and T2. This picture shows the facia of a Silver Spirit II. (Courtesy Rolls-Royce Enthusiasts' Club)

Graham Hull was chief stylist at Rolls-Royce throughout the 1980s and 1990s, and was responsible for the later development of the Silver Spirit, Silver Spur, Mulsanne, Brooklands, and Continental models. He retired from Rolls-Royce once the Silver Seraph and Bentley Arnage models were in production, both of which he designed using styling cues from the Silver Cloud. Graham has a catholic interest in motorcars, and appreciates the virtues of bubblecars and the like equally as much as larger and more powerful sports machines. Committed to Rolls-Royce and Bentley marques, he holds in high esteem stylists such as John Blatchley, Bill Allen, and Martin Bourne. (Courtesy Martin Bourne)

in their own right, were designed in some respect as a stopgap, while the new generation models were being perfected. During the Silver Spirit's gestation period there is no doubt that the Silver Shadow was used as a development vehicle and John Hollings did not hide this fact when he spoke of Rolls-Royce's engineering role during the seventies: "In accordance with our policy of introducing changes first on the coachbuilt cars, the new rear suspension was introduced initially on the Camargue and the Corniche in 1979 and on the Silver Spirit when it was introduced at the end of 1980. The new suspension was never in fact fitted to the Silver Shadow, although this car was of course used for much of the development work."

Work started on the Silver Spirit as early as 1969. In view of the huge outlay involved in the development of the Silver Shadow it was evident from the outset that the new car would use much of the technology of its forerunner. The Silver Shadow's underframe was modified at the rear to take the new rear suspension and widened in the engine compartment in order to make that for the SZ range of cars. The body styling of the Silver Spirit and its ensuing Bentley model was the work of Fritz Feller and although it enjoyed an individuality of its own, the underlying identity with its predecessor nevertheless remains. This is most apparent when studying the Silver Spirit's facia which, on first

glance looks identical to that fitted to the Silver Shadow II. The only real difference between the two is the digital display, consisting of outside temperature, clock and stopwatch in a central panel above the radio housing, and an extra 1.25 inches (32mm) in width at each end. Such was the increase in interior width over the Shadow.

In detail, the Silver Spirit was almost 3 inches (76mm) longer, 2.3 inches (62mm) wider and 1.25 inches (33mm) lower than the car it replaced. It had more window area - about 30 per cent - and a slightly longer wheelbase due to the suspension design. There was a fraction more room inside the cabin, 4 inches (102mm) wider and hardly any extra length, but the engine and transmission were all as before. The frontal styling was more modern and the radiator grille wider which helped make the car appear much larger than the Silver Shadow. Although the Silver Spirit looked as if it might be faster, its top speed was, in fact, a fraction less at 119mph (191kph).

For Bentley enthusiasts who had mourned the car's decline, there was the excitement of a noticeable resurgence in the marque. Sporting traditions were revived with the appearance of the Mulsanne Turbo, a fabulous machine with an output confirmed at a shade under 300bhp and top speed of 135mph (217.2kph), and the even mightier 328bhp, 146mph

(235kph) Turbo R. The Bentley Eight, with its mesh radiator grille, evoked memories of the marque's competitive and vintage era and was designed around the Mulsanne's specification but with simplified trim. The model was introduced in 1984 to redress the effect of a recession which had badly

After years of declining sales, the Bentley marque acquired a fresh and positive sporting image which drew new customers. Flanking the Bentley Corniche is the Bentley Eight and the mighty Mulsanne Turbo. (Courtesy Rolls-Royce Motor Cars Ltd.)

affected the market for luxury cars in the early eighties. Sales of Rolls-Royce and Bentley cars had plummeted: only 1551 cars were produced in 1983, less than half the output of 1981 (3165). The Continental R two-door coupé announced in 1992 was another model to revive a famous name and was the first Bentley in forty years not to have a parallel Rolls-Royce-badged sister car. In 1995, another newcomer, the Bentley Azure, a convertible version of the Continental R, made an appearance. For some enthusiasts of the winged B though, only the Java

concept car, unveiled in 1994, sets the standard upon the future.

The Silver Shadow and T-Series Bentley saloons were built until the autumn of 1980, so ending almost 15 years of production. Since introduction, 8425 Silver Shadow IIs left the factory, along with 2135 Silver Wraith IIs and 568 T2s, which included 10 long wheelbase cars. The price of the saloons had reached £41,959 and that of the Silver Wraith £49,447. Silver Wraiths supplied with a division between the front and rear compartments were priced at £52,138.

The Camargue went out of production in 1986 but the Corniche remained until 1995 to continue the concept of what has, so far, been recognised as the most successful car in the history of Rolls-Royce.

It was a fitting epitaph, therefore, when, thirty years after launch in the autumn of 1995, over 300 Silver Shadows and Bentley Ts gathered together in the grounds of Blenheim Palace, one of Britain's finest stately homes, to celebrate this auspicious occasion.

The Rolls-Royce Silver Spirit II. (Courtesy Rolls-Royce Motor Cars Ltd.)

Highest quality and attention to detail are integral elements of every Rolls-Royce. (Courtesy Rolls-Royce Motor Cars Ltd.)

Draped with the Union Jack, the last Silver Wraith II bodyshell has been delivered to Crewe from Pressed Steel via MPW. The car is still in its body-in-white stage. (Courtesy Rolls-Royce Motor Cars Ltd.)

The last Silver Shadow car, a Silver Wraith II, under production; an auspicious occasion and the team employed in building it is recorded on film for posterity. (Courtesy Rolls-Royce Motor Cars Ltd.)

Coachbuilt models and variants

By the time Rolls-Royce monocoque cars were being developed, the age of the bespoke carriage, painstakingly built by experienced craftsmen, was almost at an end. Almost, but not quite, because there remained a very limited market for cars such as the Continental, Flying Spur, special-bodied Silver Clouds, and exclusive Phantoms to which the traditionalist coachbuilder could apply his skills.

Before the introduction of unitary construction methods, all cars were built with separate chassis and there was no shortage of first class coachbuilders. As mass-production techniques accounted for more and more car output, so the demand for specialist coachwork declined, and many famous firms found it difficult to carry on trading. Those that did continue business, however, were affected by the recession of the thirties which plunged the industry deeper into decline, causing many established firms to disappear.

War followed recession, and with it came disruption of the motor industry, though vehicle manufacture continued in order to meet the requirements of the armed forces, and the war effort in general. When the industry resumed

Rolls-Royce and Bentley coachbuilt cars are amongst the most elegant bespoke motor vehicles in the world. This 1956 Hooper-bodied Silver Cloud (chassis number SYB 18) is owned by Harold Kay. (Author's collection)

The elegance of this Vilelm Koren-designed Park Ward S3 Continental is quite delightful. The twin headlamp design was arranged by Bill Allen, assisted by Martin Bourne, while the front indicator lenses were adopted from the Sunbeam Rapier. (Author's collection)

after hostilities ended, it was a matter of earning precious foreign currency, which meant car building for export took priority. If Rolls-Royce was to succeed, it had to adopt rationalisation if only because none of the remaining coachbuilders had the capacity to keep up with demand. With Rolls-Royce's decision to buy-in complete standard steel bodies, those coachbuilders who had so far survived were further demoralised.

Throughout the company's history, all of the most reputable coachbuilders had produced specialist bodies for Rolls-Royce and Bentley: Barker, Freestone and Webb, Gurney Nutting, Hooper, Arthur Mulliner, H. J. Mulliner, Vanden Plas, Park Ward, and James Young were all represented. Barker, after going into liquidation in 1938, was taken over by Hooper, which, in turn, became part of the Daimler company during the late thirties. In 1959, for the last time, Hooper exhibited, at the London Motor Show, coachwork intended for "royal and distinguished patrons." The Hooper name has survived,

though, and has been responsible for specialised models based upon the Bentley Mulsanne Turbo, and Bentley Turbo R. Today, Hooper & Co. (Coachbuilder) Ltd is located at Kimberley Road, London NW6, where it specialises in coachwork conversion and refurbishment.

Freestone and Webb was amalgamated into the H. R. Owen group of companies in 1955; Gurney Nutting was acquired by Jack Barclay in 1945, and Arthur Mulliner, ceasing to build private cars in 1939, was absorbed by Henly's Limited.

Vanden Plas was taken over by Austin in 1946, primarily to build the six-cylinder Austin Princess, which Austin anticipated would compete with the Bentley Mk VI. In 1967 the famous coachbuilding firm, which had once built bodies for a great many 'W.O.' Bentleys, became a division of BMC. Park Ward was purchased by Rolls-Royce in 1939 and, after the war, carried out specialist and experimental work in addition to bespoke coachbuilding for its parent company.

In 1959, H. J. Mulliner and Company was taken over by Rolls-Royce and, two years later, H. J. Mulliner, Park Ward Ltd. was formed, retaining premises at Willesden, in North London, and Chiswick, West London, respectively. James Young also survived the war years, having been acquired by Jack Barclay in 1937, and resumed production of specialist coachwork for Rolls-Royce and Bentley cars.

At the time of the T-Series and Silver Shadow launch, the only traditional coachbuilders associated with Rolls-Royce and Bentley were James Young and MPW. James Young Ltd. had been in business for 102 years when the Silver Shadow appeared, and was more famous for its bodies designed for the Silver Cloud and S3 chassis, along with some superb coachwork for the Phantom V. The latter, incidentally, is now considered amongst the most desirable and sought-after of all postwar Rolls-Royces. MPW had become the 'in-house' coachbuilder to Rolls-Royce: Park Ward which, before

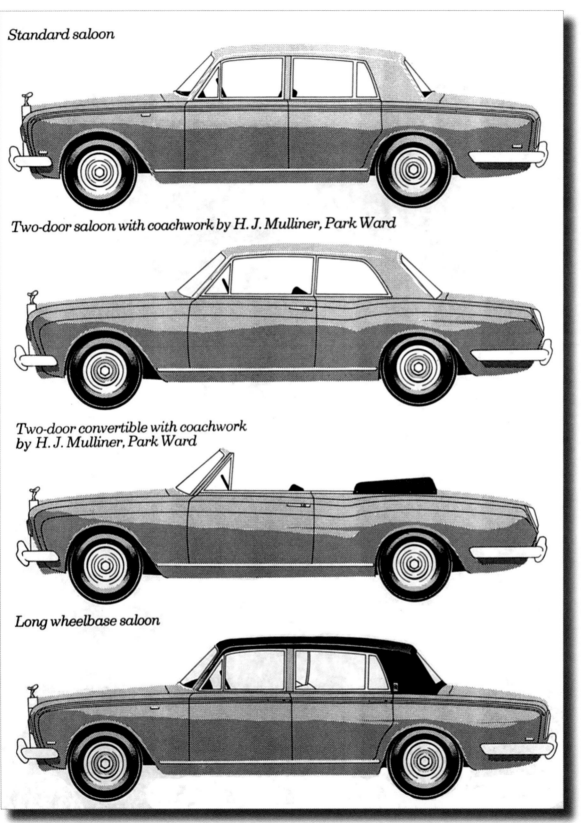

Standard saloon

Two-door saloon with coachwork by H. J. Mulliner, Park Ward

Two-door convertible with coachwork by H. J. Mulliner, Park Ward

Long wheelbase saloon

Sadly, coachbuilding went into decline and, in order for Rolls-Royce to survive, radical (for Rolls-Royce) production techniques had to be adopted. Nevertheless, there was still a demand for the bespoke carriage, hence the introduction of the two-door models as well as a long wheelbase car, constructed by MPW. This illustration, from a sales brochure, depicts the Rolls-Royce range in the late sixties. (Courtesy Rolls-Royce Motor Cars Ltd.)

1952, enjoyed a distinctiveness all its own, took on more of an identity with the standard steel products under the direction of John Blatchley; H. J. Mulliner - responsible for over half the total production of the 18 exclusive Phantom IVs - successfully managed the transition from using seasoned hardwood to metal for the framework of its bodies.

The decline in traditional coachbuilding is one of the reasons why Rolls-Royce adopted unitary construction for the Silver Shadow and T-Series models. Nevertheless, the exclusive market for coachbuilt motor cars still existed, albeit to a limited extent, and Rolls-Royce, naturally, felt compelled to satisfy this demand. Coachbuilding techniques relating to cars with monocoque construction were well understood by the time Rolls-Royce developed its two-door saloons and convertibles, such specialists as Pininfarina, Bertone and Chapron having devised some intriguing designs around Fiat, Lancia, and Citroën models. Before discussing the two-door variants, the forerunners to the Corniche and the Camargue, an important derivative of the four-door saloons must not be overlooked.

Long wheelbase saloons

The long wheelbase versions of the Silver Cloud and S-Series Bentley were always sought-after. Out of the 14,850 cars produced, just 797 (a little over 5 per cent) were constructed on the long chassis, so it's surprising that a long wheelbase Silver Shadow or T-Series Bentley was initially omitted from the catalogue. A long wheelbase Silver Shadow option was, however, intended, and it will be remembered that initial ideas for these cars were based upon designs with a longer wheelbase than the definitive prototypes.

The pressure of getting the saloon cars ready for the Paris Motor Show launch, as well as developing the two-door models, meant that any project for an alternative long wheelbase variant was delayed longer than had been anticipated. It was not until spring 1969, over three years after the standard saloon had made its appearance, that production began on a 10ft, 3.5in (3137mm) wheelbase car using chassis number 6599. A pilot batch of 10 cars, incidentally, was made during 1966/7, and included a car specially built for HRH Princess Margaret. This particular car is discussed later in the chapter.

Long wheelbase saloons were essentially standard saloons with 4 inches (102mm) added to the wheelbase just aft of the centre pillar, the B-C post, which provided a noticeable increase in space in the rear compartment. Once the floorpan and sills were cut and the new section welded into position, the body received lengthened rear doors and a new, longer roof panel. Always fitted with an Everflex vinyl-covered roof, the cars, apart from the earliest examples, also had a slightly smaller rear screen which provided a degree of extra privacy. An optional feature of long wheelbase cars was the provision of a division between the front and rear compartments which, when fitted, took up the entire extra floorpan length.

Instead of being carried out at Crewe, modifications to the bodywork were completed at the workshops of MPW, at Willesden, where the bodyshells were received direct from Pressed Steel at Cowley. Once the coachwork had been completed, the bare metal bodies (body-in-white) were dispatched to Crewe for finishing in the usual manner. All this was time-consuming, and long wheelbase cars took on average 4-5 weeks longer to prepare than standard saloons. As could be expected, the cars were fully equipped and those fitted with a division - which had an electrically operated window lift - had the benefit of two air conditioning systems, one for each compartment, the refrigeration unit for the rear passengers housed in the boot. Almost unthinkably, the cars with divisions lacked picnic tables - due to the glass screen - and rear vanity mirrors, usually built into the rear quarter panels, but now replaced by discreet air conditioning vents.

Although available from the first half of 1969, long wheelbase cars were not specified for the home market until later in the year, with early production destined for America. It is not surprising, therefore, that all of these cars were finished to US Federal safety standards and incorporated a high degree of facia padding. All long wheelbase cars received the GM400 gearbox and, apart from a few early examples, were fitted with automatic height control suspension to the rear wheels only.

Notwithstanding the fact that production of long wheelbase cars did not get under way until the standard saloon had been on the market for over three years, a pilot batch of 10 cars had been made available in 1967. Delivered on 19th July of that year through Kenning Car Mart Ltd., one of these car, which had been specially commissioned by HRH Princess Margaret and Lord Snowdon, was built on chassis LRH 2542, and incorporated several special features,

Long wheelbase cars had an extra 4 inches (102mm) added to the floorpan. Bodyshells were delivered to MPW from Pressed Steel, where the conversion was carried out, before the car went to Crewe for finishing. The car shown here is actually a Silver Wraith II. (Author's collection)

some of which were exclusive to royal requirements. Very much involved in the preparation of this particular car was chief stylist, John Blatchley, who also had responsibility for all styling matters at MPW. Together with Roger Cra'ster who, as export manager at Rolls-Royce normally conducted all negotiations between the company and the royal family, John paid two visits to Princess Margaret to discuss her specification requirements and suggestions. On the first of the two visits John recalls that Princess Margaret and Lord Snowdon knew a great deal about the car, as Dr Llewellyn-Smith had briefed them the evening before during a dinner engagement.

Features included in Princess Margaret's car were a height and forward adjustable rear seat for ceremonial occasions, extra night illumination, and the standard fitment of a special police lamp above the front screen. The usual pennant, raised when the car was used for official functions, was quite disliked by

A pilot batch of 10 long wheelbase cars was made between 1966 and 1967, and included this particular vehicle - chassis number LRH 2542 - specially built for HRH Princess Margaret. The car had several styling modifications to suit the Princess and was finished in dark green paint with special green hide to match.

Carpets were pale grey-green and the facia was made from oiled teak. Note the royal coat of arms which John Blatchley specially designed on request from the Princess. Take a look, too, at the repeater indicators on the waist moulding, which are very similar to a component used by Fiat. Note the police lamp above the windscreen. (Courtesy John Blatchley)

This Long Wheelbase Saloon (chassis number LRH 21379) was once owned by the late Princess Margaret. Built in 1975, it served Her Royal Highness for a number of years. Now owned by a marque enthusiast, the car still carries the police lamp facility above the windscreen. (Author's collection)

Princess Margaret, and John Blatchley accordingly designed a most beautiful, internally lit, 6 inch (152mm) high shield bearing the royal coat of arms, exquisitely hand carved from solid perspex. A further variation affected the repeater direction indicators, which were built into the waist moulding and were similar in design to those used by Fiat. The interior of the car was equipped with special green hide to match the colour of the bodywork, whilst the carpets were a pale grey-green colour. Instead of the usual burr walnut, the facia was made of oiled teak and the door capping rails, normally made from wood, were of leather to match the upholstery. All brightwork was given a satin finish.

The green interior colour of Princess Margaret's car was decided on by Lord Snowdon, who insisted it had to be the same shade as a piece of carpet which served as a bed for their dog. The piece of carpet was taken away by John Blatchley, depriving the royal dog of its usual bed!

Long wheelbase cars were also built as Bentley models, but only in comparatively small numbers: 2780 first series long wheelbase Silver Shadows were produced but only 9 T-Series. When the second series cars were introduced, the long wheelbase version was redesignated Silver Wraith II, so reviving a famous model name. Unlike the earlier car of the same name, the Silver Wraith II did not have a separate chassis. The Bentley version, however, underwent no such resurrection, simply acquiring the title T2 Long Wheelbase.

Series II long wheelbase cars received the same modifications as the saloon, and were immediately identified by their plastic-faced bumpers, dedicated badging upon the boot lid, the Rolls-Royce or Bentley emblem neatly positioned on the rear quarter panels, and the redesigned facias. Like its predecessor, the Silver Wraith II, when fitted with a division, lost all advantage of extra leg room for rear passengers, the centre fitting accounting for the additional 4 inches (102mm) built into the platform. Only

10 Bentley T2 Long Wheelbase cars were built, contrasting dramatically with 2135 Silver Wraith IIs.

Cars for the American market did not have the air dam beneath the front bumper, and safety regulations prevented the fitting of a central division. The reason was that, in order to install the rear air conditioning refrigeration unit, the fuel tank would have had to be relocated outside of the car's rear crumple zones.

The Silver Wraith II and its Bentley equivalent were replaced by the Silver Spur in 1980, the last chassis built being 41468. In terms of desirability, the long wheelbase cars have become much sought-after, if only because of the greater amount of rear passenger space they have. Additionally, Silver Wraith IIs are popular as they not only offer better handling with their rack and pinion steering, but also provide greater passenger comfort due to the provision of automatic air conditioning.

Conversions

Even Rolls-Royces did not escape the customising techniques applied by some specialist firms in order to 'stretch' a normal car into something much bigger. Such conversions were often carried out for publicity purposes, usually serving as courtesy transport, but some were completed to satisfy the demands of their owners.

Often bizarrely fitted out with television, auxiliary seating, and the wares of the customiser's art, these cars must surely be a far cry from what Harry Grylls and John Blatchley had envisaged. A number of cars received specialist treatment, such as the car built on chassis LRA 14837. The car's owner, John L. Hanson,

The lengthened wheelbase is evident in this publicity photograph of the Silver Wraith II.
(Courtesy Rolls-Royce Motor Cars Ltd.)

had wanted single round headlamps, reminiscent of the Silver Cloud I and II, instead of the twin lamp system; white side lamps were fitted into the tops of the front wings, and fog lamps faired into position beneath the headlamps in place of the grilles. At the rear, enclosed wheelarches gave the car a particularly heavy look. At least one estate car version was built, as Classic Coachworks of California devised a straightforward design on a

long wheelbase car with left hand drive using chassis number LRX11443. The same company also featured a pick-up style vehicle, an 'estate wagon' conversion using an early right hand drive car.

Although the Corniche was never offered as a four-door version, one such cabriolet built on an early floorpan did exist. Registered XLR 176, the car featured rear doors hinged at the rear, so as to be front opening, but it's not

known who undertook the conversion or, with any certainty, its present whereabouts.

Following a demand from the British Foreign Office, a number of Silver Shadows were equipped with armour plating to make them bulletproof. The cars were designed for use in certain countries where the embassies were considered vulnerable. Built to individual specification, this work was generally supervised by

Jock Knight at the Crewe factory, whose job it was to prepare the car according to the degree of protection required. The extra weight of these cars caused many problems and often meant boosting the car's suspension and restricting the amount of load it could carry. Jock remembers demonstrating an armoured car to the SAS (Special Air Service) at Hereford, and being somewhat concerned when an officer fired three shots directly at the car at point-blank range. Thankfully, both Jock and the car survived the ordeal! In all, no more than 10 vehicles were converted in this way.

Being a bespoke motor car, a number of vehicles were prepared to the specific requirements of owners, and it is not possible to list them all. Many enthusiasts, however, would not care to see the Silver Shadow in any other guise than that originally intended. If it was good enough for Rolls-Royce, then it was good enough for anyone ...

Two-door saloons
Less than six months after the launch of the Silver Shadow and Bentley T, Rolls-Royce unveiled an attractive two-door saloon distinctly different to that of the standard four-door car.

Eighteen months after announcing the two-door saloon, Rolls-Royce launched the Convertible, produced by MPW. Both models could be specified as a Bentley if required. (Courtesy Rolls-Royce Motor Cars Ltd.)

James Young produced 35 two-door Silver Shadows and 15 Bentley Ts. The famous Bromley firm was unable to change its coachbuilding techniques, and resorted to buying complete cars from Crewe and carrying out cosmetic modifications. The cost was enormous and the company went out of business in 1968. A James Young Silver Shadow is therefore a rarity, and a Bentley T even more so. (Courtesy Robert Vickers)

A little over 18 months later - two years after the Silver Shadow's debut - another exclusive two-door model, a convertible, was announced. These cars were forerunners to the Corniche which appeared in 1971 and, together, are now recognised as being amongst the most desirable of all postwar Rolls-Royce and Bentleys. At the time of introduction they were designed to replace the S3 Bentley Continental, which was still being produced in very small numbers.

Even though the monocoque construction of the Silver Shadow and T-Series Bentley made it difficult to produce a true coachbuilt variant, Rolls-Royce nevertheless proposed

to offer such a car to its discerning clientele. The coachbuilders that remained in business in the mid-sixties were hardly in a position to spend huge amounts on new production methods and, for James Young, the situation was critical if the company was to continue producing specialist bodies. For MPW, there was some hope inasmuch as the company was already part of Rolls-Royce, and enjoyed a great deal of support from the parent company.

It's no surprise, then, that an early decision was taken that MPW carry out the coachbuilding of the two-door models, not only because MPW was a subsidiary of Rolls-Royce,

but also because it had the capacity to produce the cars, even if it did mean a major upheaval in adapting to the techniques employed in coachwork engineering - instead of coachbuilding - building upon an already fabricated platform constructed by mass production methods.

James Young, though fully experienced in producing bespoke bodies for Rolls-Royce and Bentley chassis, was not in the same position as MPW. Its independence from Rolls-Royce placed the company at something of a disadvantage as far as the monocoque cars were concerned, but this did not deter it from trying to adapt to new methods of business. Deciding

Styled by John Blatchley, much of the Two-Door Saloon detail work was penned by Bill Allen with the full approval of the chief stylist. This example is owned by Peter Bellis. (Author's collection)

it should offer a coachbuilt alternative to the Crewe product, the company actually came up with a design before MPW. Unlike the MPW models, which had their own unique construction, the James Young cars were merely an adaptation of the standard four-door saloon. For the Bromley company there was no alternative but to buy-in complete cars from Crewe and carry out what was, essentially, a series of cosmetic modifications, which included repositioning the door pillars and fitting new doors. With traditional coachbuilding methods not compatible with the engineering of the Silver Shadow, it would not have been possible to perform any major structural operations.

At first glance, outwardly the James Young saloon looked almost identical to the four-door Crewe model. Externally, main differences affected the doors - two instead of four - which were elongated, and the provision of rear quarter windows; the chrome waist trim strip was dispensed with and the door handles were of the coachbuilder's own design. There were subtle differences to the car's interior: the rear quarter window lifts were, naturally, electrically operated and the seats, together with the wood trim, followed the style that was distinctive to the company.

The first of the James Young cars was built on chassis 1067 and the derivative was offered as a

Bentley version as well. Apart from the radiator shell and badging the cars were virtually identical, with the Bentley sporting the usual wood trim and facia found on the Crewe model. The cars were considerably more expensive than the standard saloons, commanding an additional £1214. Demand for the cars was not huge and, after having built only 50 examples, 15 of which were Bentleys, the project was abandoned in 1967.

Throughout this period when James Young was offering a Silver Shadow conversion, the company was also building bodyshells for the Phantom V which remained in production until 1968. Having produced 195 out of the 516 built,

Bill Allen, pictured in February 1996 alongside the last Corniche built. (Courtesy Rolls-Royce Motor Cars Ltd.)

James Young went out of business after producing its last Phantom, so concluding 105 years of business.

Mulliner, Park Ward (MPW) cars

The decision to build an 'official' MPW two-door version of the Silver Shadow was made during the period 1963-64. The car was styled under John Blatchley's direct supervision, to his concept and precise requirements. Some of the styling process was entrusted to Bill Allen, John Blatchley's deputy, and it was he who created the definitive shape using the wax modelling technique.

Bill, of course, was a very experienced stylist, having joined Arthur Mulliner from Towcester Grammar School, and an R-R man since 1935. As deputy to John Blatchley, Bill Allen had also been heavily involved in the standard saloon, and his work on the two-door derivatives had met with the chief stylist's full approval.

It took six weeks to complete the styling, and the most noticeable feature was the uplifted waistline above the rear wheelarch. Bill, incidentally, refers to this particular aspect of the car's design as its 'Coke-bottle' feature which was originally introduced (somewhat daringly) to suggest a rear wing.

At the time, such styling ideas were usually restricted to a few sports cars which, because of their low build, had sculptured rear wings, as in the case of the E-Type Jaguar, Big Healey and AC Cobra. This sportscar styling feature was based in tradition and was really nothing more than a hangover from the running board era. Later, chrome embellishments which suggested a wing line became popular on some saloons. The styling theme of the two-door Silver Shadow, however, successfully imitated the graceful lines of the Bentley S-Series Continentals, especially those offered by Park Ward or H.J. Mulliner with their vestigial rear wings.

A very modest person, Bill Allen claims the styling devised for the car was very simple, with a prominent

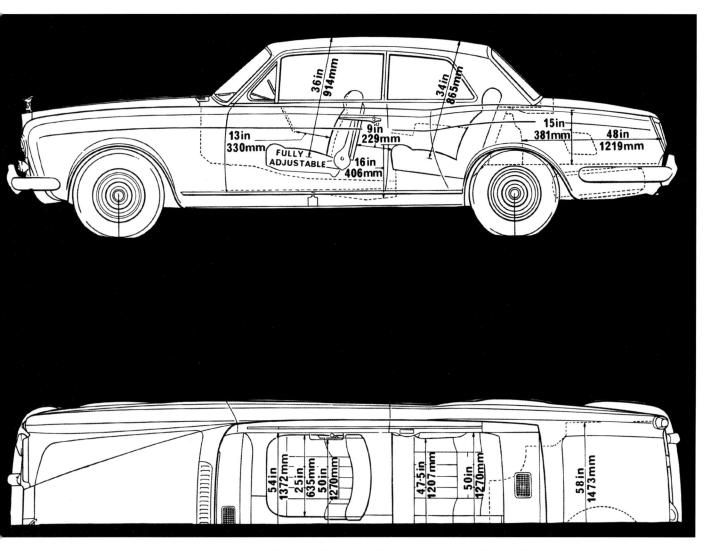

This brochure illustration clearly shows the drophead's internal measurements. Like the four-door saloon, the MPW cars were equipped with electrically-adjustable seats. (Courtesy Rolls-Royce Motor Cars Ltd.)

moulding from front to back on a surface shaped slightly to suggest a rear wing in both plan and elevation views. The moulding, he considered, also gave an impression of speed when viewed from the side, which was quite appropriate for a two-door design. The styling of the car was, therefore, very pertinent considering the model was intended as a direct replacement for the S3 Continental. Strangely, the two-door model, even though intended as the flagship of the Silver Shadow range, did not carry on the Continental nomenclature; for this customers would have to wait until 1984.

In the meantime, the two-door saloon was accompanied, in 1967, by a drophead coupé version, whose styling was, again, devised by Bill Allen with John Blatchley's approval. Everything below the waistline of the car resembled the two-door saloon version; above it, the hood was designed and built by MPW. Both two-door Silver Shadows, as a Rolls-Royce or Bentley, were completely distinctive in appearance and, although sharing a common identity with the standard saloons, nevertheless incorporated a number of subtle differences.

Auxiliary driving lamps were

fitted above the front bumper and repeater direction indicators - also a feature of the saloon cars - were positioned further forwards along the front wings, ahead and above the wheelarches. Overtaking mirrors, normally positioned at the base of the A-post, were placed on top of the front wings, while the door handles were of the style unique to MPW cars. The tail layout was enhanced by the rear wing profile, which continued the graceful sweep of the crown line down to a lower boot lid, and was much sleeker in appearance than that of the four-door models. As with

The facia of the MPW Convertible. (Courtesy Rolls-Royce Motor Cars Ltd.)

the four-door saloons, the boot lid, doors, and bonnet were all formed from aluminium alloy. The power-operated hood on the Convertible, which was finished in Everflex with a cloth lining, was superbly constructed and, as a safety measure, could only be raised or lowered when the car was stationary with the handbrake applied and the gear selector in neutral.

The passenger compartment also featured a number of differences. The front seats - electrically adjustable as well as having a manually operable backrest to allow easy access to the rear cabin - were unique to MPW design; the back seat, narrower in width than on the standard saloon, suggested a 2+2

rather than a full four-seater. There was no sacrifice in comfort: English hide upholstery, deep pile carpets, and the luxury of burr walnut for the facia and waist rails were features, while the capping rail was padded in black leather. The windows, including rear quarterlights, were electrically-operated, as was the radio aerial, and specification included cigar lighters in each of the rear armrests. As expected, air conditioning was an option.

Unveiled at the Geneva Motor Show in March 1966, the two-door Silver Shadow Saloon went on sale at £8150 (£9849 with tax), with the Bentley version £50 less at £8100 (£9789), an increase of 50 per cent

more than the standard saloon. The two-door Convertible, making its debut at the London Motor Show in 1967, attracted a further £400 with prices of £8550 (£10,511 including tax) for the Rolls-Royce and £8500 (£10,450 including tax) for the Bentley. Despite higher prices (which reflected the high build costs), there was an immediate demand for the two-door models.

Chassis numbers for the two-door MPW cars started at 1148 and 1149 (Rolls-Royce and Bentley saloons respectively), and 1698 for the Rolls-Royce Convertible. Production of Bentley Convertibles, however, did not get under way until chassis 3049. Mechanically, the MPW cars were

The interior of a two-door saloon. Note that this is a Bentley version as denoted by the emblem on the brake pedal and speedometer. (Courtesy Rolls-Royce Enthusiasts' Club)

identical to the Crewe examples: the 6.230-litre engines powered the cars smoothly and quietly; the four-speed automatic gearbox was fitted to right hand drive versions, whilst the three-speed GM400 unit was specified for left hand drive models. The constant height self-levelling suspension was also a feature and, similar to the standard saloons, offered excellent ride comfort. From 1969, as on the cars built at Crewe, the levelling device operating on the front wheels was deleted, leaving the high pressure

hydraulic rams to work on the rear axle only.

Construction of the two-door models was surprisingly complicated and necessitated the cars being transferred between London and Crewe. In essence, the platforms were built by Pressed Steel and delivered to the Willesden works of MPW, where the bodyshells were built into position before being sent to Crewe to have subframes and mechanical components fitted. Whilst there, the bodyshells received corrosion proofing

and primer coats of paint, before being returned to Willesden for fitting out and application of the finishing coats of paint. As can be appreciated, this was a costly and time-consuming performance which meant an increased price and delayed delivery.

The time taken to build an MPW car could be anything between four and a half and six months, depending upon customer requirements, in sharp contrast to the 12 weeks it took to complete a standard Silver Shadow or Bentley T. Firstly, the car would spend

MPW cars were certainly luxurious. This is a late Corniche, evidenced by the American safety requirement facia and door trim style. (Courtesy Rolls-Royce Enthusiasts' Club)

at least three weeks at Willesden before being sent to Crewe, where it remained for not less than five weeks; once returned to Willesden, several weeks of tests and checks were needed before delivery could be authorised. (The experimental department at Pyms Lane played an unusual role in this process. Frequently, during the early period of the two-door models, parts availability at Hythe Road was erratic so test drivers from Crewe, using experimental vehicles, were

asked to deliver items when there was an urgent requirement.)

Design and build of the two-door cars was quite different to that of the Crewe saloons, and entailed careful transition from the principles of monocoque construction to specialist coachbuilding techniques. As a result of the cars being built onto the standard, mass-produced platform, much new panelling was necessary. Some of this was fabricated at Willesden by MPW, but other material

had to be bought-in from suppliers such as Dowty Boulton and Paul, Airflow Streamline, and Albany Jig and Tool. The platform shells received from Pressed Steel needed sill and tunnel areas reinforced and, in the case of the convertible model, the entire floor required strengthening and cross-bracing to compensate for not having a steel roof, and the weight of the hood.

At Crewe and Willesden continual development resulted in a whole

It took between four-and-a-half and six months to build a two-door car, and sometimes longer if the customer had special requirements. By comparison, the time taken to build a standard saloon was 12 weeks. The car in this photograph is chassis DRX6539. (Courtesy Rolls-Royce Enthusiasts' Club)

raft of improvements to the Silver Shadow range of cars, and some of these were applied to the MPW models simultaneously with the standard models. Others, however, in keeping with policies dictated by John Hollings and fellow director, David Plastow, were introduced on the flagship coachbuilt models in advance of the Crewe cars, and included the General Motors GM400 gearbox and full air conditioning, which were applied to the two-door cars a few months ahead of the standard saloon. Modifications to the car's features in accordance with US Federal safety standards were,

however, synchronised between the two factories, as was the introduction of the 6.750-litre engine.

The Corniche

The events of Black Thursday, 4th February 1971, the day Rolls-Royce was plunged into receivership, did not prevent the company from announcing a new model within a couple of weeks. The events leading to the company's difficulties have been discussed, and it is clear that the receiver was resolute that car production remain unaffected, and the launch of the Corniche go ahead as planned.

The Corniche was vitally important to Rolls-Royce: the two-door Silver Shadow had, in the view of potential customers, too much of an association with the standard saloon and was in need of an identity of its own. By changing the name and introducing, in the main, a number of modifications, a certain amount of sales resistance could, it was considered, be successfully overcome. In view of the model's name it was appropriate, therefore, that the Corniche launch should take place in the South of France, at Nice, in the heart of the French Riviera.

All left hand drive MPW cars were equipped with the GM400 gearbox from the start. Home market models, and some of those right hand drive vehicles destined for export, were originally fitted with the four speed Hydramatic gearbox. This picture of a publicity car shows off the vehicle's exquisite styling. (Courtesy Rolls-Royce Enthusiasts' Club)

The Corniche was not completely new, and neither was it the first time the name had been used by Rolls-Royce. Motoring journalists also considered the Riviera venue appropriate, and the sight that greeted them as they disembarked from the plane at Nice airport generated something of a stir. Lined up outside the terminal lounge were no fewer than nine Corniches, attracting unprecedented attention: excitement mounted as the convoy of Rolls-Royces and Bentleys set off along the suitably named Promenade des Anglais. Journalists attending the launch enjoyed a spectacular event: having driven the Corniches along the coastal route to the Italian border at Menton, they went on to Genoa, where the cars were put through their

paces on the Turin *Autostrada*, before returning to Monaco.

At the heart of the Corniche was John Blatchley's superlative design styled in the mid-sixties. Now with many technical modifications, the car was given an identity which, in view of the company's difficult circumstances, was instrumental in providing a timely boost to Rolls-Royce's image. Not only did the car's name have romantic connotations, it also rekindled memories of an exotic prewar Bentley of the same title. The previous Corniche, a prototype streamlined sports saloon built by Vanvooren of Paris in 1939, was based upon the Mk V Bentley chassis and never went into production. Postwar, the Corniche name was considered for the sports

coupé which eventually became known as the R-Type Continental.

Like the two-door Silver Shadow and T models before it, the Corniche was offered in two body styles; a coupé and convertible, both of which were built by MPW, and badged as Rolls-Royces and Bentleys. Between 700 and 800 personnel were employed at the Willesden coachworks, and it was possible to build up to eight cars at one time.

Even if the cars looked similar to their predecessors, there were significant differences. The radiator shells of both marques were deeper by 15 per cent, and the interiors were given a facelift. A redesigned facia - which, apart from being very stylish and incorporating a rev counter

- pre-dated the similar type to that eventually fitted to the second series Silver Shadow and T saloons. A new steering wheel, 15 inches (381mm) in diameter, with a wooden rim and leather-covered spokes, was also a feature. All in all, the Corniche assumed a definite sporting attitude which, together with modifications to the ignition timing, valve timing and induction system which increased engine output by 20bhp, resulted in a true 120mph (192kph) luxury grand tourer.

Engine modifications couldn't be applied to American export cars because of exhaust emission controls, so these cars continued with the usual Silver Shadow unit.

First seen on the Corniche, and later on the Crewe models, was the cruise control device which could be

The Corniche was introduced in 1971, soon after Black Thursday, the day Rolls-Royce went into receivership. (Author's collection)

This elegant
coachbuilt Silver
Shadow is
pictured at a Rolls-
Royce Enthusiasts'
Club meeting. The
line-up of cars in
the background
includes some
very interesting
models. (Courtesy
Rolls-Royce
Enthusiasts' Club)

An American
specification
Corniche II. Note
the side marker
lamps; not evident
in this picture is
the absence of an
air dam beneath
the bumper. This
feature was
omitted from US
cars due, in part,
to the steepness of
ramps in American
car parks.
(Courtesy
Rolls-Royce Motor
Cars Ltd.)

The two-tone paintwork on this Corniche is particularly attractive, and the rarity of the Bentley model adds to the car's appeal. (Courtesy Rolls-Royce Enthusiasts' Club)

It's no wonder that the Corniche models - whether Rolls-Royce or Bentley - are regarded as possibly the most desirable of all the Silver Shadows. The ageless styling is a tribute to John Blatchley. (Courtesy Rolls-Royce Motor Cars Ltd.)

What better way to enjoy a summer's day than to lower the folding top of a Corniche and glide into ecstasy ...
(Courtesy Rolls-Royce Motor Cars Ltd.)

fitted at the customer's discretion.

Improved cooling was provided by a fan with a modified drive ratio, and brake efficiency was enhanced by ventilated wheel trims which allowed extra cooling of the discs. The addition of the rev counter (graduated up to an optimistic 6000rpm) showed the engine to be easily capable of about 4500rpm; on test runs in the South of France, speeds in excess of the maximum were often attained.

There was no mistaking the car's pedigree with its exclusive 'Corniche' badging specially designed by stylist Martin Bourne, based on a typeface he discovered in *Reader's Digest* magazine!

Compared with the models it replaced, the Corniche price tag showed an increase of somewhere around 10 per cent: the Rolls-Royce in saloon version cost £12,829 and the Bentley £72 less; the Convertible commanded almost another £600 at £13,410 for the Rolls-Royce and £13,332 for the Bentley.

All coachbuilt cars were built to the Corniche standard as from chassis 9770, a Rolls-Royce saloon version, while Rolls-Royce convertibles started

from chassis 9771. Bentley badged cars commenced at 10122, for the convertible, and 10420 for the saloon. Development and refinement of the models continued and resulted in a number of modifications: ventilated wheel discs, which improved brake cooling, were fitted from chassis 10500 and, importantly, compliant front suspension was applied from approximately November 1971 and chassis 12734. It was not until a couple of months later, at chassis 13485, that other models in the Silver Shadow range were similarly equipped with the new suspension. The braking system was yet again revised from chassis 13861, when the brake pedal was given a lighter feel and, at chassis 13922, export Corniches received modified rear calipers.

From 1972, North American cars received energy absorbing bumpers and a pedal-operated parking brake. American Federal safety standards brought about changes which included shortening of the radiator shell to allow horizontal movement of the bumper assembly, and deletion of the air intake grilles beneath the headlamps. Home market and European cars continued

with the traditional bumpers until styling changes dictated their demise. In early 1974 - from chassis 18563 - Corniche cars were delivered with the same 120.062 inch (3049.6mm) wheelbase as the four-door cars, 60 inch (1524mm) front track, and 59.5 inch (1514mm) rear track together with flared wheelarches. These modifications were made to suit the provision of 235/70VR x 15 radial ply tyres. Lighting was improved by fitting halogen bulbs to all left hand drive cars, except those for Sweden and the USA, from February 1975 (chassis 21104).

USA cars, commencing at chassis 21729, were supplied from early 1975 with the new automatic air conditioning unit, a revised facia and fuel emission controls. Cars for other markets, with the exception of those for the UK, however, did not receive these modifications until a little later, from chassis 21998. Home market Corniches had to wait until later, during 1975, for the same improvement, which was made from chassis 22648.

When the Series II Silver Shadow and Bentley T2 were introduced in 1977, similar styling and design changes affected the Corniche. Modifications during production - which were applied to the Crewe models also - were somewhat fewer in number as development was concentrated on the models that became the Silver Spur and Mulsanne, etc. Chassis numbers for 1977 cars started at 30003 for the Rolls-Royce convertible and 30011 for the saloon; Bentley versions commenced with chassis 31219 for the convertible and 31226 for the saloon.

Post-1977 cars were never given a

Series II designation (this arrived later, towards the end of the eighties) but these cars, apart from the American market versions, could be positively identified by frontal appearance which incorporated the air dam. Handling of these cars was improved not only by revised suspension geometry, but also Burman rack and pinion steering. Of particular interest was the convertible's dual level automatic air conditioning, the lower level of which operated with the hood down.

In saloon version, the Rolls-Royce and Bentley Corniche remained in production until 1980 when it was discontinued. By then, the price had risen to over £62,000 and the convertibles, which continued in production, commanded a figure of over £66,000. From 1979, however, an important modification affected the rear suspension but, curiously, the changes were applied without any notification. The reason for this was simple: the end of Silver Shadow II production was approaching and the Silver Spirit, with some of its technical features quite new, was still on the secret list and waiting to be announced. The rear suspension, new for the Silver Spirit, was actually fitted to the Corniche before the event!

Handling of post-1979 cars was dramatically improved, the result of a reworked suspension system which incorporated gas struts, an increased semi-trailing arm pivot angle, and slightly increased track measurements. Added to this, springing was made slightly softer, and the springs themselves a little shorter.

The convertible models survived throughout the eighties, even though proposals to alter the concept of the car had been contemplated. A plan

The exquisitely appointed Corniche Convertible was widely acclaimed on both sides of the Atlantic. (Author's collection)

Visit Veloce - www.veloce.co.uk

to update the styling to that of the embryonic Silver Spur was eventually dropped in favour of the existing traditional shape; however, not only had detailed drawings been devised, but a full-scale mock-up of the vehicle had been built. Plans for a revival of the Corniche saloon were also abandoned in the mid-eighties and, during that time, ideas for a four-door Corniche built upon an extended wheelbase were explored.

For 1986, the Corniche II was announced, though initially for America only; other markets had to wait until 1988 for the new designation. A number of modifications were incorporated in the new model, including redesigned seats and wheel trims, and colour-keyed bumpers and mirrors. The Continental nomenclature was revived for the Bentley version, which was no longer referred to as the Corniche, and revised specifications generally mirrored those applied to the Rolls-Royce version. Apart from new seats, the Continental featured a redesigned facia with separate round instruments which evoked Bentley tradition; further changes included colour-keying mirrors, bumpers and radiator shutters, while distinctive wheel trims, similar to those on the Turbo R, were available. Corniche and Continental cars for the following year were further updated and equipped with anti-lock brakes (ABS) and Bosch fuel injection.

For the 1990 model year, specification changes justified the Corniche III designation for Rolls-Royce cars; Bentleys, however, remained as Continentals. In general, changes were similar to those applied to the Silver Spirit II, but did not include, until 1992, the saloon's active

ride suspension. As a no-cost option, home market customers could choose to have both a catalytic converter and a 10-speaker radio/cassette with CD player. The electronically aided suspension system allowed settings to be automatically adjusted to suit road surface; this was, in principle, similar to the system used by Citroën for its large XM saloon. The Corniche and Continental interiors were also updated to include inlaid woodwork, revised instrumentation, and controls incorporating seat adjustment with a memory function.

Active ride suspension and 4-speed automatic transmission - together with a redesigned convertible top that incorporated a heated rear window - was sufficient for a further designation change - to Corniche IV - in 1992. Although design changes to the convertible top mechanism, and some repositioning of the rear window, followed a short time later, the specification of the cars was fully comprehensive. Not only ABS braking, but air bags for both driver and passenger were included within the safety equipment; emission controls complied with the most stringent legislation at the time.

To acknowledge the car's 21st birthday in 1992, Rolls-Royce built a special limited edition of the Corniche IV, which had features such as 4-speed automatic transmission, redesigned seats, and burr elm veneer interior woodwork with oak cross-banding and silver inlays. Each of the 25 cars produced (all finished in Ming Blue paintwork with a cream-coloured leather convertible top and sumptuous upholstery in magnolia) were identified by distinctive anniversary wheel trims and, in addition, a specially engraved

silver plaque was fitted to the inside of the glovebox lid. The finishing touch was the provision of a vanity set housed within the driver's door and, in the passenger doors, cocktail requisites.

It was no wonder that, even priced at £165,271, the cars very quickly found enthusiastic buyers, including the Sultan of Brunei who had three cars to non-standard specification. Rolls-Royce enthusiasts in California celebrated the Corniche's birthday in spectacular style and staged a convoy of 125 cars through elegant Beverly Hills. The event, noted in the *Guinness Book of Records* for the longest ever cavalcade of motor cars of one make on a public highway, not only paid tribute to the car but also acknowledged that a quarter of all Corniche Convertibles produced had been exported to that State.

Along with the Corniche, Continental and Continental Turbo, a batch of 25 of the Corniche S were built during 1995. These 25 cars were amongst the last Corniche models built, and were constructed at Crewe as the production line had already been transferred to Pyms Lane from Willesden in 1992. The MPW factory, incidentally, was closed in 1994. Special order cars were individually costed and body panels acquired from Park Sheet Metal, the company which had supplied material for the Camargue.

The Corniche concept goes far beyond a quarter century: it is now around 40 years since the car was introduced as a Silver Shadow two-door model, and something like 45 years since John Blatchley styled the car, and Bill Allen single-handedly carved the model in wax and did the

Every effort was made to ensure that each car incorporated the best and most effective developments in modern technology. (Courtesy Rolls-Royce Motor Cars Ltd.)

complete design drawings - hand-measured from the model - all within six weeks. Little did he imagine then that those drawings of a car, with its 'Coke-bottle' waistline, would evolve into one of the world's most evocative and exclusive motor cars.

An amusing anecdote which illustrates this very point is the occasion when Bill, who had suddenly become very concerned about the car's styling, especially the uplift in its waistline, confided in Martin Bourne, a fellow stylist and said "You know, this is never going to sell, it's far too old fashioned!" There is probably no better tribute to John Blatchley's original design than Bill Allen's own words, which are as modest as usual: "Production of the two-door saloon, which I always think was the better looking car of the two, eventually ceased. The name 'Corniche' was first given, officially, to the drophead car in 1971 to mark the inclusion of many engineering improvements introduced simultaneously.

"Having retired in 1977, it astonished me to discover that this car had almost reached its 25th anniversary in 1993 and some were still being sold."

Pininfarina and the Camargue

With the Silver Shadow fully established and the Corniche models in production, Rolls-Royce's board of directors began to consider a coachbuilt alternative to the existing MPW cars which, while sharing the Silver Shadow's basic platform, would generate even greater prestige. Seen by the Crewe company as its flagship, the model has suffered from much controversy which, in an odd sense, has assured its historical value. To

understand the Camargue, and how the car came about, it's necessary to look further back in history.

Pininfarina had, in postwar years, produced a number of designs for cars on Rolls-Royce and Bentley chassis; in 1948 there had been a very stylish coupé based upon the Mk VI chassis, followed by a more conventional drophead coupé a year later. For 1950, the fastback design of two years earlier was repeated, but with revisions that made the car's overall styling much more acceptable. Pininfarina had also been responsible for a delectable version of the R-Type Bentley Continental in 1954, but not before H. J. Mulliner had visited the Turin company to see how it

specialised in the use of lightweight materials for its products.

When it came to styling Rolls-Royce and Bentley cars based upon monocoque construction, there were virtually no contenders apart from MPW and James Young. Pininfarina was, however, instrumental in producing a solitary car based upon the Bentley T, and this was purchased by James (later Lord) Hanson. Displayed at the 1968 London Motor Show, the Pininfarina car was certainly controversial with its rectangular headlamps, fastback styling and unmistakable Italian flair; compared to its frontal styling, the car looked much more elegant when viewed from the rear, the detail styling of the tail

152

In February 1996 members of the styling, development and body engineering departments during the 1950s and '60s were reunited at Pyms Lane so this photograph could to be taken for this book. From left to right are: Martin Bourne, Macraith Fisher (on step) Eric Langley, Derek Coulson, John Gaskell, Jock Knight (on step), Roger Cra'ster, John Astbury, Bill Allen, George Ray, and John Cooke. The car is the last production Corniche. (Courtesy Rolls-Royce Motor Cars Ltd.)

- with its circular tail lights - having a distinctly Latin feel. It has been suggested that this car was intended as a forerunner to a new Bentley Continental but, ultimately, it was seen as a precursor to the Camargue. Never completely appreciated, those who saw the Pininfarina Bentley either loved it completely or hated it intensely.

Pininfarina's offering must have made an impression for, soon afterwards, in 1969, the styling house was approached to produce a two-door coupé of such design and proportion

it would be immediately recognised as the flagship of the Rolls-Royce fleet. In fact, the Camargue, as the concept ultimately evolved into, was revered to such an extent that it became the company's most important model, superseding even the Phantom VI and winning the accolade of most expensive car on the British market.

Code named Delta, the project as a whole began to develop at a somewhat turbulent time in Rolls-Royce history: John Hollings had taken over from Harry Grylls and John Blatchley had retired; Fritz Feller was appointed

chief stylist and, in place of "Doc" Llewellyn-Smith, who had departed the motor division, was Geoffrey Fawn, who took over day-to-day running of the company.

There were two reasons why Sergio Pininfarina was commissioned to style the Delta project: firstly, it was considered that Rolls-Royce's own styling team was too busy expanding the Silver Shadow theme and, secondly (which may have been the main factor), Geoffrey Fawn had decided the company would benefit considerably from having a

The highest quality walnut veneer is used in the interior. (Courtesy Rolls-Royce Motor Cars Ltd.)

The Rolls-Royce Corniche III.
(Courtesy Rolls-Royce
Motor Cars Ltd.)

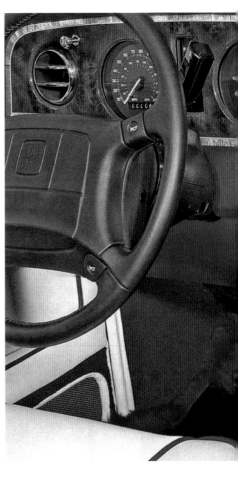

The US specification Corniche II has an air bag and front and rear seat belts.
(Courtesy Rolls-Royce Motor Cars Ltd.)

car designed by a prestigious Italian styling house. The news that Delta was being styled outside Rolls-Royce was greeted with little enthusiasm from within the ranks at Crewe. Certainly, the stylists who had achieved so much throughout the development period of the Silver Cloud and Silver Shadow felt let down at not being given the chance to offer designs. However, once the first feelings of disappointment had faded, there was a general air of excitement at the prospect of a Rolls-Royce exhibiting some of the panache of a Ferrari Berlinetta. That, of course, was not to be ...

It seems that Pininfarina encountered a number of difficulties regarding the Camargue's styling, especially when it came to incorporating the radiator shell within the car's overall size which, although the same length as the two-door saloon and Corniche, was 100mm (a fraction under 4 inches) wider. As a

Hide used in the Corniche's interior goes through a long-established process of selection, tanning, dyeing, cutting, and stitching. (Courtesy Rolls-Royce Motor Cars Ltd.)

result, the radiator on the Camargue is both wider and lower than that on the Silver Shadow. From a stylist's point of view, the Camargue's sharp-edged shape, scuttle height and huge radiator shell, emphasised its sheer size.

The styling suggested a number of novel ideas as far as Rolls-Royce was concerned, including a bonded windscreen in place of the usual type secured by moulded rubber, curved door glasses and quarter lights, and a single-piece bumper. The construction of the bumper was the same for all markets, but mounting differed for American market cars and incorporated the regulatory energy absorption. The styling of the headlamps was typical of that seen on many American cars of the early to mid-seventies, and it is clear that a similar theme was adopted on some of the prototype designs for

the Silver Spirit. At the waist, a locally dropped waistline was intended to make the windows appear larger than they actually were; Pininfarina's original proposals to finish in black all metal within this area were rejected by Rolls-Royce management - the 'black chrome' intended for the window channels was not considered sufficiently durable.

Pininfarina's brief was straightforward: the car would be a two-door coupé built by MPW, which shared the same platform and base mechanical units as the Silver Shadow. Its appointment would be even more luxurious and certainly superior to that of the two-door models currently available. Subsequently, eight sketches were prepared and Sergio Pininfarina presented his ideas to John Hollings, Geoffrey Fawn, and Fritz Feller, together with members of MPW

management, at a meeting in London at the coachbuilder's premises. From that meeting, a design was chosen and accepted, and the drawings and clay model were eventually prepared and delivered to Crewe.

Pininfarina's proposed styling followed that which was currently fashionable, and any suggestion that Pininfarina copied the design he had employed for Fiat's 130 coupé, the two-door alternative to the Turin car maker's top of the range model, has been denied. This idea appears to have originated from one of Britain's well-known motoring periodicals, where it is alleged a journalist caught a glimpse of the Delta project undergoing trials, and noticed styling similarities, and also from *Road & Track* in which Paul Frère commented that it looked "A lot like Pininfarina's 130 Coupé." Interestingly, early sketches of the

Pininfarina built this two-door Bentley T which was displayed at the 1968 London Motor Show. The fastback styling is rather elegant but the headlamps seem somewhat cumbersome. It has been suggested that this car inspired the development of the Camargue. James (now Lord) Hanson bought the car but its present location is uncertain. (Courtesy Rolls-Royce Motor Cars Ltd.)

Rolls-Royce Delta, whilst illustrating Pininfarina's contemporary styling features, are quite unlike the definitive model.

Events at Rolls-Royce during 1971 delayed the Delta programme quite severely, and it was not until the middle of 1972 that the first experimental car was made available for testing. Altogether, six experimental cars were built, four initially and two some years later using the full SZ underframe, which was not adopted for Camargue production. The last two experimental cars also helped in preparation of the Silver Shadow's replacement, the Silver Spirit. When initially seen at Crewe, the first prototype car was something of a shock, the bulk of the vehicle quite dwarfing the Silver Shadow standing alongside. An engineer, likening it to the Rock of Gibraltar, received a curt response from a test driver who, having just driven the car for the very first time, judged it to be about as fast! In fairness, as pointed out by a Rolls-Royce stylist, the change in fashion from the subtle and delicate curves of the fifties - which could disguise the bulk of a vehicle very successfully - to the crisp sharp corners of the seventies, made even a small car look big purely by emphasising its extremities. As for the interior, the mock-up was generally pleasing and was well-liked.

Testing of the Delta experimental cars was conducted using a Bentley-style radiator in common with other projects. For a time, however, the first test car was used without a radiator shell while the dummy grille was being constructed. Ironically, bearing in mind that a Bentley version of the Camargue was not contemplated, the proportions of the dummy shell seemed, to some, to suit the car's styling better than the traditional Rolls-Royce type.

A number of difficulties were experienced with the initial prototype cars: D1 (D for Delta project) suffered from excessive road noise, poor performance, and the effects of side winds; D3, the second experimental vehicle (D2 was never used for road work and performed as a crash tester) was finished in a paprika colour and was not particularly liked by the experimental department, which found it to be a poor performer at first. Enjoying something of a chequered career, D3 later served in the publicity campaign to launch the Camargue and was eventually scrapped with almost 100,000 miles (160,000km) recorded, but not before the car had been fitted with a 7.25-litre engine, which was subsequently replaced by the usual 6.75 unit. (Prior to the car's destruction it was involved in a serious accident whilst on trials in Scandinavia.)

D4, after production in 1973, was sent to France for intensive testing. John Gaskell remembers being involved in the car's 50,000 mile (80,000km) test schedule in which the only major problems were those concerning the split-level air conditioning. One of the Camargue's features was Rolls-Royce fully automatic air conditioning later fitted to the Silver Shadow II, having already been employed on the Corniche. Once the temperature levels had been selected, no further adjustment was required whatever the external temperature.

During the Camargue's incubation

Rolls-Royce considered the Camargue the flagship, and it was certainly, at the time, the most expensive car on the British market. (Courtesy Rolls-Royce Enthusiasts' Club)

Top right: This is possibly the first full-size mock-up of the Camargue. Frontal styling was particularly difficult for Pininfarina due to the mass and design of the huge radiator. The scuttle was considered too high by some. Even so, this car was especially appreciated by Rolls-Royce directors. (Courtesy Rolls-Royce Motor Cars Ltd.)

Bottom right: Several sources have suggested Pininfarina took the basic styling idea for the Camargue from the Fiat 130 Coupé. It has to be appreciated, however, that Pininfarina's then current styling trends are mirrored in this design which stems from the late sixties and early seventies. This appears to be a publicity photograph taken in 1986 for a limited edition US specification car. (Courtesy Rolls-Royce Motor Cars Ltd.)

The code name for the Camargue was Delta and the car was only ever intended as a Rolls-Royce-badged vehicle. The styling has always provoked controversy, not least from Rolls-Royce and Bentley enthusiasts and those involved in the development of the car. The date of this photograph is unknown but, looking at the bumper assembly, especially on the car's offside, the fit might suggest this to be an experimental vehicle. (Courtesy Rolls-Royce Enthusiasts' Club)

period, Macraith Fisher and Derek Coulson visited Sergio Pininfarina in Turin in readiness for the car's development programme. Pininfarina, incidentally, was very amused at the two engineers actually driving to Italy for the meeting - he was normally used to people flying in by helicopter to see him!

Like most things at Rolls-Royce, the Camargue's development programme was extremely thorough and, therefore, time-consuming. Much of the work consisted of complying with the severe emission control regulations in America, as well as that country's stringent safety requirements. The tooling process was also complicated and, like the Silver Shadow two-door saloons, building the cars was split between MPW's Willesden factory and Crewe. Pressed Steel, as with the Corniche, supplied the floorpan, dispatching it directly to MPW at Hythe Road, where it was mated with the bodyshell, itself assembled from panels supplied from the MPW factory and other sources. As with the other Silver Shadow derived models, aluminium was used for the bonnet, doors, and boot lid.

From Willesden the completed bodies were transported in pairs to Crewe for rustproofing, paint priming, and fitting of all major mechanical components before being returned to Hythe Road for completion and the usual extensive pre-delivery inspections and road testing.

Had the original plans come to fruition, the Camargue might have been ready for a 1973 launch. As it

The Camargue pictured in fashionable Chelsea in the mid-seventies; note the style of clothes then in vogue.

happened, events at Crewe dictated otherwise and, in any case, the fuel crisis of that year may well have proved detrimental to the whole project. Priced at a fraction under £30,000 with taxes, demand for the Camargue - which was almost twice the price of a standard Silver Shadow saloon and half as much again as the Corniche - was never going to be really high, hence the limited production facility. Launched in Sicily during January 1975, the two-door, five-seater Camargue was not only the most costly car in the Rolls-Royce catalogue, it was also the largest and heaviest Silver Shadow derivative.

A whole army of motoring journalists invited to test the publicity cars did allow the possibility of someone damaging all that expensive metalwork. Accordingly, to record the event John Hollings had a plaque prepared which he took with him to Sicily to present to the first journalist to sustain accidental damage to a Camargue. It had to happen, of course,

163

Bentley is back at Le Mans with a series of machines that successfully evoke the marque's sporting tradition. A Speed 8 featured at Storrs Hall near Windermere to celebrate the launch of the Continental GT. (Author's collection)

and the hapless journalist now has a permanent, if embarrassing, reminder of the feat.

As expected, the Camargue was luxuriously appointed; the softest Nuela hide gave the utmost comfort and the electrically adjustable seats even had a powered front seat back release to enable rear passengers to get into and out of the car easily. The facia was controversial and did not appeal to everybody; instead of being constructed from wood, the panels were made of aluminium to keep weight as low as possible, but covered in standard veneer in order to retain a traditional appearance. The instruments were surface-mounted, instead of being set into or behind the instrument board - a Pininfarina touch in recognition of Rolls-Royce's long association with aviation.

At the wheel of a Camargue there

was every indication that this was no ordinary Silver Shadow derivative: exclusive in all respects, the interior was surprisingly light and airy, slim roof pillars helping in this respect. Of interest are the tell-tales on the leading corners of the front wings, placed there after tests revealed that drivers were unable to accurately judge the width of the car!

From the time a platform was delivered to MPW, building a Camargue took approximately 6 months, and a customer could expect to wait up to two years before taking delivery. Initially, a single car a week was supplied and, as orders increased, so delivery times extended. Part of the reason for this long production time was the difficulty experienced in obtaining suitable body panels: Rolls-Royce standards were such that much of the material was rejected on the grounds of poor

quality. The Willesden works of MPW was already under severe pressure to produce Corniche models, as well as the other coachbuilt Silver Shadows. To ease the situation, in 1978 assembly of Camargue coachwork was transferred from Willesden and awarded to Motor Panels Ltd. of Coventry.

Pressed Steel delivered the floorpans direct to Motor Panels Ltd. at Coventry, as did suppliers of various other body components. Once Motor Panels had built the completed shells they were passed to Crewe for rust inhibiting, priming, fitting out, and road testing. The same exacting standards were applied at Crewe, and there was nothing to tell the Crewe and Willesden cars apart except the maker's plate on the door sill: Willesden Camargues can be identified by plates stating Coachwork by Mulliner Park Ward, and the Crewe cars which read

With Volkswagen investment the Bentley Arnage range has been extended to include the R, RL, and T models. (Author's collection)

Coachwork by Rolls-Royce Motors Ltd. In both cases, the words 'Designed by Pininfarina' left no doubt about the car's styling origins.

There were few major revisions to the Camargue's specification during its production span which continued over a period of eleven years; rack and pinion steering was fitted from 1977 and, from 1979, the suspension was updated to that being developed for the Silver Spirit. In 1980, cars exported to California were equipped with Bosch fuel injection and, a year later, the same modification was applied to all export models. From 1980 the Camargue was sold alongside the Silver Spirit range of cars, as well as the Corniche. Although the Camargue never received the full SZ underframe, it did get the rear end in 1979, just like the Corniche, but not the revised front end. In this way, the Camargue retained a ghostly element of the Silver Shadow well into the eighties.

Bentley enthusiasts were upset by the fact that the Camargue was only ever specified as a Rolls-Royce. However, a single Bentley version of the car was built at a customer's special request. Car D1 was built as a test car in advance of a proposal to market a high performance Bentley version equipped with a turbocharger and, in this guise, was fitted with a Bentley radiator in order to be less conspicuous. Accordingly, it couldn't really be called a Bentley as it was built as a Rolls-Royce. The project never materialised as such and the car was ultimately scrapped, but not before some incredible results had been recorded, including a top speed of 145mph (232kph). As for the specially ordered Bentley Camargue, certain styling difficulties were experienced in mating the radiator shell to the bonnet, as the same pressing as that for the usual Rolls-Royce-badged car was used.

In total, 526 Camargues were built which assures the model's exclusivity.

The last cars were built in 1986 with the final batch of 12 cars exported to the USA during the early period of 1987. Not everybody approved of the car's styling, and history records it as one of the most controversial Rolls-Royces. It was also, most certainly, one of the world's great cars.

A few words about the latter-day activities of MPW are in order before closing the chapter. The economic climate - as well as a demand for the true coachbuilt car - meant that, by the mid-nineties, it was no longer viable to retain the company's London premises and its closure was announced in May 1991, whereupon building of the Corniche, Bentley Continental, and Silver Spur Limousine was gradually transferred to a dedicated site at Pyms Lane. The Phantom VI was discontinued in 1992 and the workforce at Willesden cut back accordingly to just a handful of craftsmen in mid-1993. With work on the Touring Limousine (which was

built on an extended Silver Spur platform) concentrated at Crewe, the famous coachworks in Hythe Road, Willesden closed its doors for the last time in August 1994.

The spirit of the Silver Shadow lived on, however, and the very last Corniche enjoyed a place of honour within the gallery at Pyms Lane. As for all the other coachbuilt derivatives of the Silver Shadow and Bentley T-series cars, their futures are also assured: enthusiasts of the marques will see to that!

Collaboration and divergence

During the 1990s when Rolls-Royce and BMW collaborated over engine design and production, the Arnage and Silver Seraph models - successors to the Silver Shadow and Bentley - were introduced with BMW-derived engines, thus diverging from the familiar V8 introduced in 1959. The engine fitted to the Silver Seraph was a 24-valve, V12 unit of 5379cc, with a bore and stroke of 85mm and 79mm respectively, and maximum power of 322bhp at 5000rpm. The Arnage received an all-aluminium twin turbo 32-valve, V8 of 4398cc, with bore and stroke of 92mm and 82.7mm respectively, and maximum output of 350bhp at 5500rpm. Among Bentley customers and enthusiasts there arose some disquiet at the choice of engine specified for the Arnage, with many concerned about its ability to perform. Arnage customers, in the main, remained unhappy after taking delivery of their cars, and Rolls-Royce received a number of negative reports from customer and dealer alike.

It didn't take long for Bentley Motors (by this time Rolls-Royce and Bentley Motor Cars Ltd. had been

sliced apart and sold off in what was generally considered a controversial, contentious even, business arrangement) to address the situation and introduce the Arnage Red Label, complete with the venerable V8. The new model was enthusiastically received by customers, relieved that the trusty V8, considered to be at the end of its useful life, had gone back into production at Crewe. Thus, the vestiges of an earlier generation of cars were allowed to survive.

Bentley and Rolls-Royce today

Crewe is no longer the home of Rolls-Royce since the company was sold; Volkswagen bought Bentley, and the Rolls-Royce name was acquired by BMW. During the two decades that separate the end of Bentley T production and changes of ownership within Rolls-Royce, the Bentley revival had been absolute, with Bentley sales growing from just five per cent of total sales to outstrip Rolls-Royce demand. Policy at Crewe dictated that the Bentley name should symbolise the marque's sporting traditions, and trade on values associated with the firm's founder, 'W.O.' and his insistence on quality and proving his cars in motorsport.

When Volkswagen took over the Pyms Lane factory it made substantial investments and, as well as continuing production of the Arnage models, undertook development of a new car, the Continental GT. The new Bentley sports coupé was designed using styling cues taken from the R-Type Continental, and went into production during 2003 to great acclaim.

Volkswagen made a bold and definite statement about how it viewed the importance of Bentley by unveiling at Geneva in 1999 the 8-litre, W16 mid-engined Hunaudieres concept car that promised to return Bentley to motor racing at Le Mans. Then Bentley stole the march from Rolls-Royce by building a new state limousine that was presented to Her Majesty The Queen on the 50th anniversary of her accession to the throne in 2002.

Development of the Arnage models, begun with the Red Label, continued with the Arnage R, RL, and T. At the heart of the cars is the faithful V8, re-worked to comply with all emissions regulations and to possess such formidable power and smoothness that it can be classified as virtually a new engine. The Arnage R is the most sophisticated 'gentleman's carriage' to date, whilst the RL offers plushness with a longer platform. Possessing total sporting characteristics is the Arnage T, unveiled at the Detroit Auto Show in January 2002: capable of accelerating from 0-60mph (0-96km/h) in less than 6 seconds, the car's maximum speed is electronically governed to 170mph (272km/h).

Bentley's state limousine was commissioned in 2000 and is longer than the Arnage by a fraction under a metre. Rather than design the car around a separate chassis, it was devised as a monocoque, which, in engineering terms, gave greater strength in addition to making the most efficient use of interior space.

An intrinsic part of the Crewe factory is the Mulliner facility, which serves as Bentley's specialist coachbuilding division. Examples of Mulliner craftsmanship are the envy of rival manufacturers, and these coachbuilding skills are seen at motor shows around the world.

Bentley's return to racing has been a phenomenal achievement, due to the company's engineering commitment and the skills of Team Bentley, both coordinated from Crewe under the direction of 'Project Barnato,' a name most keenly associated with Bentley Motors and the 'Bentley Boys.' In June 2003 Bentley was victorious at Le Mans, mirroring its success there 73 years earlier. A celebratory dinner at London's Savoy Hotel marked the occasion four days later on June 18th.

The car that has made the headlines, though, is the Continental GT - the long-awaited Mid-Size Bentley. Work began on the project to develop the car in late summer 1999, the person in charge being Dirk van Braeckel, Bentley's newly appointed design director. While the Continental GT body-in-white is produced at Volkswagen's hi-tech plant at Mosel, the car was designed at Crewe, where it is built. The Continental GT's engine shares some basic family resemblance with that of the Audi A8 and VW Phaeton, but the 6-litre W12's 552bhp maximum power - at just 1600rpm, incidentally - is unique to Bentley. Maximum speed is stated at 198mph (316.8km/h) but testing prototype cars produced a true speed of 200mph (320km/h). The Continental GT offers formidable performance, with 0-60mph (0-96km/h) achievable in under 5 seconds.

What would you have to pay for a supercar like this? The launch price was set at £110,000, which, at the time, was around £40,000 less than any other model in the Bentley catalogue.

Volkswagen's investment in Bentley meant that the Crewe factory underwent change and modernisation. Many of the processes - some of which served Rolls-Royce and Bentley production over many years - were consigned to history. The very latest in technology replaced them, although it has to be emphasised that, at Bentley, some things, such as craftsmanship, are non-negotiable. Crewe skills live on, just as they did when the Bentley T and its predecessors were in production.

With BMW investment, Rolls-Royce Motors was established near Goodwood in Sussex in a purpose-designed and built factory. A completely new model - the Rolls-Royce Phantom - was developed; this, too, entering production in 2003. During the process of developing the Phantom, John Blatchley, who celebrated his ninetieth birthday in 2003, was invited to Rolls-Royce's Sussex headquarters to view styling proposals, and to select what he considered to be the most appropriate design.

While the new Rolls-Royce factory was being constructed, design of the Phantom took place at a secret location. A studio near London's Hyde Park served as the studio for the select team engaged on the project, while a short distance away in Holborn, a disused bookshop was converted into a modelling studio. It has emerged that plans for a future Rolls-Royce were discussed with BMW as early as the mid-1990s, suggested projects mirroring the BMW 9-Series. All were ultimately ditched in devising the definitive car.

The project's chief designer was Ian Cameron, who directed a select team of stylists and designers: two British, two American, and one Japanese. In its deliberations, the design team was keen not to lose track of Rolls-Royce heritage, so consulted company archives in the search for the most appropriate styling cues. The new model needed to exude that certain something associated with the marque, personified by a vertical radiator and high-mounted headlamps, long wheelbase for maximum interior space, long bonnet, long rear overhang, and strong roofline and C-post, large diameter wheels and tyres (the largest fitted to any production car). During the car's gestation period, such was the secrecy of the project that personnel had to sign confidentially agreements, and were constantly warned not to disclose any information about the car.

The Phantom is constructed using space frame technology clad with aluminium panels, with steel used for front wings and boot lid. Under the bonnet is a 6.75-litre V12 engine producing 453bhp at 5350rpm, sufficient to propel the car from 0-60mph (0-96km/h) in under 6 seconds. The car's top speed is governed to 149mph (238.4km/h). The price at launch matched that of the Mercedes Maybach at £240,000.

Living with a Silver Shadow or Bentley T-Series

There's probably no other product anywhere in the world that's as marketable as either the Rolls-Royce or Bentley. Bentley, with its famous winged B emblem, is synonymous with motor racing during the golden age of motoring, and the firm's successes at Le Mans and Brooklands are legendary. The Bentley name summons up the image of those cars built by W. O. Bentley at Cricklewood, which are the embodiment of British engineering at its best. Rolls-Royce, epitomised by the distinctive gothic temple radiator shell and the Spirit of Ecstasy, is held in the highest esteem, and the company has always been justifiably proud of its commitment to quality and excellence.

Few cars possess the charisma of a Rolls-Royce or Bentley which instantly marks them apart, and each marque jealously guards its heritage. Ownership of a new Rolls-Royce or Bentley is beyond the reach of many, but what about an older model, one that has become a recognised classic? For many enthusiasts the Silver Shadow and Bentley T-Series cars could be the ultimate classic car.

Without a doubt, the Silver Shadow and its Bentley equivalent have become recognised classics in their own right. For potential buyers the good news is that, because the survival rate of these cars is extremely high, prices are genuinely affordable and, very importantly, the supply of replacement parts is excellent.

Before rushing to buy the car of your dreams, however, remember that there is another side to ownership: running costs can be exceedingly high, some parts are hugely expensive and, unless the owner is an experienced mechanic, servicing and repairs are

Sculpted in 1911 by Charles Sykes ARBS, the Spirit of Ecstasy adorns some of the greatest cars in the world. (Author's collection)

often beyond owners' capabilities. Contrary to popular belief, the Silver Shadow range of cars requires just as much maintenance as any other motor vehicle and, due to engineering complexity, will probably require

Right: T-Series Bentleys have always attracted a particular following as some enthusiasts prefer the car's softer styling treatment. (Author's collection)

The winged B emblem was designed for W. O. Bentley by Freddie Gordon Crosby. (Author's collection)

Early Silver Shadows and Bentley Ts may have been around for some 40 years, and 25 years have elapsed since saloon versions were discontinued, which calls for care when considering a purchase. (Courtesy Rolls-Royce Motor Cars Ltd.)

Now classics in their own right, the Silver Shadow range of cars has survived in exceptionally large numbers. There are also many specialists who supply and maintain these fine cars. (Courtesy Bill Bateman)

specialist attention sooner or later. Having considered and accepted the 'for and against' arguments, ownership of these cars is a practical proposition which can be a rewarding and enjoyable experience.

Buying advice

Due to the number produced, and an excellent survival rate, there's no shortage of cars to buy (although the T-Series Bentley is not as widely available as fewer were built).

There are four obvious markets from which to purchase a car: private sale; a Bentley franchised dealer or recognised marque specialist; a second-hand (in Rolls-Royce and Bentley parlance the term 'previously-used' is preferred) car dealer, or at auction. Dealing first with an auction, only a person experienced in purchasing vehicles at a car auction should choose this route, and should have some knowledge of what to look for with a particular car. Possibly, a prospective owner could arrange for a Rolls-Royce/Bentley specialist to do this for him or her. Similarly, when contemplating buying from a used car dealer, unless the company has a good reputation, it's best to seek specialist advice.

Buying privately can be fraught with difficulty unless the purchaser

If there is evidence of coachwork repair, always ensure it has been carried out properly. When contemplating buying a Silver Shadow, it's sensible to get a specialist's report on the car first. (Courtesy Michael Hibberd)

173

Beware of cars which have been involved in an accident; damage such as this is expensive to repair.
(Courtesy Michael Hibberd)

has some experience of these cars. When viewing a car it is essential to ensure it is without damage, and has a full (preferably R-R) service history. If the history of the car is not available, it might well be prudent to have an independent appraisal of its overall condition. If major mechanical repairs are necessary, these could well be expensive to put right, especially given that the cost of an engine overhaul will run into four figures. The same goes for the bodywork; however insignificant damage may appear, it will undoubtedly be costly to repair. Always check for coachwork repairs: unless carried out expertly these are usually given away by poor quality repainting and/or badly fitting panels with uneven gaps between them. A car which has been involved in an accident and not properly repaired could be dangerous.

A safer approach - especially for the enthusiast considering their first Rolls-Royce or Bentley - could be to buy a car through a recognised dealer, or a marque specialist, who will be happy to offer a comprehensive service. A franchised Bentley agency has not only the support of the manufacturer, but also all of the technical information for a particular car. Marque specialists will be able to offer a service similar to that of a Bentley dealer but, in either case, it's best to discuss requirements beforehand to establish what support is available.

It's necessary to appreciate that the last Silver Shadows and Bentley Ts were built in 1980, and early examples have been around for some 40 years. Some Rolls-Royce dealers are therefore reluctant, unless the car is particularly special, to offer the vehicles for sale, preferring to sell through the motor trade to an independent specialist. That, of course, does not preclude them from offering specialist servicing and advice.

It goes without saying that buying through a specialist will almost certainly be more costly than buying at auction, or privately. In general, a good condition Silver Shadow or Bentley T will probably cost no more than an average, topically-priced new car.

When looking at different cars, don't be too put off by a vehicle which has changed hands a number of times. Initially, quite a number of cars were sold to companies and, usually, sold on after a couple of years. Some owners bought new cars at regular intervals - every two to three years, usually - because during the sixties and seventies it was possible to sell a car for what was paid for it - and often more - making buying a new car very attractive. As long as the vehicle has been well cared for and service schedules adhered to, there should be little problem. A word of warning, though. Silver Shadows and Ts are often purchased by motorists attracted by the cars' relatively inexpensive price, who then discover that running costs - coupled with the cost of correct maintenance - are higher than anticipated. Cars such as this are sometimes sold on after a short period and, in these circumstances, close attention should be paid to a vehicle's service history.

Just how good a Silver Shadow or T feels can only be properly appreciated by getting behind the wheel ...
(Courtesy Rolls-Royce Motor Cars Ltd.)

Prospective and existing Silver Shadow and T-Series owners will derive much benefit from joining the Rolls-Royce Enthusiasts' Club, or the Bentley Drivers Club, and it is through these organisations that marque specialists can be sourced. The R-REC does have at its disposal the complete build histories of every car, and often particular vehicles are known within club circles. Both the R-REC and BDC publish an Advertiser at regular intervals, which is supplementary to the club journal. It contains classified advertisements - trade and private - of cars for sale.

Prices for Silver Shadow and T-Series Bentley saloons can vary greatly depending upon age and condition. Coachbuilt models often command even higher prices, due to appeal and rarity factor. So, what should you pay for a car? According to John Bowling of Bowling Ryan, an independent Bentley and Rolls-Royce specialist in Bolton, Lancashire, Silver Shadows and Ts can be bought for as little as £1500 for a Series I car and £2500 for a Series II. Of course, for these prices, the car would be in need of complete restoration which, as well as being time-consuming, would also be very costly, certainly far more expensive than buying a car in first class order. To get a car to a good useable and reliable condition, expect to have to spend a minimum of £6000, rising to £8000 for a Series II car. To attain concours condition will be very expensive and, arguably, uneconomical, especially as a superior car could be bought for around £12,000 (though expect to pay more for a late model). Buying a car from a marque specialist may mean paying a premium, but any reputable firm should want to ensure that the

... or reclining in the rear compartment. (Courtesy Rolls-Royce Motor Cars Ltd.)

There are official Bentley dealerships throughout the world, and virtually all will be pleased to discuss the servicing arrangements for a Silver Shadow or Bentley T. (Courtesy Rolls Royce Enthusiasts' Club)

vehicle is supplied in the best possible condition.

A lot of people, when considering buying a Silver Shadow today, do not propose to use it as daily transport but keep it, instead, as a classic car to be driven at weekends and holidays. That does not mean that the car is not suitable for daily use, although high mileages will obviously be expensive in respect of running costs. Despite this, it does make for delightful daily transport - as a great many owners know.

Corniches and their predecessors, the two-door saloons and convertibles, along with the long wheelbase cars, make an attractive proposition. Due to rarity factor alone, prices of the MPW cars are higher than for the Standard Saloons, and cars in first class condition can command more than £40,000. A good example of a Camargue, even accounting for the car's controversial styling, can attract prices higher than £30,000, though it is

possible, as with the Corniche models, to acquire cars in a lesser condition for around a third of that price. Remember, though, any restoration of a coachbuilt variant is likely to be very, very expensive. As for the long wheelbase models (and that includes the Silver Wraith II), these cars not only provide extra comfort for rear seat passengers, but also command generally similar values to those of the Standard Saloons. Be warned, though, the extra length might mean it won't fit into your garage ...

Prices of the much rarer Bentley T and T2 are, surprisingly, mostly no higher than for the Rolls-Royce-badged cars and, according, to current published prices of classic cars, early models tend to be even cheaper. The Bentley does have a particular following, however, and many dedicated enthusiasts are keen to promote the marque's sporting image and traditions. There are those motorists who admire the engineering

finesse of the Silver Shadow and T-Series cars, yet prefer the softer frontal styling treatment of the Bentley.

Production of the Corniche and its Bentley sister of latter days, the Continental, continued until 1995. Values for these cars, which were built from the early eighties onwards, will be somewhat greater, and it can be safely assumed that the Corniche II, III, and IV will carry relatively high prices.

For anyone considering the purchase of a prestigious car as a classic vehicle, it's interesting to compare prices with alternative marques. For an Aston Martin DBS V8 of 1969-73 vintage, expect to pay up to £23,000 for a good example, and even more for a V8 from 1969-73. Daimlers and Jaguars, both of which enjoy a loyal following, carry prices only slightly lower than those of the Silver Shadow, whilst a Mercedes-Benz 450 can command much the same figure.

A two-door Saloon/Convertible or a Corniche model will, because of desirability and low build quantities, attract higher prices than the standard saloon cars. A car in first class condition can command prices of more than £40,000. (Author's collection)

When considering the purchase of a T-Series or Silver Shadow, it is important to have an idea of what sort of condition to expect for the asked purchase price. A vehicle requiring complete restoration is unlikely to be the choice of someone new to the marque, as specialist equipment will be required to do the work. Apart from the mechanical aspect, the bodywork and, more than likely, interior, will also require attention.

A more expensive car in better all-round condition may still incur some expense. Should the car require repainting, expect to pay at least £2500-6500 (depending on the car's condition and whether body repair is necessary) for a reputable job to Rolls-Royce standards; interior work to the leather or wood trim may also be expensive, especially if original materials have to be matched. Remember also that items such as tyres and external trim are easily overlooked in the enthusiasm to buy a car; tyre wear on earlier cars was always heavy, and getting more than 15,000 miles (24,000km) from tyres on those vehicles with non-compliant suspension is unusual. Tyres are expensive: a set of four can cost in excess of £800, and that doesn't include fitting, wheel-balancing or local tax. When buying tyres, it's essential to check they are correctly rated for the car; if they're not, it could invalidate your insurance.

Should the bumpers on Series I cars have sustained even minor damage, the cost to replace them, front and back, will be around £2200. Even a corner-piece section will amount to almost £250. The bumper assemblies on Series II cars are hugely more expensive and cost as much as £2500

for a front or rear section. Since the divergence of Rolls-Royce and Bentley, all parts for those cars built at Crewe - whether Rolls-Royce or Bentley - are available through Bentley dealerships and are sold as Crewe Genuine Parts. Only authorised Bentley dealers are approved to supply and fit Crewe Genuine Parts, which carry a three year warranty.

Replacement exhausts cost around £700 for the genuine article; it's false economy to fit anything other. Non-Crewe Genuine Parts systems may appear a little cheaper but usually will not fit or wear as well, which means earlier replacement and even more expense. Take a look to see whether the car's tool kit is in place and, if so, its condition. The fact that it is missing or in a damaged state could tell you a lot about the vehicle's history ...

Ideally, when contemplating buying a car, remember that, as far as Rolls-Royces and Bentleys are concerned, people are normally prepared to pay for quality; cars in lesser condition usually sell at a price which reflects the amount of money needed to restore it to good order. A car will retain its quality long after the initial cost has been accepted and forgotten. The advice, therefore, is to pay as much as you can for a car in good condition and with a satisfactory history.

John Bowling's advice is to opt for a Silver Shadow II or Bentley T2 because of the cars' refinements compared to earlier models. Handling on these cars is much better than that of the first series, and benefits from rack and pinion steering. The fully automatic air conditioning is far better than the system employed on the

first series cars and provides greater comfort. Also, once set, it never needs to be altered.

There are, of course, a great number of first series cars in day-to-day use, many of which are superbly maintained and in splendid condition. Some enthusiasts actually prefer the earlier cars to later models, and these cars will, naturally, be a first class investment. John Bowling always advocates the use of radial-ply tyres on early cars as they provide better road-holding, even at the expense of greater road noise.

John reckons potential purchasers often place too much

importance on low mileage. While this may seem an advantage, it could actually mean that the vehicle has been used mainly for short journeys, a possible cause of excessive engine wear. There's also the possibility that components could fail once the car is used more.

Most Rolls-Royce and Bentley specialists with an interest in the Silver Shadow and T-series cars will offer to survey a car and supply a written report on condition before purchase. Obviously, some agents and specialists make a charge for this service, but John Bowling's policy is to provide a free report in the interest of customer satisfaction. Unless the purchaser is confident he or she knows exactly what to look for on a car, it would not be sensible to buy without first having a survey done, which could save a lot of disappointment and expense.

For insurance purposes, the table on page 180 gives a guide to current (2004) values, depending on condition.

When considering cars for sale, it's important to determine at a glance the approximate age. This is not so easy with a Silver Shadow or Bentley equivalent because, throughout the 15 year production span, very few styling changes were implemented. To the unwary, a late Silver Shadow II or T2 can look remarkably similar to an early first series car. If the car has plastic-faced bumpers and an air dam, it is a Series II model; cars with chrome bumpers and overriders are from the first series, and those without grilles beneath the headlamps are identified as late versions. Finer identification is possible from the type of facia the car has: early first series cars have a large expanse of woodwork without a central console, while those cars complying with US Federal safety standards have greater amounts of padding, together with a V-shaped console.

Telling a car's age is a lot easier

– 2004/2005 price guide –

Silver Shadow Saloons 1965-71	£2000-12,000
Silver Shadow Saloons 1972-76	£2500-14,000
Silver Shadow Long Wheelbase	£2250-15,000
Silver Shadow MPW FHC	£5,000-17,000
Silver Shadow MPW DHC	£8000-37,000
Silver Shadow II Saloons 1977-79	£2500-15,000
Silver Shadow II Saloons 1979-81	£3000-17,000
Corniche FHC 1971-77	£5000-20,000
Corniche DHC 1971-77	£8000-37,000
Corniche DHC 1978-88	£15,000-80,000
Camargue FHC	£7000-30,000
Bentley T Saloons 1966-72	£2500-12,000
Bentley T Saloons 1972-76	£3500-14,000
Bentley MPW	£5000-30,000
Bentley T2 Saloons 1977-79	£4000-14,000
Bentley T2 Saloons 1979-81	£5000-16,000

with home market cars than those exported to the USA. American cars were never fitted with an air dam, and even first series cars had energy absorbing bumpers from 1974. To be sure about a car's age the chassis number provides positive identification.

Finally, unless buying privately or at auction, always purchase from a reputable source, even if a higher price has to be paid. Avoid any car that has been neglected or has a suspicious history.

A Shadow in the garage
Before driving home the chosen Rolls-Royce or Bentley, check that the car will actually fit inside your garage; there must be at least one enthusiast who's had to enlarge the garage, which

To the unwary, early Silver Shadows could be mistaken for later cars. Bumpers and facia styling can establish a car's age, but the way to be certain is the chassis number. This publicity photo was taken whilst the Silver Shadow was undergoing testing in wintry conditions. (Courtesy Rolls-Royce Motor Cars Ltd.)

Running costs can be high: between 12-18mpg (24lts/100km) is usual. (Courtesy Rolls-Royce Motor Cars Ltd.)

probably cost more than the car!

The satisfaction to be had from owning a quality car with one of the most desirable mascots of any marque is just the tip of the iceberg. For it to be driven and used to full potential, a Rolls-Royce or Bentley will need regular servicing and preventative maintenance. Although bought for the same sort of money as an economically-priced new family saloon, the running costs of these cars are pure Rolls-Royce.

Expect no better than 12-18mpg (24-16lts/100km) in fuel consumption, depending on engine condition and general condition. Servicing costs for a Silver Shadow and Bentley T can also be higher than for some of the more popular makes of car but, compared to a lot of 30-40 year old cars, there's no problem with parts availability as Bentley dealerships can supply all items for Crewe-built cars. Current servicing schedule prices show a difference between official Bentley dealers and independent specialists: for example, Bentley Ribble Valley,

an official Bentley dealership in Lancashire, quotes £526 inclusive of parts, labour and VAT for a 7500 mile (12,000km) service, £855 for a 15,000 mile (24,000km) service, and £1444 for a 30,000 mile (48,000km) service. The charge for the major 60,000 mile (96,000km) service is £3500, and includes a full bumper-to-bumper appraisal, as well as replacement of all serviceable items and fluids. Bowling Ryan carries out servicing at 6000 mile (9600km) or 6-monthly intervals, and charges £226 for the

Late Silver Shadows, like this Series II model, can make a fine investment. Such cars may be offered for sale through Bentley dealerships, but are more often sold through independent specialists, at auction, or privately.
(Author's collection)

minimum service, £388 for a 12,000 mile (19,200km) service, and £706 for a 24,000 mile (38,400km) service. Usually it takes one, two and two-three days respectively to carry out the service schedules. 48,000 and 96,000 mile (76,800 and 153,600km) services are major affairs, usually entailing the vehicle being off the road for a week.

Obviously, these services are expensive and, at the time of writing, minimum cost is in the region of £1500. These prices are for routine servicing only and do not take into account other repairs or maintenance that might be required. For example, should the hydraulic system need a complete overhaul, expect a specialist to run up a labour time of around 50 hours to change all the seals.

When asked what made working with Rolls-Royce and Bentley cars different John Bowling was adamant it was the quality of the original materials, together with engineering excellence. Even replacement parts, he added, are developed to the same high standard. Like official dealers, John Bowling will not fit anything other than Crewe Genuine Parts and confirmed that, in many instances, these were no more expensive than non-Crewe items. John also emphasises the need to strictly keep to manufacturer's servicing schedules. Taking short cuts is no cheaper in the long run and can result in unreliability.

The most important advice that John can offer to a potential purchaser is to have the car examined by an expert; only then can the car's overall condition be properly assessed. For an inexperienced buyer, a Silver Shadow or Bentley T could easily lead to great expense and much disappointment.

Crewe Genuine Parts

The Crewe Genuine Parts scheme has an excellent replacement parts service. Reg Vardy plc, official dealer for Tyne and Wear, can normally order any item up to 4.30pm one day for delivery by the time the dealership opens for business the following morning. In cases of urgency, customers are safe in the knowledge they can leave their car overnight and it will be ready for collection early the next day. It is not only within the United Kingdom that the company supplies replacement parts: consignments leave the warehouse by road three or four times a day en route to home market distributors, the European regional warehouse in Switzerland, to Lyndhurst, in New Jersey, which serves the American Continent, and almost any other destination worldwide. In cases of urgency, parts are air freighted on the first available flight.

To neglect a Rolls-Royce or Bentley and miss important services

Rolls-Royces do sometimes require extensive attention ...
(Courtesy John Bowling)

is, ultimately, devaluing the car, and could result in MoT failure. Even worse, neglect will pose a safety risk. All cars, including the products from Crewe, wear out eventually or need adjustment, and proper service schedules must be adhered to if the owner intends keeping the car in the condition it deserves.

Not even a Bentley or Rolls-Royce is free from corrosion, however, and the mass-produced Pressed Steel bodies can eventually show signs of rust, although the effects of rot do take longer to appear than on most other cars. Preventative maintenance is, therefore, a very serious part of owning a Silver Shadow or Bentley T-Series.

As with all cars, the Bentley T and Silver Shadow do have weaknesses. Bodily, the first signs of decay are usually to be found around the wheelarches, the back edges of the front and rear wings in particular. This is a common problem and is due to the ingress and retention of water. It's essential to ensure that all drain holes are kept clear. Michael Hibberd, a Rolls-Royce specialist in Slough, Berkshire, advises that these should be checked regularly, as he's known of cases where as much as a couple of gallons (9.5 litres) of water have been drained from the sills. In extreme cases, the floor of the car has rotted away entirely. Examine the carpets and underfelt as they act like a sponge, quietly rotting the metal beneath. Corrosion in this region is best repaired at once rather than leaving it to get worse. Regular inspections around the car are always a good idea, and periodic checks of boot floor condition and chrome trim mouldings will prevent minor

Top left: Certain areas on a Silver Shadow should be checked before and after buying. The wheelarches are prone to corrosion due to ingress of moisture. (Courtesy Michael Hibberd)

Bottom left: In this instance neglect has resulted in severe corrosion of the area around the front wheelarches, front wing lower sections, inner wheelarch filler panels, and outer sills. The wing assembly has been removed to facilitate replacement and repair. (Courtesy Michael Hibberd)

The boot floor is another area which should be checked periodically. Always use genuine Crewe components when making repairs: the cost of a stainless steel exhaust is around £700 but it will fit perfectly, whereas a non-original system will not and will require replacement sooner. (Courtesy Michael Hibberd)

corrosion from going unnoticed.

The doors on Silver Shadows and Bentley Ts are made of aluminium alloy and one effect of many winters of salted roads is corrosion; also check that salt has not affected the brightwork, door handles, and locks. Being of light alloy, which is softer than steel, doors are susceptible to even slight damage. The same, naturally, goes for the bonnet and boot. Other areas to watch, especially on older cars, are the leaded joints which can deteriorate; initial evidence of corrosion in this respect will be some cracking of the paintwork.

Coachwork quality of MPW cars is generally considered to be not much better than that of the Standard Saloons - an indication of just how well the Crewe product was constructed. This really is not surprising as the Standard Steel cars of the pre-Silver Shadow era received

All drain holes should be kept clear and the sills regularly inspected. Doors are made from an aluminium alloy and, being softer than steel, are more vulnerable to accidental damage. (Courtesy Michael Hibberd)

the same attention as their coachbuilt versions.

Mechanically, there are several points to check: rear brake discs can corrode, usually because of inactivity, and handbrake failure is not unknown because the mechanism operates on the edge of the brake disc. Brake pads tend to wear fairly quickly and, depending on the use expected

of them, may have to be replaced at intervals as short as 10,000 miles (16,000kms). Ball joints - especially on cars with compliant suspension - are susceptible to wear, if only because of the enormous amount of weight placed on them.

The hydraulic system, although well-proven, can give rise to problems. Any repairs here can be costly so it's

best to investigate troubles as soon as they occur. With the engine started, changes in weight distribution within the vehicle should be accounted for almost instantly. Any leaks from the hydraulic system, and that includes the power steering pump, should be investigated immediately.

The engine, whether the original 6.23 litre or later 6.75 litre unit, is

Leaded joints on older cars are susceptible to deterioration, which should be dealt with as soon as detected. Tyres and brake pads tend to wear quickly; rear brake discs are prone to corrosion, and handbrake failure is not unknown. (Courtesy Michael Hibberd

very reliable and should, if treated with respect, run for at least 100,000 miles (160,000km) without causing concern. Remember, though, from the driving seat there will be little evidence of a malfunction due to the unit's inherent smoothness, and efficiency of the vehicle's soundproofing material. Tell-tale signs of impending trouble may be a smoky exhaust and increase in oil consumption, as well as unusual sounds from the valve gear. (If the car has been idle for any length of time, expect some initial noise from the engine until the oil has had time to pressurise the hydraulic tappet mechanism.) If a knocking sound persists, suspect corrosion of the piston liners. Don't be surprised to see a drop of oil on the driveway or garage floor; this is a common feature, and one enthusiast reckons that most Silver Shadow owners have a gravel parking area because of this! One reason for this leak is that there's no rear oil seal on the crankshaft, and the problem is worse if the car is parked facing uphill. Another reason is that the sump is often overfilled with oil. With age, gaskets may deteriorate and allow some oil to drip down the outside of the block. Obviously, this should be rectified at once.

The engine on Silver Shadows and T-Series cars is not as quiet as is often believed, and certainly the old claim that the only sound heard at 60mph (96km) is the ticking of the clock is not altogether warranted. Under normal circumstances the engine is audible but, naturally, not intrusive.

The transmission is usually reliable; the GM400 gearbox is a superb unit which rarely gives trouble. Most

As long as it is well maintained, the engine of a Silver Shadow should provide at least 100,000 miles (160,000kms) service without major attention. The same applies to the gearbox and final drive. (Author's collection)

When considering buying a Silver Shadow or related model, it's sensible to talk to other owners about their experiences. These Silver Shadows were pictured at a vintage vehicle and steam gathering in the north west of England. (Author's collection)

Not all owners would want to take a Silver Shadow rallying! Ray Richards entered his car in the 1970 Daily Mirror World Cup Rally. This is a specially-prepared publicity photograph, taken not on the rally but in a quarry! (Courtesy National Motor Museum)

cars will be fitted with the 3-speed box and it will only be the very early home market cars that have the old 4-speed unit. Normally, the GM400 gearbox can provide up to at least 100,000 miles (160,000km) without a need for overhaul, the most common fault being a leak from the front pump seal. 4-speed boxes may need attention after 80,000 miles (128,000km), and the standard tell-tale sign of wear is usually uneven and clumsy gear changing.

The rear axle is also very reliable; early cars did suffer from some vibration but the problem was soon corrected. The unit should cover at least 100,000 miles (160,000kms) without major attention. Wheel bearings are also reliable and likely to give very long service.

Front suspension bushes should be regularly checked, especially around compliant mounts and anti-roll bar supports. Thuds from the rear end of the car - especially when pulling away - can indicate worn torque arm rubbers on the rear drive universal joints.

On vehicles as mechanically complex as the Silver Shadow and T, it's understandable that the majority of owners entrust their cars to a skilled specialist. There are enthusiasts, however, who do carry out their own

servicing and maintenance. The Rolls-Royce Enthusiasts' Club organises workshop events to explain the mechanical aspects of the cars.

It's not possible to cover all aspects of Silver Shadow maintenance here, but the following are some of the more important servicing requirements of which the owner should be aware.

The engine and hydraulic systems are the two areas of a Silver Shadow and Bentley T that warrant meticulous attention. Engine oil and filter changes should be carried out in strict accordance with manufacturer instructions, and the correct fluid used in the car's hydraulic system. There are also associated requirements such as maintaining the cooling system, checking, and - where necessary - changing drive belts, attention to the braking system, and changing brake pads when required, examining tyre condition and exhaust system: in other words, spending a little more

Customised Silver Shadows are a rarity. This example was converted by The Chelsea Workshop and is pictured at Land's End in Cornwall. (Author's collection)

This Silver Shadow (chassis number SRK 37130) has been converted for use as a support vehicle for an independent Rolls-Royce specialist in the USA. (Courtesy Bill Wolf)

time, on a regular basis, on preventive maintenance.

It has already been mentioned that the work involved in maintaining and repairing a Silver Shadow or Bentley T is probably beyond the capabilities of a lot of owners. The folly - and possible danger - of attempting any work on these cars without full knowledge of the procedure, and special tools, where required, cannot be overstressed.

Behind the wheel

The Silver Shadow and T-Series Bentley may be good to look at, but it's not until you get behind the wheel that the cars can be fully appreciated. The sumptuous interior, with its top grade hide upholstery, deep pile carpeting, and exquisite burr walnut veneer, is the height of good taste and perfectly complements the car's sophisticated engineering. Once settled into the comfortable seats - electrically adjustable, of course - which give a commanding driving position, a feeling of relaxed wellbeing is inevitable.

As the ignition is turned and the engine started, the sound of the V8 power deep under the bonnet is immensely satisfying. As the controls come alive the self-levelling immediately raises the car to its correct running height, whilst power steering makes directing the car effortless. With light pressure on the brake pedal, the gear selector is moved to the appropriate position and the handbrake released.

Even in Bentley guise, the Silver Shadow cars are far from performance machines and are most unsuitable for motor sport. Only the brave would expose such a heavyweight car with all its finery to the rigours of the rally course or track. A Silver Shadow was, however, entered in the *Daily Mirror* World Cup Rally of May 1970, for which it was extensively modified by its owner, Ray Richards. In addition to uprated suspension and a safety bar over the front of the car, extra driving lamps were fitted, and a roof rack carried extra tyres and wheels. Rather bizarrely, the exhaust pipes were routed away from the vehicle's underside, through outlets in the bonnet and over the top of the car! Richards had hoped for support from Rolls-Royce for his venture, but when this was not forthcoming, he purchased an American specification car with left

The Corniche convertible offers the ultimate in motoring, whatever the weather. (Author's collection)

hand drive. The car did not perform as well as anticipated and, in order to increase power, several modifications were carried out to the running gear and exhaust. Still the car lacked power and it was only after a cry for help from the owner that Rolls-Royce became involved in the project.

With Rolls-Royce to the rescue, the engine and exhaust were adjusted to specification settings, and a problem concerning overheating of the hub assemblies was investigated. It appears the bearings were packed with a grease with too high a melting point, which caused the hubs to run dry, so resulting in damage. The car was eventually prepared in time for the rally but it seems the going was rather tough and Ray Richards eventually arrived at the Lisbon stage in 63rd place after suffering transmission problems. Grease had leaked from the driveshafts due to the rough conditions, the bearings seized, and the shafts snapped.

A local Rolls-Royce dealer responded to the situation and cannibalised a car he had in stock, which allowed Ray Richards to continue to the next rally stage. It was in the South American section when, heavily grounding, the driveshafts

were torn away from the final drive unit and the car was forced to retire from the rally. The Silver Shadow was repaired and used as a support car for the remainder of the rally course.

T-Series Bentleys have been used for hill trial events at Prescott in a demonstration capacity staged by Rolls-Royce but, more latterly, a Silver Shadow has taken part in the Land's End to John O'Groats Reliability Trials (LE JOG). However, competitive motor sport really is not what the car's designers had in mind, and the Silver Shadow is far better equipped to be a very capable tourer, providing the highest degree of refinement and comfort.

The number of modifications made to the model throughout its production life mean that the late cars are rather different in feel and handling. Rolls-Royce accepted that there were some handling shortcomings, hence the modifications that were introduced. Series II cars have a more stable ride than earlier models, and the rack and pinion steering is also more precise than the original recirculating ball device. In fairness, however, the Silver Shadow was never intended to have out-and-out performance, but rather superior ride quality, although some

owners of the first batches of vehicles experienced rather unpleasant sensations, akin to sea-sickness, due to the car's soft suspension.

In recognition of these shortcomings, Rolls-Royce eventually offered a handling package to improve roadholding and stability. Should a car's suspension system be showing signs of wear, fitting a handling kit is well worth considering as it much improves the behaviour of the car. Taking into account the cost of replacing a set of dampers and springs, fitting a handling package, at a cost of around £1500, plus about £500 in labour (these figures do not include tax) makes economical sense.

An alternative to Rolls-Royce's own package is that devised by Harvey Bailey Engineering (HBE). Designed to cut out the pitch and roll usually associated with the Silver Shadow range of cars, the Harvey Bailey kit makes the car perform as a vehicle of its size, weight and power output should. Many owners have already fitted the Harvey Bailey modification to their cars, and the general opinion is that handling is transformed. The Harvey Bailey kit consists of specially designed front and rear anti-roll bars, as well as redesigned and uprated springs. Harvey Bailey Engineering also recommends fitting Bilstein shock absorbers, which, it says, provide greater damping ability along with enhanced ride quality. The cost of the Harvey Bailey kit is fractionally cheaper than the Rolls-Royce product; currently £1400 unfitted and £1750 with fitting, plus taxes where appropriate.

The HBE kit was developed by Rhoddy Harvey-Bailey, along with his business partner, Graham Martin. A racing and test driver, as well as Rolls-Royce devotee, Rhoddy designs high-performance chassis and suspension layouts for a number of manufacturers and vehicle specialists. An enthusiast with experience of Silver Shadows and Bentleys 'before and after' the fitting of the Harvey Bailey kit is Andrew Morris. His beautifully kept T2 now has exemplary handling and roadholding which is as good as, if not better than, any other large high-performance saloon. He well remembers, however, driving a Silver Shadow without modification, and the car's lumbering motion when cornering and negotiating bends.

Some owners do not feel the need to fit either of the handling packages, whilst others claim they make 'The Best Car In The World' even better. Bill Allen, the stylist who helped create the Silver Shadow two-door saloons and Corniche, did make the point, when asked about the handling, that the cars were prepared very much with the American customer in mind; also that, at the time of development, it was difficult to achieve superlative ride quality with high performance.

After driving a Bentley T or a Silver Shadow for a time, one becomes thoroughly spoiled by the car's effortless performance, unashamed luxury, and sophistication. The later cars do have better handling, are better equipped and will afford greater driver and passenger comfort, especially with the refined air conditioning. That's not to say that owning a Series I car is any less rewarding than owning a Series II, as each car has a special personality of its own.

For more of a sporting experience the Corniche - and especially the Convertible - may be the ultimate Rolls-Royce or Bentley. These cars, with their handbuilt coachwork, exclusive interior incorporating a modified facia layout and wood-rimmed steering wheel, enjoy a charisma all their own, and owners rejoice at being able to cruise with the hood lowered. Open-air motoring is fine in California, or on the Riviera, but in some countries the climate makes it a pleasure which can rarely be enjoyed.

The unique styling and hand-crafting of the MPW cars - and that includes the long wheelbase models - does have particular appeal and immense driver satisfaction. The same goes for the Camargue which, with distinctly different styling, has a unique attraction.

To increase enjoyment of the Silver Shadow and T-Series cars, many owners will want to join one, or both, of the recognised clubs, addresses for which can be found in the appendices. Both the Rolls-Royce Enthusiasts' Club (which equally welcomes Bentley owners) and the Bentley Drivers Club offer unique membership benefits, and go a long way towards ensuring enjoyable ownership of these fine cars. The Rolls-Royce Enthusiasts' Club was formed in 1957 and now has its headquarters at The Hunt House, Paulerspury, Northamptonshire. Along with an exhibition area and a meeting room, all of Rolls-Royce's extensive vehicle archives are housed within a specially-built library. Not only is it possible for a member of the club to obtain the detailed build history of a particular car, but research can also be undertaken. The R-REC headquarters is a Mecca for Rolls-Royce and Bentley enthusiasts worldwide, and many new owners are welcomed every year. The club, which has a number of regional sections within the United Kingdom, as well as sections established throughout Europe and Canada, has currently around 10,000 members. A superlative magazine, *The Bulletin*, is produced bi-monthly and, in addition, members receive a monthly Advertiser detailing many specialist services and cars available.

The Bentley Drivers Club, which has its headquarters at Long Crendon, Buckinghamshire, also welcomes owners of T-Series Saloons and Corniches. The BDC currently has 3500 members worldwide; there are 8 regions within the United Kingdom and approximately 30 overseas. Members receive the *Bentley Drivers Club Review*, which is published quarterly, as well as a bi-monthly Advertiser and monthly preview.

Whichever model Silver Shadow or T-Type you have (and some lucky enthusiasts have more than one) one thing is certain: there's no other car quite like it ...

Appendix 1

Production figures

ROLLS-ROYCE

Silver Shadow 16,717
Silver Shadow Long Wheelbase 2780
Silver Shadow II 8425
Silver Wraith II 2135
Silver Shadow MPW Saloon 568
Corniche Saloon 1108
Silver Shadow James Young Saloon 35
Silver Shadow MPW Convertible 505
Corniche Convertible 3239
Corniche II 1234
Corniche III 452
Corniche IV 219
Corniche S 25
Camargue 529
Total Rolls-Royce cars built 37,971

BENTLEY

T 1712
T Long Wheelbase 9
T2 558
T2 Long Wheelbase 10
T MPW Saloon 98
Corniche Saloon 63
T MPW Convertible 41
Corniche Convertible 77
Continental 433
Continental Turbo 8
T James Young Saloon 15
T Farina Coupé 1
Camargue 1
Total Bentley cars built 2585
Grand total (Rolls-Royce and Bentley) 40,556

MULLINER, PARK WARD (MPW) COACHBUILT CARS

Model	Dates produced	RHD	LHD	Chassis start numbers
ROLLS-ROYCE				
Two-door saloon	1966-71	369	199	CRH 1148
Corniche saloon	1971-76	365	274	CRH 9770
Corniche saloon	1976-77	44	97	CRH 22648
Corniche saloon	1977-79	58	95	CRH 30011
Corniche saloon	1979-80	68	107	CRX 50004
Convertible	1967-69	109	137	CRH 1698
Convertible	1969-71	124	135	DRX 6646
Corniche	1971-76	388	587	DRH 9919
Corniche	1976-77	48	206	DRH 22583
Corniche	1977-79	49	223	DRH 30003
Corniche	1979-81	116	321	DRH 50003
Corniche	1981-88	134	1167	BCX 01903
Corniche II	1986-89	60	1174	GCX 13162
Corniche III	1990-91	71	380	LCH 30001
Corniche IV	1992-93	24	90	NCX 40001
Corniche IV	1994-95	11	94	RCX 50001
Corniche S	1995	-	25	SCX 50086
BENTLEY				
T Two-door saloon	1966-71	79	19	CBX 1149
Corniche	1971-76	27	16	CBH 10420
Corniche	1976-77	2	1	CBH 24209
Corniche	1977-79	6	1	CBH 31226
Corniche	1979-80	4	6	CBK 50037
T Convertible	1967-69	24	7	CBH 3049
T Convertible	1969-71	8	2	DBH 7124
Corniche	1971-76	31	7	DBH 10122
Corniche	1976 -77	4	1	DBH 24505
Corniche	1977-79	1	6	DBG 31219
Corniche	1979-81	2	13	DBK 50042
Corniche	1981-85	3	9	BCX 02499
Continental	1985-89	43	134	GCX 13412
Continental	1990-91	67	113	LCX 30002
Continental	1992-93	8	33	NCH 40002
Continental	1994-95	5	30	RCX 50003
Continental Turbo	1992	3	-	NCH 400491
Continental Turbo	1995	-	5	SCX 50140

At-a-glance chronology

1965   Silver Shadow and T-Series launched at Paris Motor Show in autumn; a couple of weeks later the models had their British debut at the London Motor Show.

1966   Two-door saloon introduced by James Young. Shortly afterwards the MPW Two-door saloon was introduced.

1967   MPW Convertible introduced. Pilot batch of 10 long wheelbase saloons constructed, one of which was specially built for HRH Princess Margaret.

1968   GM400 automatic gearbox standard on all cars.

1969   Long wheelbase cars introduced, version available with division between front and rear seats. Self-levelling height control deleted from front suspension. Air conditioning standardised.

1970   Engine capacity increased from 6.25-litres to 6.75-litres. Central locking standardised.

1971   MPW two-door cars revised and renamed Corniche.

1972   'Compliant' suspension introduced for all cars; radial-ply tyres specified.

1973   North American market cars fitted with energy absorbing bumpers and pedal-operated parking brake; all cars have ventilated front disc brakes.

1974   Wheelbase extended, wider-section tyres fitted and wheelarches flared.

1975   Electronic ignition specified. Camargue, styled by Pininfarina, introduced complete with split level air conditioning.

1976   Corniche fitted with automatic air conditioning.

1977   Camargue and Corniche models uprated; rack and pinion steering. Silver Shadow II, T2 and Silver Wraith II introduced.

1979   Camargue and Corniche receive revised suspension. Standard Saloons continue.

1980   Bosch fuel injection introduced for Camargue and Corniche, California. Silver Shadow II, Silver Wraith II and T2 discontinued. Corniche Saloon discontinued.

1981   Fuel injection available for USA (except California - 1980). Corniche Convertible continues.

1985   Bentley Corniche renamed Continental. Camargue discontinued.

1986   Corniche II introduced for North America (rest of world had to wait until 1988).

1987   Fuel injection for all markets except California and rest of USA.

1988   Corniche II available for all markets - North America received it in 1986.

1990   Corniche III introduced.

1992   Corniche IV introduced.

1995   Corniche S and Bentley Continental Turbo available. Last Corniche and Bentley Continental produced.

Original specifications

Silver Shadow and T-Series Saloons

Coachwork
5-seat, 4-door Saloon of stressed steel monocoque construction. Separate front and rear sub-frames. Boot lid, doors, and bonnet top of aluminium alloy. Individual and electrically-operated front seats; upholstery in English hide, deep pile carpets, washable headlining, walnut veneer facia and garnish rails. Padded top roll in black Ambla (PVC), (earliest cars had top and bottom leather facia rolls).

Dimensions
Wheelbase: 9ft 11.75ins (3035mm)
Track, front and rear: 4ft 9.5ins (1460mm)
Road clearance: 6.5ins (1650mm)
Turning circle: 38ft (11,580mm)
Overall length: 16ft 11.5ins (5170mm)
Overall width: 5ft 11ins (1800mm)
Overall height: 4ft 11.75ins (1520m)
Weight (unladen, complete with oil, coolant and a full tank of fuel): 4760lbs (2159kg)

Engine
8 cylinder vee unit with overhead valves and hydraulic tappets. Bore 4.1ins (104.14mm); stroke 3.6ins (91.44mm). 6230cc; compression ratio 9.0:1 (8.0:1 available). Cylinder block of high silicon content aluminium alloy with wet liners of cast iron; aluminium alloy cylinder heads; five bearing forged steel crankshaft. Full flow oil filter; water cooling; twin SU carburettors and automatic choke.

Transmission
Home market cars 4-speed automatic transmission; lhd export models 3-speed GM400 gearbox. Ratios: (4-speed box) top: 1:1, 3rd: 1.45:1, 2nd: 2.63:1; 1st: 3.82:1, reverse: 4.3:1. (3-speed box) top: 1:1, 2nd: 1.5:1, 1st:2.5:1, reverse:2:1. Electric actuation fitted to both gearboxes.

Brakes
Disc brakes fitted to all wheels. Triple hydraulic system including two independent circuits. One power system provides 46 per cent of total braking, operating one caliper on each front disc and part of the rear brake. Second system provides 31 per cent total braking, operating the other caliper on each front disc. Direct master cylinder to part of the rear brakes provides 23 per cent of the total braking. Manually-operated parking brake.

Suspension
Independent all-round; double triangle levers, coil springs and telescopic hydraulic dampers at front; trailing arms, coil springs and telescopic hydraulic dampers at rear. Two-speed automatic height control; height sensor on front suspension and two sensors on the rear. Fast height control when doors open or neutral gear selected.

Steering
Power-assisted, Saginaw recirculating ball. 4 turns, lock-to-lock.

Wheels & tyres

15 inch, 5-stud, steel wheels, 8.45x15 low profile tyres. Tyre pressures: 23lbs/sq.in. front, 25lbs/sq.in. rear.

Electrical system

12-volt negative earth; 64 ampere-hour battery. Twin fuel pumps; rheostat on facia; 2-speed windscreen wipers; windscreen washers; electric fuel-filler cap release. Powered window lifts; electric seat adjustment; rear screen de-mister. Air conditioning optional.

Capacities

Fuel tank: .... 23.5 imp. galls., 28.8 US galls., 109 litres. (Fuel tank later increased to 24 imp. galls.)
Engine oil: .... 14 imp. pints, 16.8 US pints, 8.0 litres.
Gearbox oil: .... 24 imp. pints, 28.8 US pints, 13.6 litres.
Coolant: .... 28 imp. pints, 33.6 US pints, 16 litres.

Colour schemes

Cars were finished in either a single colour or a two-tone scheme from the following range:
Black; Shell Grey; Tudor Grey; Black Pearl; Astral Blue; Sand; Sable; Sage Green; Smoke Green; Garnet; Dawn Blue; Regal Red; Velvet Green; Caribbean Blue.

Upholstery: .... Beige; Tan; Grey; Blue; Red; Green; Scarlet; Black.
Carpets: .... Beige; Blue; Fawn; Green; Grey; Maroon; Red.
Headlining: .... Grey; Light Fawn; Pale Green; Mushroom.

Performance

Maximum speed (average): 115mph, 185kph 4390rpm
(best): 118mph, 190kph 4500rpm
3rd gear 72mph, 116kph 4000rpm
2nd gear 43mph, 69kph 4350rpm
1st gear 24mph, 39kph 3500rpm
Standing quarter mile: .... 17.6 seconds, 76mph, 121.60kph
Standing kilometre: .... 33.0 seconds, 96mph, 153.60kph
Fuel consumption: .... 11-15mpg, 25.7 lts/100km - 18.8 lts/100km; average 12.2mpg, 23.2 lts/100km

Derivative specification differed as follows:

Dimensions

Wheelbase (long): 10ft 3.5ins (3035mm)
Track: .... Silver Shadow II & T2: front 5ft (1524mm), rear 4ft 11.5ins (1514mm); Camargue & Corniche: front & rear 4ft 9.5ins (1460mm).
Overall length: .... Long wheelbase saloon: 17ft 3.5ins (5270mm); Silver Shadow II & T2: 17ft 0.5ins (5194mm) Silver Wraith II: 17ft 4.5ins (5296mm); Corniche: 17ft 3.5ins (5270mm); Camargue: 16ft 11.5ins (5169mm); North American Silver Shadow II: 17ft 3.5ins (5270mm); North American Silver Wraith II: 17ft 8.5ins (5397.5mm).

Overall width: ....Silver Shadow II/T2: 5ft 11.75ins (1820mm); Corniche: 6ft (1830mm); Camargue: 6ft 3.5ins (1918mm)

Turning circle: ....Silver Shadow II, T2 & Silver Wraith II: 39ft 2ins (11,938mm); Corniche:38ft 9ins (11,811mm); Camargue: 38ft 6ins (11,735mm).

Weight: ....Silver Shadow II & T2: 4930lbs (2237kg); long wheelbase: 5010lbs (2275kg); Silver Wraith II: 5020lbs (2277kg); Silver Wraith II with division: 5260lbs (2385kg); two-door Saloon: 4978lbs (2258kg); two-door Convertible: 5124lbs (2322kg); Corniche Saloon: 5045lbs (2288kg); Corniche Convertible: 5200lbs (2358kg); Camargue: 5175lbs (2347kg).

6.75-litre engine

Stroke:......................................3.9ins (99.1mm)

Bore: 4.1ins (104.1mm)

Capacity: ....6750cc.

Compression ratio: ....9:1. From 1975, compression ratio 8:1 and 7.3:1 for American, Australian and Japanese markets.

Performance

Maximum speed: ....Silver Shadow II & T2: 119mph (190.4kph); Corniche: 120mph (192kph); Silver Wraith II: 119mph (190.4kph); Camargue: 120mph (192kph).

Fuel consumption:.....................Silver Shadow II & T2: 13.6mpg (20 lts/100km); Silver Wraith II: 13.2mpg (22 lts/100km); Corniche: 11.9mpg (24 lts/100km); Camargue: 12.3mpg (23 lts/100km).

Chassis serial number identification

A typical Silver Shadow or Bentley T chassis number may appear as:

    S R H 1 2 3 4 5   or LBX   2 3 4 5 6
    a b c d e f g h   a b c   d e f g h

Key to identification

a   Body type..S-Standard Saloon; L-Long Wheelbase Saloon C-Two-Door Saloon and Convertible up to chassis 6632 D-Convertible from chassis 6646; J-Camargue.

b   Marque ....R-Rolls-Royce; B-Bentley.

c   Steering position ....H-right hand drive; X-left hand drive. From 1972 North American cars were given a special numbering system, X being replaced by a letter: A, 1972; B, 1973; C, 1974; D, 1975; E, 1976; F, 1977; G, 1978; J,1979; K, 1980; L, 1981. From 1980 cars destined for California with fuel injection were given a 'c' suffix.

d-h   Chassis serial numbers in batches .... 1001 - 4548; 5001 - 5603; 6001 - 8861 9001 - 26708; 30001 - 41648 (Series II cars) 50001 - 50776 (Corniche and Camargue with mineral oil hydraulics).

Appendix 2

Clubs, specialists and bibliography

Clubs

Rolls-Royce Enthusiasts' Club
The Hunt House,
Paulerspury,
Towcester,
Northants NN12 7NA,
England.
Tel: 01327 811788
Fax: 01327 811797
Website: www.rrec.co.uk
E-mail: admin@rrec.org.uk
The R-REC serves members throughout the United Kingdom, Europe, and Canada. Organised sections exist in 19 areas within the UK, in 16 European countries, and Canada. Members receive an excellent magazine, *The Bulletin*, six times a year, as well as a monthly Advertiser. The club was formed in 1957 and houses, at its headquarters, the entire build histories of Rolls-Royce and Bentley cars. Current membership is in excess of 10,000.

Rolls-Royce Owners' Club of Australia
Ian Dunn,
PO Box 163,
Lyneham,
ACT 2602,
Australia.
Tel: 0061 62545495
Formed in 1956, there are six sections throughout Australia. Magazine published six times a year.

Rolls-Royce Club of New Zealand
Tom Williams,
78 Kesteven Avenue,
Glendowie,
Auckland,
New Zealand.
The New Zealand Cub has three sections throughout the country. Meetings are arranged on a regular basis and members are kept informed of events through a magazine, which is published six times a year.

Rolls-Royce Owners' Club of America
Headquarters:
191 Hempt Road,
Mechanicsburg,
PA 17055,
USA.
Tel: 001 717 697 4671
Fax: 001 717 697 7820
Website: www.rroc.org
E-mail: rroc.hq@rroc.org
The oldest Rolls-Royce Owners' Club in the world, the American club was formed in 1951. There are 33 regions throughout the USA and Canada and members receive the journal *Flying Lady* six times a year.

Bentley Drivers Club
W. O. Bentley Memorial Building,
16 Chearsley Road,
Long Crendon,
Aylesbury,
Bucks HP18 9AW,
England.
Tel: 01844 208233
Fax: 01844 208923
The club has 8 regions in the United Kingdom and another 30-40 sections around the world. A quarterly magazine, the Bentley Drivers Club *Review*, is supplemented by a bi-monthly Advertiser and a monthly newsletter. The club currently has a membership of around 3000.

Specialists

Bentley Motors Ltd.,
Pyms Lane,
Crewe,
Cheshire CW1 3PL,
England.
Tel: 01270 653653

Fax: 01270 535450
Website: www.bentleymotors.com

Rolls-Royce Heritage Trust (ML-71)
PO Box 31,
Derby DE24 8BJ,
England.

For up-to-date information about
official Bentley dealers, contact
Bentley Motors Limited, or refer to
the manufacturer's website.

For information concerning the new
Rolls-Royce, contact:
Rolls-Royce Motor Cars Ltd
Stane Street,
Westhampnett,
Chichester,
West Sussex PO18 0PA,
England.

Other specialists (UK)

Crewe Genuine Parts – *see Official
Bentley Dealers*

P & A Wood,
Great Easton,
Dunmow,
Essex CM6 2HD,
England.
Tel: 01371 870848
Fax: 01371 870810
Website: www.pa-wood.co.uk
E-mail: enquiries@pa-wood.co.uk
*Rolls-Royce and Bentley Official
Heritage dealer. Sales of new and
previously used vehicles; restoration,
parts.*

Bonhams,
10 Salem Road,
London W2 4DL,
England.
Tel: 020 7313 3176
Fax: 020 7313 3170
E-mail: cars@bonhams.com
*Motor vehicles, motorcycles, toys,
models and automobilia auctioneers.
Branches in Switzerland, USA and
Australia.*

Denis Pilling & Son,
Old Mason's Yard,
Manchester Road,
Leigh,
Lancashire WN7 2ND,
England.
Tel: 01942 607426
Vehicle restoration.

Hunt & Keal Ltd.,
(Sales) 18-23 Radley Mews,
Kensington,
London W8 6JP,
England.
Tel: 020 7937 8487
Fax: 020 7937 1097
(Service & Parts) 53 Minerva Road,
London NW10 6HJ,
England.
Tel: 020 8838 3113
Fax: 020 8838 2800
Website: www.huntandkeal.co.uk
E-mail: enquiries@huntandkeal.co.uk

Jack Barclay,
2-4 Ponton Road,
Nine Elms,
London SW8 5BA,
England.
Tel: 0207 978 2223
E-mail: parts93@jackbarclay.co.uk
Parts.

Montague & Company,
Chinthurst Farm,
Chinthurst Lane,
Bramley,
Surrey GU5 0DR,
England.
Tel: 01483 898595
Fax: 01483 898132
Website: www.bentleyspecialists.com
E-mail: info@bentleyspecialists.com
Parts.

Sargeants of Goudhurst,
Goudhurst,
Kent TN17 1HA,
Englaand.
Tel: 01580 211327
Fax: 01580 212010
Sales, service & restoration.

Phantom Motor Cars,
Pankridge Street,
Crondall,
Farnham,
Surrey GU10 5QT,
England.
Tel: 01252 850231
Fax: 01252 850516
Website: www.pmcuk.com
E-mail: phantommotorcars@aol.com
Servicing & restoration.

Bowling-Ryan Ltd.,
Unit 5 Fishbrook Industrial Estate,
Stoneclough Road,
Kearsley,
Bolton,

Lancashire BL4 8EL,
England.
Tel: 01204 700300
Servicing, parts & restoration.

Michael Hibberd,
Unit 31 Middle Green Trading Estate,
Langley,
Slough,
Berkshire SL3 6DF,
England.
Service, restoration & sales.

Rob Jones,
Benver Services,
Unit 9 Quaker Coppice,
Crewe Gates Industrial Estate,
Crewe,
Cheshire CW1 6FA,
England.
Tel: 01270 250236
Servicing & restoration.

Hanwell Car Centre,
86/88 Uxbridge Road,
Hanwell,
London W7 3SU,
England.
Tel: 020 8567 6557/9729
Fax: 020 8579 5386
Website: www.hanwells.com
Sales.

Kearsley Pearce Ltd.,
1-5 Roe Lane,
Southport,
Merseyside,
England.
Tel: 01704 885566
Website: www.kearsleypearce.co.uk
E-mail: sales@kearsleypearce.co.uk
Sales.

Ristes,
Gamble Street,
Nottingham,
England.
Tel: 0115 978 5834
Fax: 0115 942 4351
E-mail: info@ristes.zee-web.co.uk
Restoration & maintenance.

Maxted-Page & Baxter Ltd.,
PO Box 7039,
Halstead,
Essex CO9 2WL,
England.
Tel: 01787 477749
Fax: 01787 475994
E-mail: maxtedpagebaxter@aol.com
Sales.

The Real Car Co.,
Snowdonia Business Park,
Coed y Parc,
Bethseda,
Gwynedd LL57 4YS,
Wales.
Tel: 01248 602649
Fax: 01248 600994
Website: www.realcar.co.uk
E-mail: mail@realcar.co.uk
Sales.

Introcar,
1 Manorgate Road,
Kingston-upon-Thames,
Surrey KT2 7AW,
England.
Tel: 020 8541 5642/8546 2027/5059
7639
Fax: 020 8546 5058
Website: www.introcar.co.uk
E-mail: sales@introcar.co.uk
Parts.

Frank Dale & Stepsons,
125 Harlequin Avenue,
Great West Road,
Isleworth,
West London TW8 9EW,
England.
Tel: 020 8847 5447
Fax: 020 8560 5748
Websitc: www.frankdalc.com
Sales, service, trimming, restoration.

Healey Brothers,
Irthlingborough,
Northants NN9 5RG,
England.
Tel: 01933 650247
Fax: 01933 65002
Website: www.healeybros.co.uk
E-mail: experts@healeybros.co.uk
Restoration, parts.

Stewart Walker Ltd.,
Unit 3a Crown House,
Station Road,
Thatcham,
Newbury,
Berks RG19 4PR,
England.
Tel/fax: 01653 866833
Sales, service & restoration.

Flying Spares,
Rossendale House,
Station Road Industrial Estate,
Market Bosworth,
Warwickshire CV13 0PE,
England.

Tel: 0845 1300 633 (from within UK
only); 01455 292949
Fax: 01455 292959
Website: www.flyingspares.com
E-mail, rreca@flyingspares.co.uk
Parts.

A. J. Glew Ltd.,
7 Draycott Business Centre,
Draycott, Nr Blockley,
Moreton in Marsh,
Gloucestershire,
England.
Tel: 01386 700987
Fax: 01386 700446
Website: www.ajglew.co.uk
E-mail: glews@onetel.net.uk
Specialist restoration.

Ivor Bleaney of The New Forest,
Tel: 01794 390895
Fax: 01794 390862
Website: www.ibclassiccars.co.uk
E-mail: ivorbleaney@msn.com
Sales.

Royce Servicing & Engineering,
Station Road,
Betchworth,
Surrey RH3 7BZ,
England.
Tel: 01737 844999
Fax: 01737 844855
E-mail: sales@royceservice.co.uk
Sales, service & restoration.

Colbrook,
24 High Street,
Stilton,
Peterborough,
Cambridgeshire,
England.
Tel: 01733 243737
Fax: 01733 243738
Website: www.colbrookspecialists.
co.uk
Sales, service, parts.

Silver Lady Motor Services Ltd.,
Hainault Works,
Hainault Road,
Little Heath,
Romford,
Essex RM6 5SS,
England.
Tel: 020 8599 8548/4905
Fax: 020 8599 8041
Sales, service & renovation.

Balmoral UK,
Bromsgrove Road,

Halesowen,
West Midlands,
England.
Tel: 01562 711114
Fax: 01562 711115
Sales.

Classic Restorations,
Pitnacree Street,
Alyth,
Perthshire,
Scotland.
Tel: 01828 633293
Fax: 01828 632529
Website: www.classicrestorations.
co.uk
Servicing, repairs & restoration.

R R & B Garages,
Forbes House,
Harris Business Park,
Hanbury Road,
Stoke Prior,
Bromsgrove,
Worcestershire B60 4BD,
England.
Tel: 01527 876513
Fax: 01527 877229
Website: www.rrb-garages.com
Sales & service.

Laughton Investments,
Lutterworth,
Leicestershire,
England.
Tel: 0116 240 2115
Fax: 0116 240 444
E-mail: info@classiccars-inernation.
com
Sales.

Hillier Hill,
Unit 18 Stilebrook Road,
Yardley Road Industrial Estate,
Olney,
Bucks MK46 5EA,
England.
Tel: 01234 713871
Fax: 01234 713917
Website: www.hillierhill.com
Sales, service & restoration.

Scotts,
59 Staunton Avenue,
Hayling Island,
Hants PO11 0EW,
England.
Tel: 023 9246 6592
Website: www.scottsrolls-bentley.com
Sales, service & restoration.

Fulmarques Ltd.,
Website: www.ccdata.com/
fulmarques
Sales, service, parts.

Silver Lady Services Ltd.,
64-70 Alma Road,
Winton,
Bournemouth,
Dorset BH9 1AN,
England.
Tel: 01202 388488
Fax: 01202 388288
Sales, service & restoration.

Metex Dust Covers,
Beehive Mill,
Moor Lane,
Darwen,
Lancs BB3 0EJ,
England.
Tel: 01254 704625/703893
Fax: 01254 776927
Dust covers for all cars.

J. K. Seymour,
Gillcroft Farm,
Greenmires Lane,
Stainburn,
Leeds LS21 2LP,
England.
Tel: 0113 2842442
Fax: 0113 2841087
E-mail: jkseymour.co.uk
Sales.

Hoffmann's of Henley,
Fairfield Works,
Reading Road,
Henley-on-Thames,
Oxfordshire RG9 1DR,
England.
Tel: 01941 573953
Fax: 01941 573647
Website: www.hoffmansofhenley.
co.uk
Engineering and sales.

Longstone Tyres,
Tel: 01302 711123
Fax: 01302 710113
Tyres for all models.

P. D. Gough & Co. Ltd.,
Tel: 0115 938 2241
Fax: 0115 945 9162
Website: www.pdgough.com
Stainless steel exhausts.

Hamptons Coachtrimming,
The Barn,

Grange Farm,
Hollies Lane,
Pattingham,
Wolverhampton WV6 7HJ,
England.
Tel: 01902 700733
Fax: 01902 701601
Coachtrimming.

Tregunna Electroplating,
Tel: 020 7262 5678
Fax: 020 7724 2354
Website: www.tregunnachrome.co.uk
Chromework.

Michael A. Jones & Co. Ltd.,
15 Ten Acres,
Alcester,
Warwickshire B49 6PY,
England.
Tel/fax: 01789 400011
Parts.

Kingsmill Workshop,
Unit 7 Main Valley Industrial Park,
Junction Road,
Sutton-in-Ashfield,
Notts NG17 5GS,
England.
Tel: 01623 400606
Fax: 01623 468535
Service & restoration.

P. W. Cooper Woodtrim Restoration,
Unit 6 & 7,
Quakers Coppice,
Crewe Gates Industrial Estate,
Crewe,
Cheshire CW1 6FA,
England.
Tel/fax: 01270 251432
Wood specialist.

D. E. W. Car Services (Oxford),
Unit 5 Fraser Properties,
Oakfield Industrial Estate,
Eynsham,
Oxon OX29 4TR,
England.
Tel: 01865 882789
Parts.

Stainless Steel Exhaust Systems,
Kiln Farm,
Nosterfield,
Bedale,
North Yorkshire DL8 2QX,
England.
Tel: 01677 470608

Beare Essentials Mail Order,

16 Sussex Road,
New Malden,
Surrey KT3 3PY,
England.
Tel/fax: 01306 631962
Website: www.beare-essentials.co.uk
New, used & reconditioned parts.

The London Chroming Company,
735 Old Kent Road,
London SE15 1JL,
England.
Tel/fax: 020 7639 6434
Website: www.londonchroming.co.uk
Chromework.

BCI,
16A Leinster Mews,
London W2 3EY,
England.
Tel: 020 7723 7876
Fax: 020 7258 3790
E-mail: bentleyparts@aol.com
Parts.

Paul Mackley Engineering,
50 Swains Aveneue,
Sneinton Dale,
Nottingham NG3 7AU,
England.
Tel/fax: 0115 9501063
Service & restoration.

Derby Plating Services Ltd,
148 Abbey Street,
Derby DE22 3SS,
England.
Tel/fax: 01332 382408
Plating.

Brian A. Thompson,
119 Station Road,
Warboys,
Huntingdon PE28 2TH,
England.
Tel/fax: 01487 822488
Parts.

G. Whitehouse Autos Ltd.,
Brooklands House,
Nimmings Road,
Halesowen,
West Midlands B62 9JE,
England.
Tel: 0121 559 9800
Fax: 0121 559 9885
Website: www.gwautos.com
Automatic transmissions.

Creech Coachtrimming,
Roger Condon,

55 Chatham Avenue,
Hayes,
Bromley,
Kent BR2 7QB,
England.
Tel/fax: 0208 4623425
Coachtrimming.

A. J. Hickman,
85 Worthington Road,
Fradley,
Lichfield,
Staffs,
England.
Tel: 01543 252196
Woodwork specialist.

Woodwork Restoration,
The Chalet,
Bell Road,
Rocklands St Peters,
Attleborough,
Norfolk NR17 1UL,
England.
Tel: 01953 483529

The Chelsea Workshop,
Nell Gwynn House,
Draycott Avenue,
Chelsea,
London SW3 3AU,
England.
Tel: 020 7584 8363/4, 020 7581
1761, 020 7589 1522
Fax: 020 7581 3033
Restoration.

English Automotive,
Unit 6-24 Central Avenue,
West Molesey KT8 2HH,
England.
Tel: 020 8487 3900
Fax: 020 8487 3902
E-mail: englishautomotive@btintern
et.com
Servicing.

Overseas specialists
Garage De Vaal,
Haaglanden,
Netherlands.
Tel: 0031 174 510022
Fax: 0031 174 298175
Website: www.garagedevaal.nl
Sales & restoration.

Brabo,
Arnoudstraat 17,
Hillegrom 2128DX,
The Netherlands.
Tel: 0031 25 252 78 75

Fax: 0031 25 252 79 17
Website: www.brabo-rolls-parts.nl
Parts.

Ultimate Motor Works,
895 N.County Road 427,
Longwood,
FL 32750,
Near Orlando,
USA.
Tel: 001 407 339 3443
Fax: 001 407 834 4002
Restoration.

The Frawley Company,
138 Main Street,
Parkesburg,
PA 19365,
USA.
Tel: 001 610 857 1099
Restoration, service & repair.

Madera Concepts,
55-B Depot Road,
Goleta,
CA 93117,
USA.
Toll free: 800 800 1579
Fax: 001 805 962 7359
Automotive woodwork.

E. F. Murphy Inc,
354-F Lowery Court,
Groveport,
OH 43125,
USA.
Tel: 001 614/836-3223
Fax: 001 614/836-7550
Service, repair & restoration.

Bonhams,
220 San Bruno Avenue,
San Francisco,
CA 94103,
USA.
Tel: 001 415 391 4000/(fax) 4040

Bonhams,
10 Rue Blavignac,
1227 Carouge-Geneva,
Switzerland.
Tel: 0041 (0) 22 300 3160/(fax) 3035
Sales and auctioneers.

SRS Inc,
5000 Old Ellis Pointe,
Roswell,
GA 30076,
USA.
Tel: 001 770 360 9404
Sales, service & restoration.

Albers,
360S First St.,
Zionsville,
IN 46077,
USA.
Tel: 001 317 873 2360/2460
Fax: 001 317 873 6860
Website: www.albersrollsbentley.com
Sales, service, restoration & parts.

Borla East,
24 Cokesbury Road Suite 9,
Cokesbury Road Industrial Park,
Lebanon,
NJ 08833,
USA.
Tel: 001 908 236 2820
Stainless steel exhaust systems.

Classic Auto Air Mfg. Co.,
2020W, Kennedy Blvd, Dept FL,
Tampa,
FL 33606,
USA.
Tel: 001 813 251 2356/4994
Air conditioning.

D & D Classic,
2300 Mote Drive,
Covington,
OH 45318,
USA.
Tel: 001 937 473 2229
Fax: 937 473 5433
E-mail: ddclassi@bright.net
Restoration.

Foreign Car Engineering,
75 N. Congress Avenue,
Delray Beach,
FL 33445,
USA.
Tel: 001 561 276 0114/0119
Fax: 561 274 9127
Parts, service & restoration.

Enfield Auto Restoration,
4 Print Shop Road,
Enfield,
CT 06082,
USA.
Tel: 001 860 749 7917/2836(fax)

Dennison Motors Inc,
322 South Concord Road,
West Chester,
Pennsylvania,
USA.
Tel: 001 610 436 8668/(fax) 8864
Electronic ignition conversion systems.

The latest information regarding Rolls-Royce and Bentley specialists can be obtained from the appropriate enthusiasts clubs and via the internet.

Bibliography

Rolls-Royce Silver Spirit and Silver Spur, Bentley Mulsanne, Eight, Continental, Brooklands and Azure Malcolm Bobbitt (Veloce ISBN 1 901295 84 2)

Rolls-Royce Silver Wraith, Silver Dawn and Silver Cloud, Bentley Mk VI, R-Series and S-Series Martyn Nutland (Veloce ISBN 1 874105 87 1)

British Car Factories From 1896 Collins & Stratton (Veloce Publishing ISBN 1 874105 04 9)

The Rolls-Royce Motor Car Anthony Bird & Ian Hallows (Batsford)

Rolls-Royce and Bentley Klaus-Josef Rossfelt (Haynes ISBN 0-85429 920 3)

Rolls-Royce and Bentley, The Crewe Years Martin Bennett (Haynes ISBN 0 85429 908 4)

Rolls-Royce Bentley Experimental Cars Ian Rimmer (R-REC ISBN 1 869912 00 4)

The Rolls-Royce and Bentley Vols 1, 2 & 3 Graham Robson (Motor Racing Publications ISBN 0 900549 86 6; 0 900549 87 4; 0 900549 99 8)

Those Elegant Rolls-Royce Lawrence Dalton (Dalton Watson Ltd)

Rolls-Royce In America John Webb de Campi (Dalton Watson Ltd)

Rolls-Royce, The Living Legend (Post Motor Books)

Rolls-Royce, 80 years of Motoring Excellence Edward Eves (Orbis Books ISBN 0 85613 647 6)

Rolls-Royce (Autocar archives) (Temple Press ISBN 0 600 34981 0)

The Rolls-Royce Jonathan Wood (Shire Publications ISBN 0 85263 873 6)

The Bentley Nick Georgano (Shire Publications ISBN 0 7478 0192 4)

The Life Of Sir Henry Royce Sir Max Pemberton (Huchinson)

An Illustrated History Of The Bentley Car W. O. Bentley (George Allen & Unwin Ltd)

Bentley Past & Present Rivers Fletcher (Gentry Books ISBN 085614 082 1)

Bentley, The Cars From Crewe Rodney Steel (Dalton Watson ISBN 0 901564 45 1)

Rolls-Royces - Hive's Turbulent Barons Alec Harvey-Bailey (Sir Henry Royce Memorial Foundation)

Bentley R-Type Continental Stanley Sedgwick (Bentley Drivers Club Ltd)

W. O. Bentley, The Man Behind the Marque Malcolm Bobbitt (Breedon Books ISBN 1 85983 352 7)

Bentley, The Story Andrew Frankel (Redwood Publishing ISBN 0 9517751 9 7)

Illustrated Rolls-Royce & Bentley Buyer's Guide Paul R. Woudenberg (Motorbooks International)

Postwar Rolls-Royce and Bentley, A Concise Buying Guide Barry D.Cooney (Cooney-Taylor Publishing Inc ISBN 0 916117 00 6)

Bentley Heritage Richard Bird (Osprey Automotive ISBN 1 85532 187 4)

Bentley Cars 1940-1945 (Brooklands Books)

Bentley, Fifty Years of the Marque 3rd Edition Johnnie Green (Dalton Watson ISBN 1 85443 135 8)

Bentley, Cricklewood to Crewe Michael Frostick (Osprey ISBN 0 85045 376 3)

Rolls-Royce Silver Shadow Gold Portfolio, 1965-1980 (Brooklands Books ISBN 1 85520 2298)

Road & Track on Rolls-Royce and Bentley (Brooklands Books ISBN 0 946489 59 9)

Rolls-Royce Silver Shadow 1 & II (Transport Source Books ISBN 1 85847 298 9)

Rolls-Royce Silver Shadow - The complete story Graham Robson (Crowood ISBN 1 86126 116 0)

Rolls-Royce Corniche, Camargue & Silver Spirit (Transport Source Books ISBN 1 85847 299 7)

Rolls-Royce Silver Dawn, Cloud & Phantom (Transport Source Books ISBN 1 85847 281 4)

Rolls-Royce and Bentley - Sixty Years at Crewe Malcolm Bobbitt (Sutton ISBN 0 7509 1623 0)

Rolls-Royce, The Magic of a Name (3 volumes) Peter Hugh (Icon Books ISBN 1 84046 151 9/1 84046 284 1 1 84046 405 4

Original Rolls-Royce and Bentley 1946-65 James Taylor (Bay View Books ISBN 1 901432 18 1)

From The Shadow's Corner Cal West (Rolls-Royce Owners' Club Inc)

The Motor Car 1946-56 Michael Sedgwick (Batsford ISBN 0 7134 1271 2)

Britain's Motor Industry, The First Hundred Years Georgano, Baldwin,Clausager & Wood (Haynes ISBN 0 85429 923 8)

Rolls-Royce Enthusiasts' Club Bulletin

Bentley Drivers Club *Review*

Motor Magazine

Autocar Magazine

Autosport Magazine

Motor Sport Magazine

Classic Cars Magazine

Queste Magazine

Index